# Sunnyside ...
# Unconditional Love ....
# And Sweet-Smelling Dirt

*My Story*

**Lyn Maxwell**

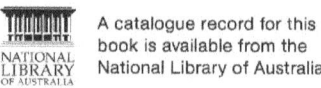
A catalogue record for this book is available from the National Library of Australia

Copyright © 2025 Lyn Maxwell
All rights reserved.
ISBN-13: 978-1-923174-58-0

Linellen Press
265 Boomerang Road
Oldbury, Western Australia
www.linellenpress.com.au

# Dedication

To Dad and Mum
William Whistler Sainsbury and Margaret June Sainsbury
(Bill and Peg)

# Contents

Dedication ................................................................... iii
Contents ....................................................................... v
Strongest thread ......................................................... 1
About My Book ......................................................... 3
Please Note ................................................................. 4
Cultural Sensitivity Warning ..................................... 4
Introduction ............................................................... 5
The Beginning … Part 1 ........................................... 7
The Beginning … Part 2 ........................................... 16
Two Hearts Collide ................................................... 24
Starting Out ............................................................... 32
Pitter Patter of Little Feet ........................................ 36
Pitter Patter of Little Feet 2 .................................... 41
Earliest Memories ..................................................... 45
Young Childhood ...................................................... 55
After Ploughing ......................................................... 70
Down Nan's ............................................................... 72
The Humble Wheat Bag .......................................... 86
Home from Nanna's ................................................. 88
Shearing ...................................................................... 93
After Shearing ........................................................... 96
After Shearing – House-building ............................ 98
Summer on the Farm ............................................... 100
School Days ............................................................... 108

| | |
|---|---|
| Fun and Friends | 117 |
| Scripture at School | 123 |
| Christmas at Sunnyside | 126 |
| Summer Holidays | 131 |
| Holidays at Nanna Jess's and Pop's | 137 |
| Dark Clouds Gather | 141 |
| Later Years at Primary School | 144 |
| A Message in the Form of a Letter | 147 |
| Goodbye and Thank You | 150 |
| High School, Life-changing Times | 155 |
| Development into Life's Journey on my Web of Life | 158 |
| Wrong Decision Made | 163 |
| First marriage | 164 |
| The Wedding | 172 |
| Married Life Begins | 176 |
| Married Life with First Child | 181 |
| Baby Number Two | 185 |
| Family Life Continues | 198 |
| Holiday Happiness at the Farm | 208 |
| Too Many Storms | 210 |
| Love, Laughter and Happiness | 218 |
| Newfound Happiness | 223 |
| Snippets of Memories | 227 |
| Second Marriage: Life Begins Again | 229 |
| Our Life Together | 232 |
| More Snippets and Memories | 234 |

| | |
|---|---|
| Kindness, Always | 239 |
| Busy Times | 245 |
| Dad and Mum's Retirement | 247 |
| Dark Clouds | 248 |
| Time to Move | 250 |
| Don't Tell Mum | 253 |
| Our Life in the Fast Lane | 255 |
| Holiday Snippets | 256 |
| Snippets of Memories | 257 |
| The Darkest of Clouds, Never Forgotten | 260 |
| More Blessings and More of Life's Storms | 263 |
| Battering Storms Ahead | 270 |
| Rebuilding With Love | 273 |
| Second Marriage, Happy Holidays | 285 |
| Why? Dear God, Why? | 294 |
| New Opportunities | 296 |
| Messy, Stormy Times | 299 |
| Christmas Heartbreak | 300 |
| The Strength to Rebuild my Web of Life | 302 |
| Back to Work | 304 |
| Nine Little Words | 306 |
| Life Changes Ahead | 308 |
| Could a Wish Come True | 313 |
| Gentle Arms of Future Happiness | 315 |
| Magnetic Attraction | 317 |
| Catastrophic Pain and Suffering | 322 |

| | |
|---|---|
| A Loss Like No Other | 330 |
| Balhill Water Gardens | 331 |
| More Fun than Golf | 334 |
| Gentle Changes | 338 |
| Our Wedding | 343 |
| Holiday of a Lifetime | 348 |
| Balhill Water Gardens continues | 359 |
| Goodbye to Balhill | 368 |
| Fun Parties and Dress-Ups | 374 |
| Happy Memories Waikiki | 377 |
| Walkabout Again | 386 |
| Blast from the Past | 397 |
| Dark Clouds Approaching | 399 |
| A Wish Comes True | 401 |
| Life Has Many Twists and Turns | 408 |
| Relentless Storms | 414 |
| Building New Threads in My Web of Life | 418 |
| Tip-Toeing Past Threads | 423 |
| Quick Glance at my Favourite Things | 433 |
| Time Waits for No One | 441 |
| Revisiting Some Precious Threads 50 Years Later | 444 |
| Reflections of My Book … Closing Chapters? | 446 |
| My Web of Life | 448 |
| My Queer-Odd Way of Writing | 450 |
| The Depths of Emotion, Love | 451 |
| Dreams Do Come True. Shhhh Moment | 452 |

## Strongest thread ...

Unequivocally, the strongest thread in my life, and one for which I am now able to be writing this book, was the blessing to be born to my beautiful parents, Bill and Peg (William and Margaret), their love for each other, teachings, strengths and wisdom in life, but most of all, the unconditional love bestowed on my brother and myself was a foundation from which I based my life.

This enabled me to question situations as they presented themselves; to know right from wrong, even though, like most finding their way on this journey, I, from time to time, deviated and failed to stay within the boundaries, finding myself balancing on weaker, finer threads, coming very close to being unable to keep my footing.

Fortunately, the many invaluable teachings and love instilled by Mum and Dad played the part it was designed to do. I am eternally grateful.

# About My Book

I have written this book in the hope that some of my life's memories, along with a small glimpse of our family's history, will not be lost in time but be passed on through the next generations, with a desire that they, too, will one day enjoy telling their own stories.

My book was never meant to be a word-perfect account of my life, but simply memories, written from the heart, as accurate as my memories (and memories of my darling mum) can provide. Certainly, some of the things I have written about are controversial or, unfortunately, sad, touchy subjects. I have, however, tried to write with the utmost respect whilst being truthful with my story. The book was never written to place blame, make fun of, or be hurtful. Although I have tried to be as accurate as possible, some inadvertent discrepancies with dates and times may occur. My intention was to ensure utmost respect to all persons named throughout the book, (both living or now in God's care.) I hope you enjoy reading my Web of Life.

I would sincerely like to thank all those who have helped me to write my story.

My not only a valuable proofreader and spell-check provider, but my wonderful husband, Paul.

My beautiful mum, Margaret (Peg), who provided me with many accounts of her life. I feel extremely blessed.

All of my adored children, family and friends, who not only provided me with the substance of my book, but helped me with the 'computer bit' which enabled me to type my story. Thank you!

*Lyn.*

## Please Note

This story is based on true facts. However, some names have been changed, and some events have been glossed over to protect the privacy of the individuals involved.

## Cultural Sensitivity Warning

Aboriginal and Torres Strait Islander people are warned that this book may contain names and pictures of people who have passed.

# Introduction

Some people have described their 'life's journey' as a turning wheel, rolling along through the ups and downs of an ever-changing path.

I feel, however, my life can be best described as a balancing act upon a beautiful spider's web.

Although perfectly joined by a myriad of tiny threads to ensure a long, lasting and enduring web, my Web of Life has encountered some very strong storms which have, from time to time, torn the delicate little fibres. When this has occurred, I have always been blessed with the strength to rebuild and not fall.

There have been many times, however, when my strength to hold on has been tested to the limit, but with the love of God and the unity of family (life's most precious gifts), I have been able to patiently wait for the strong wind and heavy rain to subside, allowing the sun to shine again. Happiness and high spirits!

The most precious of times (and I have been blessed with more than my share) is when the sun glistens through my 'Web of Life', bringing so much joy and happiness to my heart.

My story begins …

## The Beginning ... Part 1

As early as 1910 and 1912, Sainsbury brothers, Felix, Severin with his wife Annie, Lilo and Stanley migrated to Australia from their home in the countryside of Hampshire, England.

The nine Sainsbury brothers and two sisters had worked with their parents on many different farms and flour mills in that vicinity, the last of which was a farm located close to the picturesque, quaint village of Overton. This beautifully preserved little part of England would one day appear as one of the very strongest threads in my Web of Life's journey.

On the other side of the globe, over 9,000 miles away, the Australian Government had just introduced an initiative to increase the production and export of wheat and wool, thus bolstering the farming industry in Australia. Production of these commodities suffered badly as a result of the cruel 1914–18 war. Tragically, it was during this war that William and Susan's fifth-born, Felix Edmund John, was killed in action in France. Sadly, they were not the only parents suffering as many 1,000s of treasured sons perished during this terrible war, leaving many farms in Australia without a workforce and putting extreme pressure on the farming industry throughout Australia. The Australian Government advertised in England and other countries offering conditional purchasing of land in country areas, which would be a win-win for anyone taking up the offer, and, of course, a win for the Australian economy.

With what must have been tormenting mixed emotions of sadness and excitement, Violet, with son William, and two more of the Sainsbury brothers, began their long, arduous voyage to Australia, arriving many months later at Port Fremantle in Western Australia.

Not all of the brothers decided to take up the offer in the country. Severin established himself school teaching in Perth and decided to leave the farming to his other brothers after the painfully long and, more times than not, extremely nauseating voyage by ship to Australia.

Violet, and Willie, as he was referred to as a child, and three Sainsbury brothers alighted at Fremantle, only to then board a steam train to commence the 180-mile train journey required to reach their destination, eventually arriving at the small, somewhat isolated, Wheatbelt town of Nungarin. What a shock this must have been.

I can only imagine the anguish they felt leaving behind beautiful green pastures, close-knit communities, extended families and friends, with the comforts of a large brick homestead to be confronted with a very small, humble, tin and hessian dwelling with no running water, summer weather conditions that could melt the hat off your head, and of course, the incessant flies.

There was, however, no time to ponder, as the land had to be cleared and farmed to produce wheat, which it goes without saying, was an enormous undertaking. Aside from the extreme elements and isolation, they had to work with the use of minimum tools and machinery, thus encountering many setbacks and heart-wrenching hardships against all odds, but by the grace of God, Lavington Farm, fondly named, slowly began to emerge from the red-brown, sun-parched dirt into a progressing farm. Willie was only nine years of age when he arrived in Australia, but he worked willingly with his uncles, learning all the while.

The main diet for the family was rabbit, not surprisingly, as there were 1,000s of them. Hattie's ability to 'vary' the way she cooked rabbit was possibly an inherited gift from her own mother, but by adding flavour with the vegetables, she managed to grow, using carted dam water and much hard work, her large family did not go hungry. Rabbits, however invaluable as a food source, were vermin, and it was imperative if the crops were to survive, that they be eliminated.

Will/Bill, as he was referred to as he grew older, joined his uncles on a nightly basis to help with this almost impossible task of getting rid of those of crop-munching, continually breeding rabbits. Along with the many wonderful 'story-telling' old photographs I have in my possession, I found a wonderful photo of Dad as a young man in his Scouts uniform, standing beside a very large mound of dead rabbits, presumably taken after one such night.

Violet (Hattie, as her brothers called her) had the unenviable and almost impossible tasks of not only cooking, washing, cleaning, mending, milking the cow, tending the horses, and producing vegetables, along with a myriad of other duties, but also to the best of her ability, had to maintain a harmonious working and co-habitat environment in which to live. This was not easy with so many people, all with different opinions, living in such a small house. There were, to be sure, some very loud 'west country' accent discussions from time to time. Thank goodness for the survival of Hattie, 'if nothing else'. The farm was a stepping stone for the family, and as time went by, some of the brothers moved on to take up different opportunities.

*William Sainsbury and wife Susan (nee Lyle), early 1900s with their 11 children.*

*Ticket used by two of the Sainsbury family to come to Australia.*

*Family photo: Violet Harriet Valentine standing centre top, William and Susan seated with Tina leaning on her mother with their St Bernard family dog proudly seated in front. Many tales, heard from Uncle Monty, were about this dog 'barking' to put out the candles at night.*

*Violet Valentine Harriet Sainsbury,*
*14/02/1890 to January 1973*

This beautiful photo was returned to my dad after Uncle Monty passed away in 1996. How wonderful for me to read the inscription on the back of the photo, handwritten by Nanna Hattie herself, which read: To Lynette, I too loved my doll ... seven words that filled my heart with loving memories of time spent with Nanna Hattie. Always remembered, never forgotten.

*William Whistler Sainsbury,*
*my dad,*
*Born 21st July, 1918,*
*died 22nd February, 1989*

This amazing photo is of my dad before he was breeched, as it was called, meaning put into britches pants. Young boys were dressed in skirts in England in the early 1900s.

Christmas lunch outside the original Lavington Farm home. Left to Right: Uncle, Monty Uncle Aub, Nanna Hattie, person unknown, Bill/Dad.

*Dad as a young man in his Scouts uniform standing behind a mound of dead rabbits. Lavington Farm, 1920s.*

*Dad (William Whistler Sainsbury) reading in the sun outside the original Lavington farmhouse, 1920s. Book, possibly the Bible.*

*Nanna Hattie, Uncle Aub, unknown driver of amazing looking motor vehicle, dog and Dad/Bill*

*Uncle Lilo and Auntie Doris's Tent (home) at Elabbin siding, children sitting on mat so no snakes will get to them - Roy Hazel and Bill/Dad.*

# The Beginning ... Part 2

In Western Australia, the Goldfields Water Supply Scheme commenced in 1898, with Engineering Chief CY O'Connor needing an enormous workforce to achieve what most at this time thought impossible. Ralph Taylor, accompanied by his wife and family, arrived in Fremantle from the United Kingdom the early 1900s. Ralph immediately commenced work as a surveyor, draftsman, joining the hundreds of unsung men and women who made this now world-renowned achievement possible. Water was pumped through the pipes at Mundaring Weir in the hills of Perth to Kalgoorlie in the Goldfields in 1903.

Alan Walter Taylor, son of Ralph Taylor and Rose Ellen Taylor (nee Hill) was born on the 29th of October 1895. At a young age, he began an apprenticeship as a watchmaker/jeweller. Alan's artistic skills could be seen in his many handcrafted pieces of jewellery. This was a wonderful trade, which he thought would take him throughout his working life. Tragically, the event of the First World War in 1914 changed this, and many other plans, for Alan and 1,000s of young men worldwide.

Alan volunteered to join the Australian Army and serve his country. He, again, like many others, was not actually old enough, but with the need being so great for soldiers, managed to join as a stretcher bearer. He served tirelessly in the trenches in Europe alongside his comrades, venturing out on a cease fire to retrieve as many of the wounded as possible before the horrors of war began again. He was one of the fortunate to return home from war, but not without evidence of what was. He was wounded, and until just recently, our family was under the impression he was also gassed in the trenches with the extensively used mustard gas. He certainly suffered severe lung problems, and later in life, received a TPI pension. On returning from the war, he returned to his chosen profession as a watchmaker, jeweller.

Jess Watson, daughter of Robert George Watson and Agnes (nee McNeil), was born on the 25th of December, 1899. Robert George went to the WA town of Wagin in 1902 and farmed 'Eastfield' Nallian. Agnes was the first school teacher in this community.

Unbelievably, this part of my family's history reappears much later in my story as one of the ongoing Threads of Life.

Alan Taylor married Jess Watson on the 28th of December, 1920. They lived in Subiaco in Perth, and had four children, Rosellen Jess Blanch, who, from what Mum has always told me, was miffed that she was given three names when all her siblings only had two. Margaret June (Mum) was second-born. Then James Allen was the eldest son, followed by Donald Leigh.

Alan and Jessie ran a watchmaking jewellery business from the little corner shop in Rokerby Road, Subiaco. The family lived in the house upstairs from the shop. This building, although without its balcony, still stands today. Only a few years ago, Aunty Rose, Mum's sister, visited the house and told Mum how very small it was and how she could not ever remember as a child the stairs being so narrow and the rooms so small.

As children do, Mum spent many hours watching her father skillfully designing and creating beautiful and unique diamond rings and brooches. This love and appreciation of the fine jewellery is evident today with Mum's treasured collection, much of which being originally inherited pieces handmade by her very talented father.

Church and Sunday school was an important part of their upbringing, and walking to and from there was almost a part of life. In fact, Mum tells how, as children, they walked for miles and miles. From what I can gather, there was a very normal amount of sibling rivalry between Mum and her elder sister, Rose. One particular time, Mum's dad insisted Rose take Mum with her on an outing with a few girlfriends, as the girls intended to walk to the river. Strict instructions were given. Alan instructed his eldest daughter, "You be sure to look after Margaret June, (Peggy for short)" – such a cute little nickname). Reluctantly, Rose did as she was told. What he didn't know was that, on the other side of the river, a group of young, handsome Boy Scouts would be frolicking and calling out for the girls to join them.

It goes without saying that, within a very short time, all the older girls were swimming to the other side, all except Mum. Mum was not able to swim, but didn't want to be left behind either. It was an extremely fortunate one of the scouts noticed Mum drowning and came to the rescue. I don't think the day's events were ever relayed to their parents.

Alan's health was deteriorating. The fumes from the blowtorch used all day increasingly hampered breathing, so Alan had no choice but to give up his trade and commence a job that would hopefully allow an improvement in health. The family moved to the Maylands area. They moved a few times more until settling in Drummond Street, Inglewood. Alan was by then working as a tram conductor, which his children thought was just wonderful, especially when they caught the same train their dad was working on.

The Methodist Church was within walking distance from their home, and religiously every Sunday, Jess would dress the children in their Sunday best, and off they would go. The children would go to the Sunday school, and Jess would join her friends in the church choir. Mum enjoyed Sunday school and made many friends, including some with the surname Sainsbury.

# Marriage Through the Generations

*Marriage of Robert George Watson to Agnes Leishman McNeil, 5th November, 1896, with Florence William and George Watson.*

*My great-grandmother on my mother's side, Agnes Watson, pictured here with my grandmother, Jess Watson, standing on the left.*

Agnes Watson migrated to Western Australia from Scotland to become the first school teacher in Wagin, WA, in the late 1800s. Her grave has since been recognised and the headstone renewed at the local Wagin cemetery.

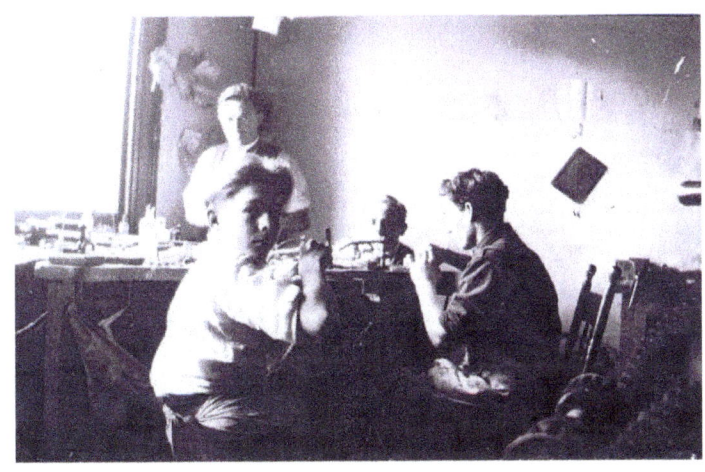

*Treasured photo of Alan Taylor (my grandfather on my mother's side), early 1900s. This photo shows him (blond hair) left and front, working as an apprentice watchmaker jeweller at a young age.*

# Marriage Through the Generations

*Marriage of Alan Walter Taylor (son of Ralph Taylor and Rosellen Hill) to Jess Watson (daughter of Robert George Watson and Agnes McNeil). 28 December, 1920. Married in Wesley Church, Subiaco, WA*

*Jess Taylor, (nee Watson)
born 25th December, 1899
Died 15 February, 1982*

*These photos show proud mum Jessie with daughters Rosellen Jess Blanch, born July 1922, left, and Margaret, born Margaret June, born 31st January, 1925*

*Left: Alan Taylor with his sons Donald and James.*

*Right: Siblings, James left, Margaret, centre, with Donald on the right.*

*Much later family photo.
Left to right: Margaret, Don, Jess, Alan, Rose and Jim*

# Two Hearts Collide

## Dad and Mum 1945

*William/Bill as a young man,*

*Margaret/Peg as a young lady.*

*Dad during Second World War. He served in New Britain, New Guinea, and was also posted to Darwin to repair the bridges and infrastructures which were damaged during the bombing of Darwin. Dad, seated, second from the right second row.*

*Dad, squatting right front*

*Dad, during Second World War.*
*Great photo. Dad, far right.*
*(Golly, I know where I get my knees from).*

Dad and Mum met in 1945. Dad had just been discharged from the army on compassionate grounds as he was needed to work on the family farm at Nungarin, as only two of Nanna's brothers remained on the farm by then, and both were aging and unable to cope with the heavy work involved.

Dad had served in the army for approximately six years, training at Puckapunyal and many army training bases in WA, including Northam and Cunderdin. During the Second World War, he was sent to Darwin to rebuild the bridges after the bombing of Darwin harbour. He also served as an engineer and driver in New Britten for some time. As far as the war went, Dad never spoke much of it. That was how it was – respect and solidarity. He did, however, speak very highly of the native people of New Britten, who the Australian soldiers affectionately called the Fuzzy Wuzzy Angels because of their abundance of fuzzy, thick hair. Dad would often tell of how these ever-willing men were always there for them, and the assistance they provided was invaluable. Indeed, they were thought of as angels. Being very clever with his hands, Dad would, during his leave time, carve beautiful pieces of jewellery from Mother of Pearl shell found readily on the wave-washed beaches of New Britten. He would send these lovingly carved pieces home to his mother and cousin Hazel. One of these very precious pieces was a heart made into a neck chain with Hazel carved on the back. To this day, I wear this heart neckpiece with much pride. I am only able to do so due to the kindness of my special Auntie Hazel (actually Dad's cousin).

It was respectful to call older people Auntie or Uncle in those days. Thus, I have always referred to Auntie Hazel in this manner.

Not long before her sad passing, I made a visit to her home, as she had been quite ill. We always had mutual things to chat about, one being our love of cats. This day, Aunty Hazel, while sitting patting her adored cat, said she had something special that she wanted me to have, saying that she knew I would be the one to appreciate it, and she handed me the beautiful hand-carved Mother of Pearl necklace.

My love for Auntie Hazel, and appreciation of this gift, I will treasure forever. Another very special item Dad made is a jewellery box. This piece he crafted from an empty cannon shell with diamond shaped Mother of Pearl inserts around the outside and on the lid. This jewellery box sat proudly on a linen doily in the centre of Nanna Hattie's dressing table for many, many years. Now it is situated in the middle of my dressing table, another of my most treasured possessions.

Mum was still serving in the Australian Army Medical Women's Service, AAMWS, attached to Hollywood Hospital in Perth. Here, Mum worked as a medical records clerk in the Engineers Department. She also worked from an old Salvation Army boys' home opposite the hospital. Mum was involved with the Scouts' organisation, which assisted with air raid precaution work during wartime. Boy Scouts, including Mum's brother Jim, escorted people to the many air raid shelters located in the streets of Perth. Thank goodness these blood-curdling alert sirens turned out to be precautionary, not actual.

Prior to her time in the army, Mum worked for Gibney & Sons, who were proprietors of a printers and advertising company in Perth. Mum commenced her working life as a lettering artist. Art, in many forms of the word, had been a big part of Mum's younger life, not only with her dad being such a wonderful jewellery designer but also having an uncle who was an amazing artist. Edwin (Ted) painted in oils, and his many landscapes were to be admired. Thus, Mum's talents of having the ability to draw, paint and create may have been inherited, who knows.

Whilst at Gibney & Sons, Mum would often commence work early to map out the most recent advancement of the German and Russian armies, then carry on with her normal working day as a commercial artist. Newspaper advertisements (whether it be hats, shoes, clothing and of course, cigarettes) were all drawn by hand with pen and ink.

I still proudly have in my possession many of Mum's amazing ink drawings which appeared in the daily newspapers during the 1940s. Mum often tells of the many intrusions to normal life the war brought with it. The city shop windows were replaced with boards; lights of any description were not to be used; even motor vehicles had to cover the headlights with tape, with only a small slit of light being permitted.

The air raid shelters were many in Perth, some of these remained until well after the end of the war. With all the sadness of the war came the blessing of kindness and the looking out for each other, and as Mum would say, many enjoyable social times spent with friends. It was during one of these happy social times that Kathy, a mutual friend of Mum and Dad, eventually convinced Mum that she should meet Sainz, as he was known. It just so happened that Kathy's father was the policeman at Nungarin. It must have been even a small world back then. Mum had never visited Nungarin, but knew of it as her dad at that time was a sergeant with the five BOD army camp based in the town of Nungarin.

Kathy arranged for them to meet on the 10th of March. In Mum's own words, it was love at first sight. They then became engaged on the 7th of April and married on the 30th of June 1945. They honeymooned in Bunbury and then commenced their wonderful life together at Lavington Farm in Nungarin.

Mum and Dad lived with Nanna, Uncle Monty and Uncle Aub for the first year. The adjoining farm, Sunnyside, was purchased from Mr Barstow in 1946.

Although there was a small house on the property, it did need work done on it to make it livable. Mum and Dad would spend all their spare time happily creating the tiny four walls they called home.

# Marriage Through the Generations

*Marriage of William Whistler Sainsbury to Margaret June Taylor on the 30th of June 1945 at Mount Lawley, WA*

*Dad and Mum's Wedding Party.*
*Left to right, Auntie Hazel, (Dad's cousin), Uncle Jack, Dad's best friend), Dad, and Mum (wearing the same wedding gown as her sister wore). Uncle Monty, (Dad's Uncle), and Auntie Rose, (Mum's sister). How beautiful were the bouquets?*

*How very fortunate to be able to revisit the threads of our life many years later with this most amazing photo of Dad and Mum's 40th wedding anniversary, showing their complete wedding party standing in the exact same sequence altogether after so many years.*

*I love this photo.*

*Left to right: Auntie Hazel (Dad's cousin), Uncle Jack, (Dad's best friend), Dad, Mum, Uncle Monty (Dad's uncle), Auntie Rose (Mum's sister).*

# Starting Out

Like all newlyweds, Dad and Mum didn't mind not having much. In fact, as Mum tells it, they had everything they needed. They had each other.

Farm commitments always came first, but nevertheless, and with much enthusiasm, they found the time to renovate a simple little weatherboard and hessian (ex-miners hut from Kalgoorlie) into a wonderful home filled with love. My *Web of Life*'s journey has allowed me to see the following generations in our family repeat much of the same process as they, too, delight in renovating their homes as their grandparents had done before them.

Mum was from the city, so I can only imagine how difficult it must have been for her to adjust to being so isolated, away from her family and without all the then thought of as the mod cons of city life. By the middle 1940s most city homes had a wash house inside and a separate bathroom and even an ice box to keep food cool.

Without complaint, Mum's first wash house was a copper in the back yard. I can best describe a copper used extensively in the country at that time as a 44-gallon drum on its end with a cut-out hole at the bottom for a wood fire. The copper itself was a large, round tub with a lip which then fitted into the open end of the 44-gallon drum, which held it from falling through. The copper was hand filled with water from the tank and a fire lit on the grate under the copper. Thank goodness clothing was tough back then, as everything was then pushed down into the boiling water with a wooden prod until the water resembled thin pea soup, at which time the sheets and clothes would be lifted out, wrung out by hand before being hung on the clothesline to drip dry.

Mum's first bathroom consisted of a large oval tin tub placed on the kitchen floor. Dad always positioned it in front of the Metters stove for a little warmth on a cold winter's night.

Let's also not forget Mum's first refrigerator, the Kalgoorlie Safe hung on the back veranda, being the only food cooler Mum had for many years. The Kalgoorlie Safe was also used extensively in the outback, and did, at least on a cold day, prevent the butter from turning completely into liquid. I can describe this best as a small tin cupboard with a door and the sides were fine mesh tin. The top was flat with a small lip creating a water tray. A hook was secured to the top so it could be hung at different sites to catch as much breeze as possible. A hessian bag was hung over the tin mesh sides. Water from the lid dripped very slowly through the tiny holes, keeping the bag damp. Thus, as the breeze blew through the wet bag, it had a cooling effect on the contents of the safe. Unfortunately, more than a gale force wind on a winter's day was needed to keep meat fresh enough to avoid that ever slightly greenish tinge. Never mind. It was simply amazing what a long, slow cook, after a quick wash in vinegar, will do to a 'just on-the-turn' lamb chop.

Over the years, one little story Mum has mentioned was of her first time on the back of Dad's motorbike during a wet, stormy, dark night. Farm bikes were mechanically sound, but little things like working headlights were not always on the need to have list. It was a cold, dark night and was raining heavily, so Mum rugged up and put a warm scarf around her head and nervously boarded the pillion seat of the bike. Dad was checking on some sheep which had broken through in to the new country. This was a concern, as the area had not been checked for any poisonous bushes. Dad explained to Mum that it would be much safer for her to stay with the bike as he hurried off to find the escapees. Mum said she remembered being cold, wet and so scared as the wind was blowing and she could hear all the different unexplainable noises coming from the bush. Mum explained how she had even imagined being eaten by wild animals.

By the time Dad returned, Mum was in a terrible state, crying uncontrollably, so much so Dad thought she had been physically hurt in some way. He quickly struck a match, only to get the fright of his life when he saw blood running down Mum's face. After burning his finger on the first match, he hastily lit another and, to his relief, realised what he first thought was blood was only red dye from Mum's scarf running down her distraught, tear-drenched face. Fright and fear quickly turned to relief, laughter and love as they headed home with a new story to tell.

*A wonderful old photo of Uncle Monty playing in the Nungarin band with Uncle Aub playing the piano. Mum painted the front of Uncle Monty's drum.*

*Dad in his tennis gear.*

# Pitter Patter of Little Feet

Mum always told me that she and Dad had planned to have two children, one boy – definitely a boy first – and one girl, which would be the second born. These were very high expectations, considering Mum was still very thin and still unwell as a result of suffering peritonitis just prior to being discharged from the army. The doctor had not drained the affected area after her appendix burst on the operating table; this caused blood poisoning and many infections, which reoccurred for some time. Thus, as you can imagine, Mum and Dad were delighted and over the moon with joy when the doctor confirmed they were expecting their first baby, with Mum's emphatic mind set on having a boy, and with no positive way of knowing the sex of an unborn child in the 1940s, it was no wonder that Mum's mother, Jess, was somewhat concerned, just in case this plan for a son didn't come to fruition.

With joy in her heart, Mum's amazing sewing skills were put to work, happily designing and making many beautiful baby outfits, including the bedding for the cot and pram and yes, all in blue.

Dad, being ever the diplomat, gently reassured Mum that a healthy boy or girl would be a blessing. Just prior to Mum's due date to give birth, a new doctor took over the practice in Merredin. Mum and Dad made the 30-mile trip to Merredin to meet the new doctor, Bill Gray, and for Mum to have her final check-up. Like most women, Mum always worried about her looks, particularly her nose. So, when her new doctor said,

"Hello, are you due?" Mum quickly put her hand on her face and said, "No, I might look Jew, but I'm not."

In the midst of laughter, Dr Gray reassured Mum he was only asking if she was due to have her baby. At least it did break the ice and Dr Bill Gray became a great friend of Mum and Dad's for years to come.

It was the month of June, and seeding was in full swing, which meant Dad was on the tractor day and night. Fortunately, they were working in the house paddock. Uncle Monty worked with Dad to get the seed in as quickly as possible, to take advantage of the forecasted pending rain. It was nine o'clock at night when Mum's labour pains reached the stage where she needed to signal Dad that it was time to take her into hospital. Dad had set up a special light for Mum to turn on when the need arose.

Mum was all packed and ready for the arrival of their baby boy. Things were done very differently back then: husbands would drive their wives to the hospital and then be told, "Go home and we'll telephone you after your baby has arrived."

Luckily, Nanna and Uncle Monty did have a telephone. Not many farmhouses had that privilege, and of course, Nanna was at the ready for this joyous news

Telephone exchanges were manned, and as the calls went through the switchboard, it was quite usual for lines to be left open, allowing more than one person at a time to hear what should be private conversation. It was all a bit of fun, but could cause a lot of angst, especially if someone, for example, knew how much money you had left in your bank account. There was a way of hearing if someone else was 'on the line', and as this was special and private news, Nanna was at the ready to ask the switchboard lady to make sure no one else could hear the news before Dad.

As Mum tells it, she was taken to the delivery room, which seemed to be miles away from the rest of the hospital, and was made *comfortable* on an icy cold, very narrow steel delivery table with a starched cotton sheet, her only defence against the bitterly cold winter's night. Mum tells of a very long, freezing, cold, painful night with only two visits from the midnight nurse, which failed dismally to relieve her pain and ever-present fear of what to expect. Dr Gray was called at 8:30 am to deliver Mum's first baby, after a few attempts by the sister to push the baby's head back. Dr Gray arrived to deliver, and with God's much-needed blessing, a boy, Brian William, was born at 9 am on the 18th of June, 1946. Elation and sheer joy, a son to carry on the name and one to take over the responsibilities of the farm. Dad and Mum could not be happier.

The rain on the tin roof of the hospital couldn't dampen everyone's elation, but the rain did make it difficult to dry nappies. Mum would stand for hours in front of the open fire in the small Nursery Ward drying nappies, remembering they were all cloth nappies with safety pins back then. Sadly, with Mum already being weak from the delivery of Brian, she quickly caught a chill from the damp air, which developed into pneumonia. Brian lost weight in hospital, and because Mum was so sick, he had to be put on cow's milk, which did the trick very nicely, with a plentiful supply from not the local supermarket, but from Daisy the cow in the tea tree cow shed. With love and help from Dad's mum, Hattie, and Mum's mother, Jess, both mother and baby gained strength gradually, and soon the joy of motherhood was being cherished to its fullest.

Mum tells of how Brian was a delightfully inquisitive baby and an outside child, always wanting to be 'doing' and following Dad everywhere, copying his every move. Not that we want to mention it, but unfortunately, many men smoked cigarettes, usually rolled tobacco. Dad would often relax beside the open wood fire at night and smoke a pipe. Brian wouldn't take a dummy, even when he was teething, but he did – don't tell anyone – suck a pipe. Fortunately, nobody made a fuss, and most people just thought it was cute. Yes, 'empty', of course. Dad and Mum loved being parents and loved being together in their home sweet home.

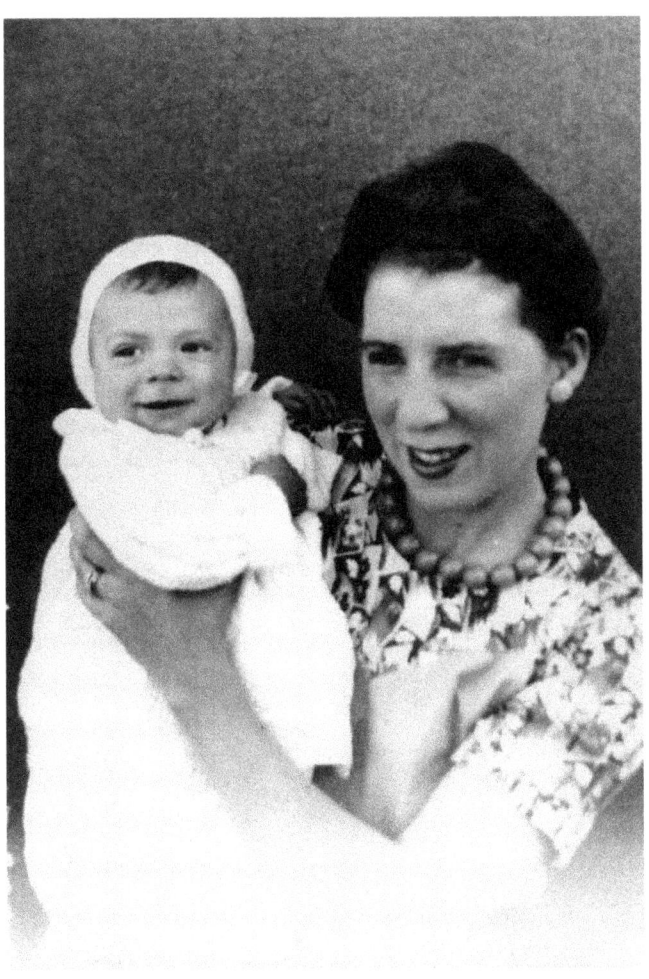

*Brian as a baby*

*Brian smoking his pipe. Don't tell anyone.
Tea Tree shed in background and even a glimpse of the dunny, oh,
sorry, lavatory down the back.*

# Pitter Patter of Little Feet 2

Brian was almost two years of age when Mum fell pregnant with their well-planned second child. Of course, the 'Jonesie' was put to great use once again, only this time the cotton used in the sewing machine (and every fabric sewn with it) was, you guessed it, PINK. Mum lovingly designed and made many new beautiful baby girl clothes. All the time, once again, Dad and Nanna Jess tried very hard to convince Mum that she just might have another boy. Mum wouldn't hear of it with this pregnancy. She even went so far as to buy a little doll ready for their much-wanted baby girl. This little rubber doll was a cream colour with light brown painted glass eyes, and was impregnated with a wonderful vanilla perfume, which lasted for many, many years. Now, just a few years later, (sixty-seven to be precise), this now dark brown, perished and smelly doll has joined the far too many items that I just can't bear to part with.

Kununoppin was the hospital of choice this time, as it was considerably closer – only fourteen miles from the house gate, but mainly because Mum had gained much confidence with Dr Samuels, who was the GP at Kununoppin.

With this birth, Mum was two weeks overdue when Dad drove her to the hospital, kissed her goodbye and was quickly hurried off home to await the news. The sister, the only one on duty for the night, walked Mum all the way around the open verandah to the very isolated delivery room. 6 pm that evening, Dr Samuels called to check Mum, and a decision was made to put a binder on Mum's stomach to help move the baby into position for delivery. He then left. The sister settled Mum on the very firm, narrow, cold, delivery table, and with reassurance in her voice, told Mum that she would be a long time yet and not to worry! With that, she very kindly gave Mum a kerosene lamp and said, "When you need me, come around to my room and I will walk across the road, let the Dr Samuels know, and then wake the caretaker so as he can start the engine for the lights."

As with most homes in the country during the 1940s, the hospital's only power source was a 24-volt generator or a kerosene lamp. Poor Mum! As instructed, she waited until she felt she couldn't last much longer without giving birth alone. Between contractions, she managed to struggle off the delivery table, then carried that little flickering lamp all the way around the long, very long, verandah to alert the sister that she was ready to give birth. Certainly slightly primitive by today's standards, but the doctor arrived in time. The binder did the trick. The lights were on, and lo and behold, I, Lynette Margaret Sainsbury, was born 30/01/1949. And so began my 'web of life', ever turning, ever twisting.

*Mum with me as a baby*

*Dad with me.*

*Mum looking very cute, always a trendsetter of her time. Dad just handsome Dad, with Brian standing and me in the beautiful cane pram.*

*Granita biscuits were around then, and are still a favourite for me.*

*Brian and me*

# Earliest Memories

Quite clearly, I can remember the cane pram being put on the back of the old, flat tray Ford truck, which was Dad and Mum's only means of transport at that time. Luxurious or what? The seat of the truck had a 4-6-turn soft spring base, but unfortunately, most of these springs had rusted off the wooden frame, popping through the very rough and itchy, wheat bag seat cover, making luxury a thing of the past. The pram handle was tied securely with binder twine to the wooden railings at the back of the cab, and then, with a little squeeze, we all piled into the ridiculously small cab, including tennis rackets, balls and, of course, a thermos of tea, cut sandwiches with a dusty water bag hanging on the front bumper of the truck being the most important necessity for any outing.

With Dad's whites pressed hard against the driver's door, Brian squashed in the middle, gear stick between his legs, and me on Mum's knee, off we tonked to tennis. Dad was a great sportsman. He loved his tennis, golf and rifle shooting, and was a member of all the clubs in the town. Mum hadn't had the same opportunities to play sport when she was growing up, but with the encouragement and support from the man she loved, she also came to enjoy tennis. She did, however, enjoy golf much more.

I was not a young baby, but children were put in prams up to the age of two or even older, remembering the country sporting grounds were mainly red, dusty dirt sticks and stones with many undesirable ants and critters ready to bite – not exactly suitable for young children dressed in their lovely, clean going out clothes to be crawling around on. I actually remember snuggling up in that cane pram with its lovely, powdery smell and soft pillow arranged comfortably for me to sleep on. So nice. I also remember when Mum and Dad brought a new lay-down burgundy pusher. I was obviously too big for the cane pram by then.

When there was a dance at the town hall, all the younger children were put into the side room to sleep whilst their parents enjoyed dancing to the music of one of the local bands, which was quite often Uncle Monty's band. The canvas pram was also very comfortable, but it did have the new canvas smell.

The safe cot was something I also remember (with somewhat of a feeling of affection). Safe cots were used extensively in the outback areas for as the name suggests, it was considered one of the safest cots to protect babies and young children from all sorts of invaders, such as the pet cats, flies, of which there were many, bugs, spiders, mosquitos, and even the occasional flying bat or too. It was a wooden-framed cot with a folding lid (as high as the cot itself), all completely covered in fly-screen wire. The lid could be folded back so the cot was an open cot, or folded over to ensure the baby child was safe from all creepy crawlies. I don't know why, but from a very early age, I developed a strong sense of smell, and even today, I can 'smell a fire a mile away', as the saying goes. Possibly, it was just the freshly washed bed clothes, baby powder and velvet soap combination, but that cot had the most beautiful smell.

As our home only consisted of four rooms and a small front veranda, when we were young, my brother and I shared a bedroom. I think I slept in my safe cot until the age of two or three.

One night, I remember uncontrollably vomiting everywhere in my special bed. What a mess! Within minutes, Mum and Dad were there. They were just the most loving, caring parents. Mum gave me a soothing, much-needed wash with lovely, warm water, which certainly would not have been easy to do in the middle of the night. Thank goodness for Dad's trusty Primus.

Working as always together, Mum and Dad sorted out the wet mess, changed the bedclothes, and before I knew it, I was once again wearing lovely, clean pyjamas tucked safely back in my warm, sweet-smelling bed.

Although I must have been very young, maybe two or three, when this occurred, I remember so vividly the day a big snake had slithered into the Tea-tree walls of the shed, which was only a stone's throw from our house. The shed was constructed from local Tea-tree branches placed vertically, bundled closely together, then using horizontal wire secured to a large strainer post to form the walls of the shed. This type of building material was commonly used for sheds and even some homes. Not only was it easily accessible due to the clearing of land for farming, but these types of buildings were extremely strong, waterproof, and as the breeze could blow through the walls themselves acted as a cooling system. Very environmentally friendly.

Unfortunately, these walls were perfect hiding places for snakes as well. One summer morning, I heard a lot of commotion going on outside. Mum was shouting 'Be careful!' and telling Brian and Dad to come away. Although I was still in my pyjamas and dressing gown, I ran outside, only to be confronted with another yell from Mum to 'Stay away! A snake!'

I clearly remember a saucer of milk being placed strategically to entice the snake to come out; we all waited at a distance, Dad much closer, with axe in hand. I might add here that death from a snake bite was a genuine reality back then due to the methods used for a snake bite, which was to place a tight tourniquet above the bite, cut with anything available at the time, a small slit through the fang bite and suck out the poison, making sure not to swallow. The distance from any medical facility was, of course, the biggest problem.

Eventually, the saucer of milk did the job it was intended to do, and so did Dad. The snake met a quick death and lay motionless in many little pieces, a sight I have never forgotten. We saw many snakes on the farm – under the back step, near the tank stand, on the road, in the chook pen, and, in fact, just about everywhere. To this day, I always remember Mum saying every time we went out of the house, 'watch out for snakes!' I must admit, I still have a very genuine fear of them.

Children spent much of their time playing outside. When we were growing up, Brian and myself were no different. We would either be with Dad in the shed, watching and learning how to build, repair and create, or simply playing on farm machinery, all being fun things to do. One of our most favourite pastimes was catching taddies in the creek. Sunnyside Farm was, as I always remember it, a very pretty farm, especially in the winter months. Our home was situated about a quarter of a mile from the main road into Nungarin. This main road was, however, just dirt and gravel, like most of the roads to the farms.

As a child, dirt roads were so much fun, especially when the school bus became bogged on our way to school, giving us exciting (usually a little exaggerated) news to share with the other bus kids, but more importantly, the townies. We were the envy of the whole school. We were not only lucky enough to be late for school without getting into trouble, but we also enjoyed the fun of getting muddy and playing on the side of the road while waiting for the bus to be pulled from the bog. Yes, dirt roads were fun.

This main road passed the top entrance to our farm, which, like all properties with livestock, was secure with a rusty but effective gate. Our driveway followed down an incline winding past the large, low-lying blue granite rock, past an avenue of Mallee gum trees along a well-worn track that ended at the gate to the house. In winter, the rock created a runoff into several little creeks, one of which ran down past the cow shed, down the side of the race to the bottom dam, as it was known.

The little catchment holes in the creek became ideal places to find tadpoles. The water was like ice, but it was such fun to see who could catch the most. Not so for the tadpoles. The rock also gave us a wonderful place to play, as all the little holes would have water in them, proving very handy for the poor little taddies when Mum refused to let us keep them in jam jars in the house. Moss grew over the rock, creating a soft velvet-like carpet of green. Tiny pink flowers would appear through this moss to create the perfect setting for a fairy's castle. I would spend hours making little houses for the fairies out of different shaped rock pieces and placed my tiny little plastic dolls on the chairs I had created. And when the day's play was over, I imagined the fairies enjoying the little houses I had made for them.

Milking old Daisy, as our milking cow was fondly named, was possibly an early morning job that my darling Dad could have done without, considering his very long working day on the farm. But somehow, he seemed to enjoy everything he did. With a metal bucket in hand, beret slightly tilted, and, of course, his 'little chicken' (me) right at his heels. Off, we went through the metal gate, down the incline, past another avenue of dew moistened Mallee gums, through the little creek and up the bank to the cow shed. Dad would happily whistle or sing funny little ditties all the way. These precious little tunes remain special to me; although I have forgotten many of the words. I am sure it doesn't matter too much, as Dad made a lot of them up as he went along. However, I can recall the words to one of my favourites. It went something like this, 'Down in the middle of the itty-bitty dam swam three little fishies and the mumma fishy too. Swim, said the mumma fishy, swim, if you can. So they swam, and they swam all over the dam'. The remaining forgotten words I now make up when singing with my great-grandchildren.

The cow shed was built with Tea tree and strainer posts, as was used to construct our house shed. And once again, my sense of smell comes to the fore with clear memories of the wonderful smells of the cow shed. I know it may be hard to believe, but cow manure mixed with straw, wheat, oats and dirt isn't unpleasant.

Dad always reminded me of the dangers of standing behind the back legs of a cow being milked. But like most children, I am sure I walk closer than I should have, as I can remember the flick of Daisy's long straw-like tail in my face a few times. Happily, I climbed over railings, went out into the yard to assist dragging a bale of hay back to the old cement bathtub, which had been put to good use as a cow feeder. The hay, coupled with a sprinkle of oats, kept Daisy contented while being milked. It was also exciting to see just how many mice would run out from under the stacks of hessian wheat bags when disturbed. I had no trouble keeping myself amused while Dad's labour of love, almost always three-quarters filled the bucket with fresh, warm milk. Over the years, Dad did teach me to milk the cows, but it is actually harder than you think, and if the cow becomes unhappy, as they often did with beginner milkers, understandably, they would move around, accidentally treading on little toes. One would learn very quickly just how heavy a cow can be.

Getting the milk home to Mum without any little bush flies dropping into the froth was quite a task. If milking took a little longer than it should, the warmth of the early morning sun would quickly bring them out. Most mornings, luckily, it was still nice and cool, and once home, the milk was quickly put into jugs for the cream to settle on top. We were very fortunate, being a sheep and wheat farm by this stage, as well as having one or two wonderful milking cows and an amazing vegetable garden, nurtured to perfection by my adored Nanna, both Lavington Farm and Sunny Side Farm were almost self-sufficient.

*A photo of me dressed warmly, standing under the clothesline,*

*Wood heap to the left, pepper trees behind. Age one to two years.*

*Me with one of my Cupid dolls. I always loved my dolls*

*Photo of me and Brian taken in Perth, our clothes, all lovingly sewn by Mum.*

*Me at the beach during our annual holidays at Palm Beach.*

*The only photo of me with both my nannas, Nanna Hattie, Nanna Jess and me*

*Uncle Monty's twin spinner Ford in the background.*

*Nannie Hattie dressed to go to Merredin to shop*

*This is one of those pictures where the true meaning of every picture tells a story. As you can see, I was not happy. Stephanie was allowed to dress in a pretty dress for Auntie Shirl's and Uncle Don's wedding. I, on the other hand, had to wear my pyjamas.*

*How embarrassing.*

# Young Childhood

Our house, which will always be home to my heart, was situated on a half-acre block of land, fully enclosed with, wishful thinking, a rabbit-proof fence.

I will try to paint a picture for you.

The back of the house faced east; if sitting on the back step – watch out for snakes – to the right of me was the wash house, behind which the main large water tank sat on a very high tank stand to enable gravity-fed water to flow to the house. The tank stand, along with almost everything else that was or could be built, was cleverly designed and built by Dad.

For this project, he used recycled piping and metal. Dad was a perfectionist; thus, after many weeks of work and many more coats of silver-frost paint, the tank stand was not only finished, but it was there to stay for years to come. Looking about 15 yards straight in front was the clothesline. Clotheslines were constructed using fencing wire strung tightly between two posts with a prop in the middle of the wire, used to stop the clothes dragging in the dirt or, more upsetting, in the grass seeds. Much to Mum's horror, the combination of Dolly pegs, slippery fence wire and strong easterly winds, we were regularly confronted with the unenviable task of picking the grass seeds from woollen socks and clothing. Behind the clothesline was an impressive wood heap piled high with mainly Mallee roots. The axe was wedged firmly into the large chopping block.

Directly behind stood a row of large peppercorn trees that graced the back fence. Thank goodness for these very attractive trees with an abundance of brightly coloured seed pods and most of all, fresh, clean-smelling perfume, which, thanks to the ever-present easterly winds, gave slight relief from the other odour in the backyard. The outside lavatory was in the left-hand corner, as far away from the house as possible, which was a good thing. This is one smell I can honestly say I have never missed. Although Mum used gallons of fennel, a strongly scented liquid used to deodorise, the very unpleasant odour was always there to greet you when you had to go outside.

Lavatories were renowned for being home to many spiders. Ours was no different. The trick to getting rid of the many spider webs, and hopefully spiders, was a little highlight to the task. An old rag was wrapped around a green branch just long enough to reach the pitch of the lavatory roof, dipped in petrol, and then, when Dad was in position, which included us being well enough away so as not to be burnt, but close enough to see, Mum would light the rag.

We always wondered how Dad could manage to burn all the spider webs inside the lav without burning the wood structure to the ground. Getting away from that smell, to the north left of the house was the Tea tree shed and a separate fenced-off garden area. Mum didn't have to grow many vegetables, thanks to Nanna's ever producing garden. But I can't forget how proud she was when the fenced garden boasted an abundance of ready-to-pick watermelons and rock melons. Usually, this mouth-watering treat was only experienced while on our annual summer holiday in Rockingham. How extremely upsetting for us all, but particularly Mum, when on her return from town, she was greeted with the garden resembling a cow's picnic. The gate had been left open, and the cows didn't need an invitation. Poor Mum.

I can remember Dad trying so hard to console a distraught Mum, reassuring her unsuccessfully, I might add, 'that one or two melons with only small hoof prints embedded in them will be fine to eat'.

Moving on … the front of the house faced west and was pretty bare, with only a well-remembered never-to-be left-open gate leading down to the cow shed.

*Photo of the lavatory down the back. We were not permitted to call it the dunny That was not nice. Peppermint trees along the fence.*

*General Grant tank in the chook pen. Lavatory to the right.*

*Happy memories of me holding Fang Woo the Claw cat, and Brian holding Speck, the magpie. How big is that cat!*

*Brian and me sitting on Dad's Ariel motorbike*

*One of my favourite photos, because I felt so proud and warm wearing my pink fluffy jumper, which Mum had knitted, and burgundy corduroy jumpsuit, which, of course, Mum also made for me.*

One of the most delightful aspects of being brought up on a farm was the enjoyment of always being involved with animals. Pets to love and care for, farm animals to learn about, and even the opportunity to learn about the not-so-nice animals and reptiles. Most children could only dream of having so many pets and animals to interact with. We were truly blessed.

As young children, we were able to experience the happiness that came from little things such as feeding the chooks, collecting the eggs, patting the dog, cuddling the cats, and so much more. As early as I can remember, we had at least one or two cats. Still, my favourite pet by far.

Although Dad named our cow Daisy, a pretty predictable name for a cow, he somewhat extended his imagination with the naming of his cat. Fang Woo the Claw was a very, very large, dare I say it, slightly ugly tabby cat. He had large, fang-like top teeth, which protruded down over his bottom lip, giving the impression of anger. Luckily, this was furthermost from the truth. He was, in fact, a loving, placid cat, only ever showing those claws as he lay in the sun, rolling in a lazy stretch.

Although Woo was Dad's cat, he shared himself around to suit his own needs, as clever cats do. Mum's love of cats wasn't quite as evident as ours, to say the least. Poor Mum, we found out later that she just couldn't handle the feel of the fur. Cats are very smart, of course. Woo knew where he stood with Mum.

Bedtime for Brian and me was a routine. Go to the toilet, wash our face and hands and feet, clean our teeth, kiss Dad Good night, and into bed. Right on cue, Fang Woo the Claw would scramble under the blanket straight down the bottom of my bed as Mum walked through the door to tuck us in and say goodnight.

Cats may be smart, but of course, Mums are smarter, and every night, Mum would pat the bed heavily and make the same statement: 'I hope you haven't got that cat in the bed with you,' knowing full well he was. Without a doubt, the extra loud purring didn't help my cause. Mum would remind us to say our prayers, kiss us goodnight and leave to join Dad for some quiet time. Woo would stay only as long as it suited him.

In the morning, whilst Dad was getting wood for the kitchen fire and making a cup of tea, Woo was, once again, Dad's cat. He would jump on his back and lay around his shoulders, seemingly not even hanging on.

Our dog's name was Sandy. I'm not sure what breed he was, but of course, that didn't matter a hoot to us. He was our dog, and we loved him. He did help work with the sheep, but was not a trained sheepdog; he was just a wonderful pet. He would follow us around as though keeping an eye on us. He was such a lovely dog.

The gate to the chook pen was behind the shed. We were given the task of feeding the chooks, making sure they had water and collecting the eggs. However, there were many repeated instructions to follow prior to these very responsible daily duties: 'Put your boots on, don't leave the gate open. Watch out for the rooster, check the snakes before you put your hand in the laying box, and don't drop the eggs.' Now that's a lot of pressure for a kid, especially as I did have a tendency to be a little clumsy.

Lambing season was by far the best time. The survival of the newly born lambs was of the utmost importance as sheep, including the wool they produced, were a major source of income for the farm. During lambing season, the sheep were checked two to three times a day to ensure the ewes weren't in trouble whilst giving birth. There were no vets within coo-ee of us. Thus, farmers had to possess many more skills than one could imagine. Many times, the ewes would, for one reason or another, leave their lamb soon after birth. Blind to the sadness of this, and if I could prove to Dad that the lamb's mummy wasn't allowing it to feed, I was able to take it home and look after it. So exciting!

Little lambs are adorable, but of course, lots of work. We only had cows' milk, which was not really suitable for lambs. The milk had to be scalded, and then a hot iron bar would be put into the milk to provide the lamb with iron, then cooled to perfect feeding temperature. Thank goodness, when we were children, the good old King brown beer bottles were readily available.

In those days, they were used for everything, including bottling tomato sauce, homemade ginger beer, garden path edgings and feeding bottles for the lambs and any other animals that needed a bottle of milk. The next little problem was the teat, which, in fact, was not a problem at all, as Nanna had almost perfected making feeding teats from old bike or car tyre tubes. How clever! The teats were black in colour, and I'm sure they tasted like rubber, even to a lamb. But after Nanna carefully rolled a triangular piece of tube into shape and stitched it together using a darning needle and string, lo and behold, a teat sat proudly on a brown feeding bottle.

Brian and I were delighted watching little lambs' tails flick back and forth and see how their once flat tummies puff out to being fat tummies so quickly as they drank. Most lambs were put back with the flock as soon as they were able to survive on their own. But I was, for some reason, allowed to keep Bubby, as I called him, just that little bit longer.

Bubby grew quickly, maturing into a young ram, and in doing so, he grew horns, literally. One morning whilst playing in the fenced enclosure where Bubby was kept, he decided to show his maturity and began bunting me. At first, it was funny, but after baling me up against the corner post and a few more heavy bunts, the fun went out of the game, and to my embarrassment, I had to call out for Mum's help.

We were never allowed to scream or cry wolf, as it was commonly referred to, unless we really needed help. Mum came to my assistance quickly. With Dad's reassurance that Bubby would not come to any harm – tongue in cheek – he was put with the rest of the flock.

Bulls can be very large and not so friendly animals, but they also had their place, which was to reproduce and provide our farm with wonderful milking cows. But later, Dad did experiment a little with beef. Once again, everyone became involved when a calf was born.

Most births went as nature designed. However, I do recall one time everyone having their vet's hat on to help a young cow deliver her calf. We watched with mouth and eyes wide open with the wonderment of a calf being born – all in a day's life on a farm. Calves are so very cute, but to experience a calf lick your hand with its sloppy, wet, very sandpaper-like rough tongue is enough to delight any young child. Their big eyes and eyelashes can just melt your heart.

Some of the not-so-nice animals were fox, as they would target the sick and injured animals. Horrible to see! Although we had many different birds on the farm, crows, however, were disliked by all farmers. They, too, would prey on the sick and vulnerable, even pecking the lamb's eyes out as they were being born.

Snakes were my greatest fear, and that fear has remained with me always. We encountered many sightings of snakes – under the back step – in the chook pen – under the tank stand – in the Mallee heap – under the clothesline – and in more places than I wish to remember. Bobtail lizards were plentiful also. They looked scary, but weren't as dangerous. Nanna would feed the 'bobbies', as we called them, with a saucer of milk, as she claimed they kept the snakes away. Good enough for me! Little Mountain devils were also scary looking, but after a small amount of coaxing, I would enjoy watching them change colour when placed on different parts of my clothing.

Kangaroos, rabbits and emu were considered pests. Unfortunately, they could, and did, do an enormous amount of damage to fences and the crops; being the farm's main source of income, many ways were used to eliminate these wild animals from ruining the crops, including trapping, baiting and shooting. Rifles were part of the farm's necessities. We were all taught to use the .22 rifle. Mum was a very good shot. But no matter how hard she tried, those destructive crows avoided the bullet every time, flying off into the distance with a gawwwww.

Dad was, without a doubt, the kindest, most gentle person ever, and shooting an animal was only done to avoid suffering or if anyone was in danger of being hurt. Dad taught us that guns were to be treated with the utmost respect. The .22 rifle stood on the back verandah at all times, never loaded, but always ready.

The weather, particularly rain, was always uppermost on everyone's mind. Outlying farming communities such as Nungarin had a paltry average rainfall of 10 inches per year. Therefore, to have rain at the right time of the season was extremely important. Rain, by far (and/or the lack of it), was the most talked about, prayed for, argued over, worried about, thought of and watched out for element ever. Subsequently, the most rejoiced blessing was its eventual arrival; at last, this precious, long-awaited gift would make a gentle entrance with tiny drops just enough to release an amazing perfume of rain-moistened stubble mixed with dampened, parched dirt.

Then, before you had time to enjoy the moment, down it would come. Very quickly, water flowed from the rock, down the creek and into the bottom dam. With the good day's downfall, all the dams on the farm would have their supplies replenished. Unbelievably, with the first rains, fresh green grass seemed to appear almost instantly, and so did the mushrooms. We loved mushroom season, as short and sweet as it was. Mushrooms were plentiful, especially around the cow shed; there has to be something said for natural fertilizers. The only small problem was that Dad was the only one in our family who actually enjoyed eating them. I suppose it worked well. We loved finding and picking them. Mum enjoyed preparing and cooking them. And Dad, well, I'm sure he was just a little glad mushrooming was a short-lived event.

With the arrival of rain, playing outside was curtailed for a short time. Dad had built a bench on the back verandah with a cupboard underneath in which we kept our toys. We were very fortunate children and had many wonderful toys to play with, keeping us amused for many happy hours. Toys were very different when we were young. Boys' toys, as they were called, consisted in the main of cars, bikes, trucks, tractors. Girls' toys, on the other hand, were dolls, prams, tea sets, kitchen items and more dolls. This suited me, as from a young age, I developed a strong affection for dolls. Any doll would do – even poor Fang Woo the Claw suffered the indignity (for a male cat) of being wheeled around in my doll's pram, dressed in a baby's outfit and bonnet.

Although we did have many beautiful toys to enjoy, we were taught from an early age to appreciate what we were given. And this did not only refer to our toys. Mum and Dad taught us to look after our things and anything that was damaged in any way was repaired immediately. This very simple but ever so important teaching by our parents has proved so beneficial throughout our lives. Many of my dolls, including Blinky Bill, a very special mohair teddy bear I received from Nanna on my fifth birthday, now sit proudly in a purpose-bought glass cabinet for my own grandchildren and great-grandchildren to enjoy, although, because of the sentimental attachment, these are 'look but don't touch' dolls.

Dad and Mum used the bench top for a myriad of projects, including punching a new hole through a leather belt, stamping a metal eyelet into the corner of a golf towel, preparing pickling onions, cleaning mud from shoes, fixing a bike tube, and, most importantly, repainting golf balls.

Golf balls were very different back then. They were constructed with a small sack of liquid in the centre, surrounded by yards and yards of rubber bands, which would be wound tightly around and around until the correct size of the ball was achieved. The balls were also slightly smaller than we know now. An extremely hard, stippled white casing was then moulded over the rubber, finishing the golf ball. 'Waste not, want not' was a common expression and most times, ours was no different. Nothing was thrown away that could be reused, mended, painted or changed to serve another purpose; golf balls were no different.

Golf played a big part in Mum and Dad's social life. Winter was the only season suitable to play golf in most Wheat Belt areas. Golf balls were of value, like everything else in those days. People didn't just throw them out when they became damaged and old. No, no, no, they were repainted many times before they were then retired to the practice bucket to be used at home. Dad would stick sewing pins into the dirty, scuffed golf balls, then dip them into a correctly textured white paint and hang the balls on a taut string to dry. Presto, shiny new white golf balls!

*Dad driving one of the earlier metal-wheeled tractors.*

*Dad driving on one of the rubber-tyred tractors, as I knew them.*
*The sweet-smelling dirt, a never-forgotten delightful smell.*

*Dad repairing a tine or two, with Keith and Brian also enjoying being face down in the damp soil.*

The first rains also signalled that seeding season was very close. Most paddocks were seeded every second year, as the leftover stubble from harvest was the main feed for the sheep and cows. It was done on a rotation basis to allow nutrient and oxygen-producing weeds to grow. The types of soil on our farm varied considerably, which was a great benefit, as even with a bad-yielding year, at least one type of soil would usually produce enough seed for the next year. The remaining dry stubble and weeds were ploughed into the paddocks prior to seeding.

I was always very excited when Dad was working in one of the house paddocks, as we called them. Mum would be able to carry the morning tea out to meet Dad as he was working. Of course, Dad's 'little chicken' would stumble along behind

Mum, ever so hopeful that Dad would allow me to ride on the Fordson tractor with him. Mum would always wait patiently for Dad to complete a lap of the paddock so he could enjoy a well-earned cup of hot soup and sausage roll. Mum was a wonderful cook, and always ensured Dad had meals on time, even when he worked all through the night. It was extremely cold during seeding, but we all dressed accordingly, thanks to Mum's sewing abilities. And besides, when you're a kid, as long as you're doing something, you don't seem to feel the cold.

Yes, I was allowed to do a couple of laps. For me, it was an exhilarating feeling bouncing along propped up on a purpose-built metal seat with the icy cold easterly winds almost cutting through my face, the only part of me exposed to the elements. Then the turn of the corner with an instant burning heat from the engine, accompanied by that wonderful smell of diesel. Dad would whistle while he worked, always checking if I was okay, patiently stopping for me to do a wee behind the tractor tyre. And this was no easy feat. Just finding the buttons on my trousers through all the layers of clothing was difficult enough without making sure I didn't get my shoes wet. Oops. Oh well, they will blow dry. Back on the tractor and away we went, icy cold breeze on my face. Dad would do a few more laps, and then it was time for me to go back to the house. The furrows left by the plough discs were quite deep, and whilst trudging all the way home, I would often stumble and fall into the dirt – not that I minded one little bit. In fact, to this day, I still love the feeling of just-turned-over soft, damp, ever-so-sweet-smelling dirt.

# After Ploughing

No rest for the wicked, as Dad would often say; no sooner ploughing had finished, seeding began in earnest, and the never-ending conversation about rain would once again grace every smoke break, morning tea, afternoon tea and meal break. It was, however, so important to get the seeding done as quickly as possible to capitalise on any rainfall, no matter how little.

Seeding was done using a combine seeder. Wheat grain and super phosphate (Supa) was transported in hessian bags by truck to the paddock being worked, and loaded by hand into the Combine. The Combine had a narrow railing to walk along with separate compartments (bins) in which the wheat and supa was poured. This was a back-breaking job, not only because of the weight of the bags, but then maneuvering to drop the bags into the correct position without any spillage, including cutting the binder twine and trying to open the bag, made this task very difficult indeed.

At a very early age, Brian was driving most of the machinery and vehicles on the farm. In fact, he commenced his farming apprenticeship at a very young age, excelling not only in farming crops and sheep but in all aspects of farming, including motor mechanics, welding, fencing, plumbing, shearing, wool classing, carpentry, metal work, electrical and so much more. Dad was an amazing teacher, and Brian enjoyed learning this; coupled with a wonderful father-son bond enabled them to not only always work harmoniously but also share happily many sporting and social interests together.

Driving the tractor during seeding was taken very seriously, especially the cornering, because as much ground as possible had to be planted for maximum return of crop. This became a challenge to get it just right, and Brian loved to please Dad with his work. On the other hand, whilst enjoying the ride, I just loved the even pattern the tines made in the corners of the paddock.

Between the time of ploughing and seeding, plovers, a beautiful little native bird of the Wheatbelt areas, would nest on the ground in deep plough furrows, sheltering from the cold winds and other birds of prey. Unfortunately, when the machinery once again entered the paddocks to commence the seeding process, the dear little birds were often still waiting for their chicks to hatch. This became one of the most loved and important jobs. The little plovers depended on me! My eyes could be watering with the cold, but Dad had entrusted me to watch out for the nests. Surprisingly, it was quite easy to spot the nest as the mother bird, on feeling the danger of the approaching tractor, used her instinctive survival tactic; she would leave her nest and drop her wing to appear wounded, and the predator would be attracted to the wounded bird, not her chicks. So clever.

As soon as I saw this cleverly executed charade, I would gleefully alert Dad, who, of course, was already aware of the situation, but Dad, being the wonderful dad he was, thanked and praised me for my efforts as he brought the tractor to a stop. Very quickly and gently, we moved the two or three eggs or chicks to an already worked part of the paddock, hopefully enabling the chicks to one day join their mother in flight.

# Down Nan's

Over time, most of Hattie's brothers left Lavington farm to pursue their own chosen paths in life. Lilo, accompanied by wife, Doris, and two small children, Hazel and Roy, moved to Elabbin, a small railway siding where Lilo worked loading wheat onto the goods train to be taken to the city. Here, their house was a very basic tent, which was harsh enough without all the other almost impossible conditions they faced daily. Doris was given one kerosene tin filled with water for the day's usage, which included drinking, cooking, bathing and washing. Quite a feat for anyone, especially during the searing hot days of summer. Doris cooked many a rabbit stew on an open fire, and managed to cover the dirt floor in their tent with an old carpet mat to give the tiniest of home comforts. They had to suffer freezing cold winters, extremely hot, dry summers, bush flies, bull ants, wild fox, mosquitoes, and, of course, venomous snakes. The tale has it, Lilo, endeavouring to alleviate the ever-present fear of being bitten by a poisonous snake, explained to his anxious wife, "Don't worry, Doris. Just sit the kids on the carpet and they will be fine. Snakes don't like carpet."

After many years of blood, sweat and tears and many moves from one town to another, they finally relocated to the suburb of Inglewood in Perth, astonishingly, with their three children, Roy Hazel and Colin, safely in tow. Much later in my story, this lovely lady, Doris, will rejoin my Web of Life, guiding me towards one of the most unbelievable and special threads of all, resulting in sheer joy with the sunshine once again glistening through my web of life. Garnet had already settled in Perth to take up his chosen field of school teaching. Aub (Albert) remained on the farm.

The remaining brothers, from what I can remember being told, also moved to other towns, mainly in the southwest of WA. Nanna, Uncle Monty and Aub moved into a newer farmhouse, which was much closer to the main Nungarin to Knungajin Rock road.

Sadly, Aub passed away in this home in 1947.

Not many years later, and after I was born, Keith, Nanna's great-nephew, came to live with Nanna to finish his schooling at Nungarin. As was the case with most young boys of that time, Keith left school at an early age to work on the farm with Dad and Uncle Monty. Years of hard work and more hardship than imaginable was beginning to pay off, as the farm had become a fine wheat/sheep property, possibly as a result of careful planning and being very frugal.

I remember with a light heart the many discussions over a cuppa while sitting around the kitchen table about how to best improve, rebuild or buy a new whatever, fix the old whatever, replace it, don't replace it. And of course, within these many conversations, Uncle Monty's predicted comment in his very broad West English accent, "We'll all be ruined if it don't rain." Such fun.

Dad and, of course, his little apprentice would spend their time working evenly between Sunnyside and Lavington, which by this time, was one and the same farm. Nanna and Uncle Monty and Keith, lived together, but for as long as I can remember, their house was always referred to as Nan's or Down Nan's. I adored my Nanna and just loved spending time with her. So as soon as Mum would even breathe a word about 'Dad's going down Nan's', I would, like a shot out of a gun, have my boots on and be waiting near the old Ariel motorbike ready to go. Brian, resembling a miniature dad with his matching beret tilted to one side and a cheeky grin, was allowed to ride on the pillion seat. Dad would lift me onto the petrol tank of the motorbike, feet tucked up, cradled by Dad's arms, and hanging on for grim death, off we would go Down Nan's.

Memories of the many times spent with Nanna are those of happiness, excitement and of learning new and different things. These special and precious memories are to me, as vivid today as they were yesterday. Being allowed to sleep at Nanna's on the weekend or school holidays was even more wonderful.

Brian was the gate opener and closer as Dad, Brian and I bumped along happily on the old but very reliable farm bike through the adjoining paddocks towards Nanna's, checking each sheep trough as we went, with Dad whistling all the way. There were many gates to open and close on the way, but finally, the back house gate was closed, and the motorbike slowly tonked over the crackling clay dirt, coming to a stop near the water tank at the end of the back veranda. After ensuring Dad that I didn't burn my leg on the hot exhaust pipe, he lifted me off the tank, and before my feet hit the ground, I was off to see Nanna. Nanna would quite often be sitting on the back veranda, mending wheat bags with binder twine, always singing or humming as she worked. Her eyes lit up when we arrived, and after showing Dad the pile of bags ready to be used again, she would say, "Come in, my son, we'll have a cuppa."

Squeak went to the fly-screen door as we wiped our feet on an old wheat bag recycled as a doormat before entering the warm kitchen. The kitchen was the hub of the house with so much going on all at the same time. Uncle Monty would be checking the bank statements. Keith would be fixing a part of his bike. Nanna checking a pie or tray of biscuits in the wood oven. Nevertheless, everyone stopped for a hot cuppa.

The centre of the kitchen had a large square wooden table with turned legs, always with one or more seersucker tablecloths covering it. The wooden chairs had high backs and were painted cream using a lead-based paint, as was the case with all gloss paints in the 1950s. Although Brian and I spent most of our time with adults, it was still a time when, for the most, 'children were to be seen and not heard'. We would love sitting listening intently to all the loud – sometimes very loud – morning tea chatter as Nanna would pour another cup of tea for everyone. The teapot was large, made of baked enamel with a flip-top lid. It was placed on the hearth of the wood stove to keep hot, being refilled with boiling water as the need arose. Brian and I were permitted to have a cup of tea with sugar, but the adults made sure that the sugar wasn't overdone. The diamond-cut glass sugar bowl was the attraction for me, which, as fortune has it, I still have the privilege of admiring this same sugar bowl as it sits prominently in my glass cabinet.

Uncle Monty was so funny, as he would saucer his tea and slurp it down while still talking in his fascinating West country accent. Dad and Keith would be working out when to get the shearers in; Nanna would be reading a letter which she had received from Auntie Doris as she passed around the biscuits. Oh, yes, now I realise these morning tea sessions must have been the wonderful training ground, and the very reason Brian and I enjoyed talking so much. This is my story, and I'm sticking to it.

The pipeline from Knungajin Rock, the local water catchment, ran past Nanna's front gate, which allowed her to access this most valuable commodity, thus enabling her to have an even bigger and more amazing garden. As you walked out from the kitchen door, you would look through an archway covered in grapevines, under which, placed on the ground, were two or three saucers of milk, being nourishment for Nanna's pet Bobtail lizards. To the left of the grapevines was one garden enclosed in corrugated tin and boasting lush Cape gooseberry bushes and strawberries. To the right was an even larger corrugated tin enclosed garden with, when in season, lettuce, tomatoes, carrots, cauliflower, beans and peas, in fact, you name it, Nanna grew it. There has to be a lot said for the value of sheep poo and water.

*I've always loved this photo of Brian, Nanna Hattie, Mum and me with Uncle Monty's pride and joy car at that time. I think we were all dressed up to go shopping in Merredin, possibly to go to Atkinson Drapery, where Mum purchased most of the material used for making our clothes. Taken at the side of Lavington Farm homestead, early 50s. I noticed Brian's home-sewn beret, just like Dad's. I'm not sure about Mum's design of my hat, but I think it kept the sun out of my eyes.*

The telegraph line drooped proudly between the not-so-upright poles, also leading past the front gate all the way to the Knungajin telephone exchange. To have a telephone was such a privilege, and no one took this privilege for granted. The phone itself was a large, rectangular-shaped wooden box attached to the wall with a metal handle, Bakelite fixed mouthpiece and a lift-off earpiece. Nanna's telephone was on the passage wall next to the front door. How fortunate we were to have access to this modern equipment.

Afternoons we were as busy as mornings on the farm. However, Nanna was always willing to let me help with the daily chores. Washing the dishes was one of my favourite jobs, not for any other reason than that of using the automatic soap dispenser. Velvet soap was cut in half and one half placed into a small, rectangular fly wire case, which had a six-inch long wire handle. The little wire case was then clipped shut, and dipped into the hot water whilst vigorously moving it back and forth, creating much froth and bubbles. What fun! I'm sure more soap than necessary was used, and maybe the kitchen windows didn't require the washing they received, but darling Nan would just wipe up the water and hand me another plastic bowl to wash.

We also needed to get the wood in ready for the cold night ahead. My arms were almost at full stretch as I struggled independently with the very large homemade wheelbarrow through the grapevine archway to the wood heap. I would always try to go a little faster when passing the old gum tree because of the smelly fly bait, which hung precariously from one of the lower branches, abuzz with trapped blow flies. Yuck. These types of fly bait systems were not only a common sight, but they were also reasonably effective. A small amount of raw meat was placed in a large glass bottle with a funnel secured into the neck of the bottle. With the warmth of the day, the meat would soon rot and presto, the flies couldn't resist crawling into the bottle, unable to get out.

Once again, Nanna would wait patiently as I endeavoured to show just how capable I was of manoeuvring the wheelbarrow into position. Nanna could split the kindling so finely. How clever! We loaded the barrow and, without a to-do, Nanna wheeled the wood back to the house. No time to waste, the wood was placed onto last night's blackened coals in the sitting room. The fire was set ready for that night, and we were off again to put the chooks in before dark. Hand in hand, off we walked past the machinery shed, through the back house gate, towards the cow shed. Chooks were very clever, so by the time we reached their pen with the food scraps from the day, they were already perched up on their roost, settling in for the night. Foxes were a big threat to the defenceless chooks, so the gates needed to be securely fixed to avoid any flying feathers to add to Nanna's feather mattress.

The meat pie was cooked to perfection, ready for our tea, as the evening meal was called, when Dad called into the house to give Uncle Monty a rundown of the day's events and say his good nights. Then Dad headed off through the paddock home.

The house was always cozy, warm, with both kitchen and sitting room fires burning, and I fondly remember the wonderful mixed smells at Nanna's house of burning wood, baked apples, velvet soap and chrysanthemums, which, when in season, graced the sitting room table.

Nanna always washed the dishes after the evening meal, as there were too many heavy pots and pans for me to manage. What a lovely way of saying, 'because I don't want to mop the floor again today'. Unaware of the subtle aversion, I was just happy to pull a kitchen chair up to the sink and dry or attempt to dry the dishes. I do recall, however, I was asked to leave the cups and plates and just wipe the cutlery and plastic bowls; maybe the cups without handles Nanna used in the flour and sugar bags were the reason I was restricted to certain items. Who knows.

After the evening dishes were finished, it was time to have

a bath and get ready for bed. To get to the bathroom, we had to go out through the kitchen door to the end of the enclosed side verandah where it was situated. This all sounds perfectly fine, but not for me. As a child, I found getting from the kitchen to the bathroom quite scary, actually. Even now, when I think of walking out through that door, I think of poor great Uncle Aub. Uncle Monty, in his wisdom and loud voice, always thought there was a need to point out to everyone who visited, whether it be family or friend or even the travelling salesman, that poor old Aub died in that house. He would say, 'Poor old Aub, there he was lying right in the doorway, stone cold dead. Yep, stone cold dead! That's as true as I can stand here, isn't it, Hattie?'

Darling Nanna, forever the peacemaker, and without even looking up from what she was doing, would quietly say, 'Yep.'

I, of course, after hearing this story many times, the gruesome picture of this sad event was very vivid in my mind, and therefore, every time I had to use that door, I quickly ran, trying not to allow my feet to touch the floor where I envisaged he had died. Once reaching the bathroom, things were fine, except for the leather cutthroat razor strap, which hung dauntingly on the side of the hand basin, always a visual threat. Fortunately, it was never used on children who didn't do as they were told.

Chip heaters were very modern and exciting. Sometimes steam and not much water would spurt out and spit through the pipe into the concrete bath. We were told of the danger of being scalded with boiling water so always ended up sitting uncomfortably on the plug, facing the heater, ready to jump out if need be. After a wonderful hot bath and liberal dusting with Johnson's baby powder, clean pyjamas and warm slippers, it was time to listen to the wireless and sit beside the warm fire. The sitting room was such a special memory. Nanna would poke the Mallee roots in the open fire, creating a wonderful red glow, and with a bit of luck, sparks would noisily fly out into the room. We then had the important job of making sure the carpet wasn't on fire. My heightened sense of smell came in handy many times, as burning carpet was one of the unpleasant ones. Adults were so clever – they could lick their fingers and quick as a flash, pick up the burning ember from the carpet and toss it back into the fire without burning their fingers. Uncle Monty sat comfortably in his special wicker chair in the corner with a large table alongside generously covered with the Countryman magazine and many old newspapers. I snuggled up next to Nanna on the lounge waiting to see just how clever she was, being able to peel an entire apple with a small vegetable knife without breaking the peel once. This was one of the highlights of the night, especially as Miss Independent, me, had to try to do the same with the next apple. Thank goodness for the old, torn-up sheet made into small bandages. The most enjoyable part of the evening was when Nanna made me a hot arrowroot, as we call it. Nanna would mix arrowroot, cocoa and sugar to a paste, then stir in hot milk until it resembled thin custard. It was delicious.

Uncle Monty was so proud of his wood veneer wireless, jumping up every few seconds, endeavouring to tune it into the ABC News, twisting the Bakelite knobs, reassuring us that the new static was much clearer than the last.

Bedtime in the winter was great, but for me, a little scary also. Nanna would light the kerosene lamp, and I followed closely at her heels into the inside bedroom, jumping quickly into the already hollowed-out dip lovingly created in the feather mattress just for me. Nanna would settle the kerosene lamp safely on the dried-out timber bedside as she knelt to say her prayers, encouraging me to join in with her. Unfortunately, in the very dim light of the bedroom, the two large paintings situated on either side of the wooden wardrobe would not allow me to shut my eyes for a second.

One was of the crucifixion of Jesus, and it showed the crown of thorns pressed into Jesus's head and blood dripping down his face. I was always glad when Nanna finally got into bed and held my hand to go to sleep – so warm, half buried in the feather mattress and covered with a matching feather doona. Sheer bliss. It was still quite dark when Nanna stirred to get out of bed, kindly reassuring me that, because it was a very cold morning, it would be okay if I wanted to stay in bed until she returned from milking the cows. Not realising that Nanna really meant it'll be a lot quicker and easier without you, I bounced out of those feathers and dressed as quick as a flash. I wasn't about to miss out on the day's adventures. No way.

All the extra warm clothes needed to venture out on a frosty morning, including Nanna's very well-worn woollen coat, green hand-knitted bonnet and milking apron hung behind the kitchen door, ready for the many daily chores. Nanna would quickly rekindle the embers in the Metters wood stove before enjoying a hot cuppa and Granita biscuit, which would tide us over until breakfast. Then off we went, metal milking buckets in hand; we walked bristly past the machinery shed, through the back gate with the crisp easterly wind in our face, listening to the ice on the grass crackle beneath our wellies. As we approach the chook pen, the cluck-clucking noise of the hens waiting not so patiently to be released to roam for the day drowned out any other sound, including Nanna's happy tune. After many minutes of untwisting the fence wire which held the gate shut, Nanna's girls, as she called them, scrambled out of their coop, scratching and pecking the icy grass as chooks do. On we went towards the cow shed, Nanna humming all the way. Wellington boots are very handy around a cow shed, especially in winter as the ever-present abundance of cow pats are very soft and smelly and slippery. The best way to avoid the added chore of cleaning the poo off your boots is to walk very carefully looking down. I enjoyed wandering around the large cow shed, which was, before I was born, the horse stables. Fascinated with the old horse bits and dried-out leather harnesses, which hung lifelessly on every strainer post in the run-down shed, I was kept amused for hours.

The big rule in the cow shed was never to walk between a cow and its calf. Nanna, unfortunately, found this out first-hand, almost dying when she was gored by an overprotective cow. At that time, the only means of transport was horse and cart, which was a very slow way to get to Kununoppin Hospital, 15 miles away.

Fortunately, the bleeding did stop, thanks to some homegrown doctors and many old sheets; Nanna, although a little apprehensive, was back milking her cows only a few weeks later. By the time I was old enough to help with the milking, the only reminder of that terrible time was a large scar on Nanna's arm, but I'm sure there were a few hidden scars as well. Happily, I wandered around until I noticed a difference in the sound of the milk entering the bucket. At this point, I would sit on the railing watching the steam rise from the frothy milk as the last few squirts of warm milk disappeared into the bucket. The milk was distributed between the two buckets to make it easier for Nanna to carry home. I had the important job of carrying, without spilling, a small bucket of wheat to toss to the chooks as we passed on our way back for breakfast. Nanna and her little helper carefully collected the day's eggs from the back of the nesting boxes, and then, full of importance, and under the watchful eye of Nanna, I carried the valuable eggs home. By the time we reached the back veranda, the pet lambs were bleating repeatedly for their morning bottle of milk. And cocky, the pink and grey pet galah, was screeching for his wheat bag night cover to be removed.

Keith was still in his bed on the side veranda. Nanna advised me not to wake him as 'he got home at all hours of the morning. And I'm not sure, but I think he and his mate, Dougie, must have got up to all sorts of tomfoolery last night'. I wasn't sure what up to all sorts of tomfoolery meant, but it didn't matter to me, I was off to feed the lambs. The experience of feeding a little lamb is that of sheer joy, and it would be a wish come true for every child to experience watching their little tails wagging so fast and their little flat tummies growing bigger and bigger with every suck. The hardest thing to do is to stop the lamb from pulling the handmade rubber teat off the recycled beer bottle. Many times, there was spilt milk.

Walking inside Nanna's house after returning from milking, especially during winter, was so, so good. The warmth accompanied by the smell of toast being cooked on the open fire was enough to take the chill off your toes instantly. After removing her milking apron to reveal her day apron, Nanna, once again, hung it along with her slightly damp woollen bonnet and warm coat on the horse nail behind the kitchen door, ready for the next cold morning start. I'm not sure, but I think (tongue in cheek) that my Nanna must have been responsible for inventing layered clothing as, under her day apron, was yet another 'in-case-someone-calls-in' apron. Not many people did actually call in, but Nanna would have been just fine if they did, as I remember her 'in case' apron being the prettiest of all, reflecting maybe that they all just kept her a little warmer. Yes, loving memories.

Breakfast was such fun. Balancing a piece of bread on a homemade fencing wire toasting fork was difficult enough, but knowing the precise moment between perfectly cooked toast and 'oops burnt it' toast was another thing again. After breakfast, it was time to make butter from the plentiful supply of milk. This was exciting, as I was given the all-important job of turning the handle of the separator. The separator itself was quite a contraption, to say the least. It was made of shiny metal with one basin-like container with a spout fitting into another, stacked up onto another until there were spouts at all angles. Milk flowed from one spout, thick cream from another, and this cream was then transferred to the butter churner to make the final product, butter. This took quite a long time, as I remember it, but helping with the final process to form the butter was well worth the wait. If there was a tiny bit of butter left over after Nanna had painstakingly pitted and patted for hours, I was allowed to make a piece of butter. The wooden butter bats had patterns already grooved into them, but of course, I wanted to make different patterns. I think by the time that little piece of butter was finally put to rest in the kerosene fridge, its likeness to butter was far from evident.

Cake making was a little easier for me, especially if I just watched, as most of the requirements needed to make a cake were stored in the kitchenette, being the least visited cupboard from the ever-scrounging mice.

The kitchenette was painted cream to match the chairs, and had a special Nanna's kitchenette smell. I'm not sure how to explain it, but similar to a mix of fresh vanilla, flour sacks and velvet soap. I'd know that smell anywhere. Perhaps I am a bit queer-odd. Cutting open a new flour sack was done very carefully to avoid waste. The old sack would be emptied with a dusty shake or two, then put into a basin of water to soak until wash day. These empty flour sacks were then hemmed on all sides, converting them into fantastic flour-stamped tea towels.

Cracking the eggs into the creamed butter and sugar can be a little tricky, especially for children who were just learning. How spoilt I was. Patiently, Nanna would help me break the eggs and then, even more patiently, help me take the shell out of the mixture before finally being able to complete the much-appreciated-by-all butter cake.

Sunday afternoons were spent in the sitting room. Nanna would either be mending or reading letters from back home, as she affectionately called England. Often, we looked at old photographs of the many beautiful two-storey stone houses that the Sainsbury family had once lived in. Photos were only black and white back then, but I never tired of imagining the lush green fields and pretty colours of the beautiful Hollyhock flowers, as she explained to me. This far, far away place seemed so amazing that I would drift off into a child's happy place, wishing with all my heart that one day I'd be able to visit this place called England, where it snowed at Christmas, but most of all, to see where our dad was born. This little but very strong thread of my Web of Life will, thanks to a special blessing, be revisited much later as I travel my journey. Thoughts of a snowman came to a sudden halt as the familiar noise of the bike took over. Dad was here to take me home. Can't wait to see Mum.

# The Humble Wheat Bag

It's the year 2015, as I write this story, and I still possess an old wheat bag. I don't NEED it for any reason, but I just have a strong affection for the humble wheat bag. Paul, my wonderful and much-loved husband, always tells me, "You're a bit queer odd, you know," and I probably am, but those little wheat bags have a big story to tell.

They have, in their day, not only carried thousands and thousands of tons of wheat all around the world, boosting the Australian economy by millions and millions of dollars, they have performed many other 'nothing else could ever have done as good' duties. After years of being dragged over hundreds of double-gee-covered paddocks, pulled across splinter-ridden truck trays, dropped from shoulder height into the sharp metal combine bin, their duties on the farm have just started. There's the drip rag for the leaking tractor, truck or car sump, the lining for the dog's kennel, the much-needed door mat, and, of course, the perfect bag to cart a couple of laying chooks to a neighbouring farmer who's had a bad experience with a fox the night before.

Wheat bags actually make me sneeze, and they are rough and itchy, but among the myriad of amazing uses, the humble wheat bag often played a huge part in saving many a sheep's life during a straw fire. Straw fires were, unfortunately, quite common in the extremely hot summer months; the fire would burn very rapidly, racing across the paddock, burning everything in its path, including confused, frightened sheep.

Electrical storms were responsible for most, but of course, just a small spark from machinery, or sad but true of that time, a cigarette butt that had not been put out correctly could also start these dreadfully destructive fires. The wheat bag would be soaked in water and used to beat out the flames, being backbreaking, to say the least, but a very effective way to extinguish all sorts of fires. This sort of firefighting also relied heavily on the theory that 'many hands make light work' to ensure its effectiveness.

Uncle Monty had lots of other really good uses for the old wheat bags. He was very proud of his 1949 twin spinner, light brown Ford, and spent many hours cleaning and polishing every single part of his much-loved motor car, including the shiny chrome wheel trims. One wheat bag was put on the floor of the driver's side to stop any dirt from getting onto the carpet. Plus, quite a few were put into the boot for the same reason. But most importantly, one wheat bag was hung down over each tyre to make sure that when old Boots, the dog, lifted his leg, the chrome wheel trims didn't become victims of the abuse. Yes, I just love wheat bags.

# Home from Nanna's

Brian was waiting excitedly as Dad rode through the house gate with me perched between his arms on the petrol tank of the motorbike. Sandy, our much-beloved dog, enjoyed his fun for the day by biting at the bike tyres all the way to the back door. Brian quickly showed me what he was excited about. Dad had made us some stilts. What fun! They weren't stilts as we know them today, but they were sure loads of fun. Dad would make them from old jam tins. He would drill holes on either side of the tin, just under the enclosed bottom of the tin, then thread old electrical wire or any other strong rope through the holes, looping back through to make waist-height handles. We would stand on the upside-down jam tins, pulling the looped wire tight whilst trying to walk without falling off, or more to the point, without breaking our ankle. Not as easy as it sounds.

Children's fun games often result in a fall or two, and this was no different. We caused poor mum a bit of grief with the inevitable bumps, scratches and sprained ankles, and, of course, a little blood from time to time, but it was so much fun. The stilts not only made a wonderful noise on the hard dirt, but they made fantastic ring patterns wherever we walked as well. Mum was very happy when it was too dark for us to play outside anymore, especially if we had managed to avoid injury.

Our house always smelt wonderful. If it wasn't Mum's amazing cooking, it was the Marveer cleaning polish she used regularly, or maybe it was just the smell of home. Whatever it was, I was always glad to be home. There was also another surprise in store for me with this homecoming. Whilst I was down at Nan's, Mum had managed to complete the sewing of a very special dress for me to wear when we next visited Nanna Jess and Pop in Perth. This dress was the most beautiful dress Mum ever made me, and believe me, Mum was a talented seamstress, making me many beautiful dresses over the years, but this one was special. I will always remember it. Not only was it soft and very comfortable to wear, but Mum had also gone to all the trouble to lovingly embroider the nursery rhyme, Little Bo Peep on it. The lost sheep were stitched onto the bodice using white fluffy wool with a little path running down to a perfectly drawn and satin stitched Little Bo Peep. Mum had also carefully hand-stitched many pretty-coloured flowers onto the skirt of this never-to-be-forgotten pretty pale pink dress. Mum made all of our clothing using a treadle sewing machine at first, then a machine she referred to as Jonesie, which was the most hard-worked hand machine ever. That little machine made everything from curtains to bridesmaid dresses to pyjamas to leather boots for the sheepdog. Dad often helped willingly with things such as intricate pleating, heavy curtain and bedspread making and times when there were yards of material to be held as Mum's little sewing machine worked a treat for as long as I can remember. Mum and Dad always worked as a team to achieve some amazing results. Brian and I were truly blessed to have such wonderful parents.

As water was very precious, bath time was planned carefully. If Mum had used the copper during the day, the hot water would then be bucketed into the bath from the wash house. Dad would bathe first when the water was the hottest, then Mum, then Brian, and last but not least, I would hop into the slightly less hot, slightly more-gritty, but nevertheless enjoyable Lifebuoy soap-smelling bath.

Thank goodness that the soap we used back then didn't have too much caustic in it as, after this precious little bit of bath water had completed its duty in the bathtub, the water was then bucketed back out of the bath and poured into the thirsty geranium plants. It was, in fact, an era where nothing was ever wasted. When we were growing up, recycling, as we know it today, was just called waste, not want, and played a very important part in everyone's life, just to survive. For example, empty jam and fruit tins were not only used to give children fun as stilts but were also recycled for many other valuable uses in the kitchen; they made great egg boilers and steamed pudding tins, dripping tins and multiple other uses, including scone cutters. Most work sheds boasted rows of these tins, proudly holding nuts, bolts, screws and nails of all sizes, drill bits, washers and many more 'We may need these one day, things', Clothing was never thrown out., oh no! Old dresses were made into aprons, doll clothes, pot holders, and, dare I say, worn-out undies were cut up and used for dusting cloths. Washed first, don't panic. Worn sheets were cut and turned with the size changing according to the amount of wear, from double sheets to single sheets. These poor sheets didn't finish their work there; they were, after another couple of years as single sheets, sent to the shed as rags. Rags polished cars, washed mud from golf buggies, cleaned motor engines and, when finally in total tatters, were dipped in petrol and used to burn out the spider webs from the lavatory down the back. Food was never wasted. Any leftovers were fed to the appropriate pets and then to the chooks. The chook manure was then put on the veggie garden, and it all started again. Life on the farm was always busy, and each day brought a new adventure. The shearing team were arriving the next day, which meant busy times ahead for all you.

*Me with Dad's cat, Fang Woo the Claw. The dress I'm wearing was my favourite ever, with nursery rhyme Little Bo Peep embroidered on the front. Mum was extremely artistic.*

*Me with my doll Julie, named after my cousin Julie. This doll still has pride of place in my doll collection.*

*Me with Sandy, the dog, in front of our new green FX Holden.*

Dad had just driven from Perth in this much sought-after, thought about, discussed and then talked over again demo model FX Holden. He purchased it from General Motors Holden, where his cousin Felix Sainsbury was the salesman. Such excitement.

# Shearing

Mum's day commenced very early during shearing, Dad's even earlier, ensuring firstly that the old Metters stove was fully stoked up with Mallee roots before briskly heading off to the shearing shed, fingers crossed in the hopes that all shearers had turned up for work and at least recovered slightly from the night before a drink or two.

It was no trouble for me to get out of bed early during shearing time, as I didn't want to miss out on any of the action. Besides, Mum needed me to help. Before very long, the amazing smell of homemade sausage rolls, pies and pasties engulfed the kitchen. The Hawkins pressure cooker hissed gently on the stovetop, allowing another wonderful smell of pea soup to escape. It is quite amazing that we do revisit our threads of life, no matter how insignificant they may have seemed at the time. For example, whilst writing this little part of my Web of Life, I have just checked on a pot of pea soup hissing on the gas hot plate in a very old but identical Hawkins pressure cooker. Getting back to the story, after packing a mountain of sausage rolls, pies and pasties into a carry tray, Nanna's apple slice was last to be carefully put into a cake tin, ready to transport to the always very hungry shearers, with all of this food supplied just for smoko (morning tea).

Being a little clumsy as I was, had its disadvantages. I wanted to help so much, but most things were seen to be too hot, too heavy or too breakable for me. However, I was given the task of opening the car door to enable Mum to strategically place the 12-cup teapot on the floor of the car. I also had the important job of carrying the salt and pepper and tomato sauce to the men up the stairs through the never-forgotten very smelly shearing shed, where somehow everyone except me seemed oblivious to the pungent, mixed odour of sheep urine yoke and dags whilst munching on their second meat pie. Time was so important, but Mum always seemed to arrive at the shed just as the bell went for smoko.

There were three shearers, with Dad and Uncle Monty wool classing, Keith and Brian working on the wool press as well as rousting to make sure the pens were full of dry sheep. The enormous amount of food seemed to disappear very quickly, and we were off home again to make sure lunch was ready for exactly 12-midday. The men would come in for lunch, (boots all at the back door). No matter how wonderful the roast dinner was, the underlying odour of sheep yolk lingered in the house for hours after they all returned to work. Afternoon tea was at exactly 3 pm, and once again, the tea leaves from lunch were emptied onto the always-thirsty plants, and the teapot was reloaded for the next run down to the shed. Nanna helped with baking homemade biscuits and slices, which she sent up with Uncle Monty in the morning. These delicious biscuits were a great help in Mum's busy day, and the shearers, once again, enjoyed an afternoon tea fit for a king.

I would sometimes be permitted to stay and watch the shearing, as long as I didn't get in the way. This wasn't easy as everywhere was in the way. Dad would occasionally let me stencil the wool bales with a special blue ink according to the grade of the wool within the bale. I'm sure that even this was tedious for Dad after a long day's work, but Dad, being Dad, showed complete patience and always praised me for a job well done. Such a beautiful person.

After their evening meal, which was also eaten 'up home'. as eating inside the house was referred to. the shearers would then travel to Nungarin for a few drinks at the hotel. Quite often, one shearer – in fact, the ringer – would not arrive with his team for work the next morning. I wasn't sure what happened, but I do remember very clearly that the chatter was about the same shearer getting on the metho! Later in life, I did learn that it was true. This shearer did actually (from time to time), drink methylated spirits. No wonder he found it difficult to get to work. Fortunately, this particular day, someone found him and drove him out to Sunnyside, where he quickly cleaned his well-used shearing combs, bent his back and, as always, well and truly earned his day's pay yet again.

## After Shearing

With the past very busy weeks of preparation and shearing now over for another year, Dad would sometimes have a day or two to rest. Well, that's not exactly true, as the word 'resting' didn't come into Dad's vocabulary. As far back as I can remember if Dad wasn't at work on the farm, he and Mum would be working together, pulling down walls, putting up walls, painting, renewing and generally building the home we all love so much.

One of the most exciting times was when the new toilet was being built at the end of the wash house. It was not only a very flash pull-chain toilet, but it was inside the house. Redback spiders didn't come inside the house very often, and if they did, they were met with a quick, painless of course, departure. How exciting. No more running all the way down to the lav in the rain and freezing cold. No more calling out for Dad to kill, sorry, relocate the spiders, and best of all, no more holding our noses because of that smell. Waiting for the completion of this newest room to be added to our enlarging home was unbearable. When was that cement going to set? Who was going to be the first to pull the chain? Has Dad finished the toilet roll holder?

Toilet was the new name for our inside lavatory, as it was so much more upmarket. We were almost as modern as the townies now. With the privilege of having this new inside pull chain toilet came, of course, a few new rules. Our water was carted from Nungarin by truck to the house water tanks. It was still a very precious commodity. Therefore, we were only permitted to pull that magnet-like attraction of the chain for the daily constitutional sits, not for the ever-increasing need for a tinkle trip to the inside toilet. Real toilet paper in a roll quickly superseded the many previously used lavatory varieties, such as old newspaper cuttings in squares and wrapping from the granny smith apples, as well as butcher's paper, all of which, as I remember, were pretty rough and certainly not suitable for our modern, new toilet.

# After Shearing – House-building

Planning, the next extension of the house was always on the drawing board. Everyone wanted to show their drafting skills, with many sketches being passed around the laminex kitchen table and studied carefully until one was chosen to achieve the best result. Brian's new bedroom and enclosed side verandah seemed to take forever to design, but eventually, the master plan had the seal of approval, and work could begin.

Dad decided to cement the floor. This meant a huge area needed to be filled with rocks and sand to attain the same level as the rest of the house prior to the cement being trowelled smoothly over the top. How to kill two birds with one stone, or what! Our dad was not just a pretty face, you know! It just so happened that the two house paddocks made hard work of ploughing and seeding with damage being done to the discs and tines on the machinery because of the amount of small and not-so-small rocks scattered all over these paddocks. Problem solved!

Load after load of rocks of all sizes were picked from the paddocks and carted on the back of the Austin truck to be unloaded into the designated verandah area. As children, and possibly as our workload was slightly less than everyone else's, we thought it was just a lot of fun. To enable Dad to pick rocks with us, he would put the truck in low gear, face it towards the north, jump out of the cab, and join us behind the driverless truck. Not exactly job-safe practices as we know them today, but I think it was called improvisation to get a big job done.

Large rocks were squared off then cemented together to form the edge of what appeared to be a bottomless pit. Slowly but surely, and with Dad's 'never give up' motto, the rock height reached the desired level, and it was time to fill in the very large rectangle area with sand. This was another chance for Dad to solve two problems at the same time: the bottom dam was refilled each winter with runoff from the rock. This much-needed water meandered down the creek into the thirsty dam below. Digging out the loose sand from the sometimes not so free-flowing creek not only enabled us to acquire building material, but it most certainly helped with water flow into the dam.

Work on the farm was very demanding, and this building project took more time to complete than expected, but nevertheless, we all managed to enjoy the work in progress.

With the summer months well on the way, and all of us still feeling hot from a long, hard day, it was decided we all sleep on the unfinished, still sandy veranda. Sleeping under the stars with the cool breeze blowing over your face is such a magical experience unless, of course, you have a pet lamb named Bubby. Lambs are not like cats and dogs, and they don't respond accordingly when you say, lay down or snuggle up on the end of the mattress. No, they just walk all over you with their sharp little hooves digging in, bleating loudly all the while.

Harvesting was fast approaching, which meant the building would have to be put on the back burner for a while, at least.

# Summer on the Farm

The hot summer months in the outlying wheat belt area can be a real test for anyone's endurance, not only with the extreme opposites in temperature from the bitterly cold winter months, to months of unbearable temperatures of 110 degrees in the water bag, as often described, but also the almost immediate visual changes to the landscape. The once sea of green with rich brown paddocks quickly and dramatically turned to a dusty light yellow, almost white, endless horizon, so dry it beggars belief for it to ever resemble some form of life again.

Summertime not only brought with its searing temperatures, snakes, bats, millions of moths, and of course, those damn blowflies, but it also brought with it the ever and continual real fear of fire. All farmers had a compulsory firefighting water tank stand, usually situated to one side of the entrance to their farms, as close to the main road as possible. These stands were truck tray height, with two or more 44-gallon drums standing in a row on top, resembling Silent Sentinels full of water and at the ready, as there were no mobile phones and very few landline phones either to alert everyone of a fire. Thus, God's precious gift of our senses worked extremely well. Sight and smell worked a treat to detect a straw fire, even if it was miles away. Everyone dropped what they were doing and headed towards the fire with drums of water rolled hastily onto the truck, knapsacks and, of course, the old trusty wet wheat bag.

One of my many favourite smells is what I call perfume rain, created by a summer storm as heavy raindrops hit the dry straw and dusty paddocks, creating such a delightful perfume; there is nothing like it. But unfortunately, these summer electrical storms were one of the main causes, along with sparks from machinery and occasionally a cigarette butt, for many of the destructive fires.

It was not all bad during summer, in fact, I have many happy memories, one of which was when Mum's sister, Aunty Rose, Uncle Ron, and our much-loved cousins, Leigh, Stephanie and Phil, were visiting from Perth. It was a very hot day, and poor Aunt Rose was feeling the heat so much that Dad decided to cheer her up with one of his best cheeky grins. He asked her, "Would you like a nice cold shower?"

Knowing full well that our bathroom consisted of a bathtub only, she questioned how. Dad and Mum both chuckled a little, grabbed the old Lifebouy soap and a few towels, and with an added cheeky grin, Dad told us all to jump in the back of the truck, and off we went, bumping along the side track, around the base of the rock with Aunty Rose, I'm sure, having many doubts. Nevertheless, Dad always delivered, even if it was a slight variant to the actual.

They slowly pulled the truck to a stop in the middle of a flock of thirsty sheep drinking in procession, as sheep do, from the slightly smelly water trough. This trough was fed from the only soak well we had on our farm – such a wonderful bonus. After waiting for quite some time for the remaining sheep to quench their thirst and waddle off, Dad moved a piece of corrugated iron nearer to the soak for us to stand on. After all, no one wants fresh sheep droppings under their feet while showering. With Mum's help, Dad primed the pump several times, eventually enjoying the screams of delight as we all ran under the icy cold water. After the initial shock of the icy cold water spurting out from the pump onto our overheated bodies, sheer relief was evident on everyone's happy faces, which are memories I will never forget.

Our much-needed shower was sadly short-lived, as water was precious, and the sheep would be back the next evening to quench their hot summer thirst. No one wanted to dry the cool moisture drops from their body, so the towels were used merely to sit on to avoid splinters in our bums from the tray of the truck as we headed off home to enjoy one of Mum's yummy tea.

With a restless, hot, sticky night had by all, Mum and Auntie Rose decided to go to into Nungarin, not only to replenish some very quickly diminishing food supplies, but to spend some valuable sister time together. Dad and Uncle Ron had left early for work down Nans and would be away for the day. So unfortunately, Sister time became Sister and Kid time after a fleeting, not realistic thought of maybe leaving us at all home alone, was replaced by another almost unbearable thought of what could and probably would transpire if five excited, often mischievous children were left home. This was not an option.

So, into the FX, we all clambered. Cars weren't fitted with seat belts during the 50s, and not many rules applied. Although we weren't permitted to put our shoes on the vinyl seat or put our heads out the window, another rule also applied. If the car door hadn't closed fully, we had to wait until Mum stopped the car before re-closing it.

Nungarin was seven miles from our top gate with a dirt road until just before our neighbour's driveway (Mr and Mrs Young) then it was bitumen the rest of the way. We all chatted as we passed the golf course entrance and then passed Uncle Jack's abattoir road, finally rounding a half-circle bend, slowly bumping over the railway line, and we were there.

Nungarin town was typical of most small West Australian Wheat Belt towns. However, Nungarin boasted an added and much-appreciated population boost because of the high-security army ordinance depot. This very big military complete complex was built in 1942. In 1943, a displaced persons camp, which housed 1,000 Europeans, was also built in Nungarin, increasing the population immensely. After the war finished, much of the machinery and buildings from this camp were sold. Dad and Uncle Monty decided to purchase one of the many General Grant tanks, which they used successfully to clear much of Sunnyside. This very large piece of machinery was eventually put to rest in the chook yard, providing some very interesting nesting boxes for the laying hens, but more importantly, providing a wonderful play toy for us kids.

I'll try to describe the main street of Nungarin as I remember it. The Freemasons Lodge was located on the Merredin end of the street, then the entrance to the 'everything sport and more' oval, after which was the Town Hall. This building was used for many and varied events and was a hub of activity throughout the year. It was used for shows, dances, concerts, badminton, fancy dress balls, school dancing, pictures, CWA activities, flower shows, weddings, and you name it, the Town Hall was where it took place. The two-storey brick hotel was next, followed by a vacant lot, then Uncle Jack's Butcher shop. Uncle Jack and Auntie Jean were Dad and Mum's best friends. We spent countless happy, fun times with them and their children, Trish, Jenny and Kathy, enjoying countless memorable times, including family holidays at the beach in Busselton, golf days, sleepovers and, of course, those unforgettable Christmas Eve parties listening to Auntie Jean play the piano with everyone singing along.

This special bond and friendship is one thread of my life that I will treasure always. Forgive me if I missed some of the buildings along the way, as things have changed, not a lot, but certainly a little since then. Mr MacLernon's garage was next, followed by the Road Boards building. Mr Wog Waterhouse's hardware/farm needs shop was next. No offence meant whatsoever with using the name 'Wog', it was just his name as we knew it. When I think of it, his business could have been a forerunner to Bunnings. Anything and everything needed for drenching, tailing, feeding, welding, machinery fixing and or building, was somewhere on that 'shiny' tiled floor. Further down the street was Mr Cairn's grocery store, followed by Nungarin's famous Auntie Jim's Lolly shop. The post office stood alone further towards Mr Harper's bakery.

Back to the story, Mum and Aunt Rose were more than happy, I'm sure, to leave us kids to spend our pocket money and occupy ourselves as Mum had much to do with not only grocery shopping, as there were all other things to check on, pick up, post off before Mum even began shopping. Aunty Jim, a nickname given to her as a child, was a very well-loved and special part of the community. Her original shop, the one I'm referring to in this part of my story, was a long, narrow building with a counter each side at the front, and some tables and chairs further back in the shop. What a wonderful lady. She knew everyone and never forgot a name. Even our cousins were greeted with 'Hello, Stephanie. Are you having a good holiday?' Brian and Leigh ran straight to the comic book stand, hoping the latest Dick Tracy and Phantom comics had arrived, while Steph and I pondered how we would best spend our money. Auntie Jim had the patience of Jobe waiting for, not only us as children to make our minds up, but also for our children and grandchildren, who followed many years later to make up their minds whether they would get a red lolly or a blue one.

We happily wandered all around the town making our own entertainment as children do. Mum and Aunty Rose finally made time to enjoy a well-earned cold drink and quiet chat in the lounge of the hotel. Women were not permitted in the bar, being strictly men-only. Running all around the town did make us kids thirsty. With noses pressed against the hotel's lounge window, followed by an anxious tap or two, the sash window slid upwards, not only allowing clouds of cigarette smoke to escape from its confines, but to our delight, five little ponies of Sarsaparilla drinks were placed on the windowsill. Soon after, Mum and Aunty Rose appeared with a couple of King brown bottles peering out from the top of the paper bag, completing the 'had to gets' whilst in town.

It was about dusk as we travelled home, so we all had to be on kangaroo watch. Sure enough, just as we approached Young's corner, a mob of roos came into view, and Mum immediately slowed down as they pounded off into the bush. Kangaroos are, sadly, very unpredictable and fast, and just as Mum thought the road was clear, *bump*, the very gamey smell of kangaroo was immediate throughout the car – another one of those smells never forgotten. After a 'be careful' instruction, we tentatively gathered around a very dead kangaroo. Surprisingly, the good old Holden only had a small dent in the front bumper bar as a result of the awful ordeal. 'Waste not, want not'. With quite a bit of energy exerted and a lot of "Ooh, yuck" explanations, the now 'wonderful pet meat' was bundled onto a wheat bag in the boot. How proud we were to be able to tell Dad that we had not only picked up the spare parts he required, but we had also acquired enough pet meat for months to come.

*The General Grant tank with tea tree shed in the background. Nanna Jess and Pop were visiting from Perth with a friend*

*Left to right, friend, Pop, Nanna Jess, Dad, Me on bike, Mum in Brian's tin car. Our beautiful home behind, in the eyes of the beholder.*

*Nanna Jess and Pop Taylor with their grandchildren. Pop standing, Brian, Leigh, Lynette, Stephanie, Julie, Nanna Jess with Annette on her lap, Darcy, Susan and Philip.*
*Sadly, not all of their grandchildren are in this photo.*

# School Days

I was six years of age when I commenced school at Nungarin Primary School. In the 1950s, a child was required to be six years of age or turning six within the first year of school to commence Bubs, as it was then called.

Leaving the secure arms of Mum and Dad to go to the unknown, frightening place called school was bad enough, but having to catch that big orange bus with all those strange kids on board was just too much for me. Fortunately, my big brother had paved the way, and Brian was always there to comfort, support and protect his little sister. Of course, within a very short time, all the tears, fears and hanging on to Mum's tartan skirt disappeared, and the fun began. I was going to and from school, and that big orange bus became one of my favourite times of the day. Every child would be greeted with a "good morning" as they clambered, school case in hand, up the stairs onto the bus, and every child would respond with gusto, "Morn-nin, Mr Har-pa." This never changed in the entire seven years we rode the bus to school.

During winter, the bus seats felt like ice. The windows were all fogged up, and every child would be hoaring as they yelled to each other above the noise of the bus engine, bumps in the dirt road and the many yells from Mr Harper to "Sit down, you kids, I won't tell you again." We were even sometimes fortunate enough for the bus to become bogged. Yay.

Naturally, we all loved the slip-sliding of the bus as Mr Harper carefully navigated the water-sodden, muddy roads.

We watched with glee as the mud flicked up higher and higher with every effort to move the bus forward. Usually, within a short time, a nearby farmer would bring his tractor to pull the bus to firmer ground, and we would be on our way again.

Summertime on the bus was an entirely different kettle of fish. The ride to school wasn't much different. Mr Harper still kept an eagle eye on us through the rear vision mirror and the bumps in the road still vibrated the entire bus, but the once-foggy windows were replaced by thick, red, dusty ones. On the way home from school, however, with 20 or so sweat-drenched, sticky, smelly, 'I've been running around at school all day' children, things were very different. The temperature inside the bus could be horrendous, well over 100 degrees Fahrenheit. The burning, hot wind blasting us from the open windows, accompanied by the 1,000s of Bush flies literally sticking to our faces, seemed to have an effective way of quietening even the noisiest of children.

*Fun on the haystack with cousins visiting Sunnyside on school holidays.*

*Julie at the top, then me, Annette and Darcy in front.*

*Straw isn't as soft as it looks in photos. It is actually very scratchy, but a little bit of itch never gets in the way of fun.*

*Me with Speck, our pet magpie, on my head, one of Percil's kittens on my lap.*

*Cousins Julie with some of my dolls, Annette holding Blinky Bill and Diane holding Percil, the cat, 1950s*

Without a doubt, one of the most vivid memories of my time at primary school is one that my keen sense of smell has never allowed me to forget. I feel confident that most people of my age would also remember the very pungent smoke odour of smouldering orange peel, apple cores, sandwich crusts and everything in between drifting across the playground from the rusty chimney of the 44-gallon drum incinerator.

Fortunately, not all smells I remember were bad. A gentle breeze blowing through two large peppercorn trees on the side of the dirt playground was one of the more pleasant smells, as it sent a fresh mint perfume all the way to the lunch shed. I clearly remember the odour of the oil-stained floorboards on the well-worn school verandah and the 'old leather' smell wafting from the sports equipment cupboard. It goes without saying that everyone remembers that 'school classroom' smell, neither good nor bad, but never forgotten.

During the 1950s, the government introduced the supply of quarter-pint bottles of milk to all schools as an initiative to ensure all children had at least a drink of milk to start their day. Sadly, in the country areas, the milk was delivered to the roadside near the school gate, where it remained cooking in the sun until it was collected by one of the students and placed in the shade of the lunch shed. I can assure you that by the time we peeled off the little tin foil gold caps, the almost hot milk under a thick, smelly cream layer was very unpleasant.

Ringing the metal School Bell was one of the most sought-after duties to perform. Due to the sheer importance of this duty, only the older children were allowed to ring the bell. Everyone hoped that one day they would be chosen to perform this task. Come rain, hail or shine, as soon as that first bell of the day rang, we would all run from every corner of the playground and assemble in front of the three-room weatherboard school. Our teachers would ensure we were all standing bolt upright in our designated lines, with eyes forward when the headmaster arrived. We always commenced the day with the Lord's Prayer, followed by the National Anthem (being God Save the Queen). After a small talk by the headmaster about personal hygiene, we were required to participate in a brief physical exercise before filing into our classrooms. Each room had mixed classes to enable us to all fit into the three rooms. Our lift-up desks were in neat lines and not a water bottle inside.

Toilet breaks were permitted in emergencies, but as a new first-year pupil at school, it was frightening and embarrassing to have to put your hand up in front of everyone and ask, "Please, may I go to the toilet?" Sadly, due to this dilemma, I found myself in a more embarrassing situation, having to sit in the corner of the room with a jumper wrapped around my legs whilst my corduroy long pants dried.

During winter, there was a wood fire burning in the corner of our classroom. However, it seemed to have little effect during the very cold winter months. During the summer months, we were cooled by the searing hot puffs of air, which occasionally drifted through the open sash-drawn windows. We were, however, permitted to go home if the temperature reached over 110 degrees Fahrenheit. During lunchtime, we would quickly retrieve our almost cooked, very crisp turned-up at-the-edge sandwich from our even hotter school case, gobble it down, and then off to play. We played hopscotch, doogs (marbles), cricket, chasey, and if we wanted to risk it, we climbed the only big tree in the playground. It was great being the first up the tree, and when that bell rang, it meant you were the last to get down from the tree, or worst of all, late back to class.

Playing marbles was one of my favourite games, especially if I managed to take a favorite doog from a boy. We all had a pouch, or in my case, a tobacco tin, in which we carefully kept our taws. Checking out the array of colours in the cat's eyes and counting our winnings was one of the exciting activities done during the bus ride home. Many of my beautiful school friends remain to this day, part of my Web of Life, each with their own memories and stories to tell. We had so many happy times together, not only at school but with the many outside school activities held in the town.

School faction sports day was a big event each year, with weeks of training going into the preparation of every event, including tunnel ball, hop-skip-and-jump, flag races, sack races, high jump, handball and different length races. Running races were by age. This meant, however, that there were always only three in my age group. Lyn, Pam and I would line up every year, knowing full well that a much faster, (much slimmer) Pam would win. The two Lyns seemed to take it in turns to come last, but fortunately, there was a first, second and third place in all races. We had over 100 pupils at Nungarin School during this time, as the army camp didn't disperse until later. Sports days were held on the town oval, as did every other event of the year.

I remember, prior to one particular inter-school sports day, Mum spent days making each pupil at Nungarin School a name tag. They were sewn in blue material with each student's name pencilled on by hand and then painted in white lettering. In fact, thanks to Mum's ability to keep and not throw it out, I proudly was able to wear my original name tag to the recently held century celebrations of Nungarin school.

Who could ever forget the school dentist? Not me, that's for sure. To this day, my wonderful as she is dentist, sadly bears the brunt of an embedded fear of even so much as a visit to the dentist. That dreaded clove-smelling dental caravan would unexpectedly appear every year, parked in clear view as we arrived at school. Our expectations of just another happy day playing with our friends ground to a rapid halt as we realised this confronting monster was back. Waiting for your turn to be called was bad enough, but walking up those very narrow caravan stairs, I felt like my heart was making more noise than my brown school shoes hitting the metal steps. It was very cramped inside with the nurse on one side and the devil – oops, sorry, the dentist – on the other.

Dentistry was quite primitive. In the 1950s, they did not have X-ray machines to check for any decay or problem. They just used the probe. Yes, that nerve-hitting probe. The drill was a foot-pumped conveyor belt contraption, which rotated so slowly, the smell of the drill bit burning tooth away was enough to make you vomit. Anaesthetic wasn't wasted on a filling. Thank goodness they did spare some for an extraction.

Inter-school sports were held annually with all pupils from the surrounding country schools, including Mukinbudin and Trayning travelling by school bus for this prestigious event. Mums and dads (seeding permitting), Nannas and Pops all came to cheer on their up-and-coming athletes of the future. All students had to march to their designated holding areas, where, unless participating in an event, remained screaming for their team or just generally mucking around. I loved the marching music, scratchy as it sounded, blaring out from an old stereogram. Lyn and I didn't seem to do very well in the inter-school running races. Thank goodness we had Pam to beat those Training kids. Happily, many children went home with blue, red or yellow ribbons pinned to their shirts with stories to tell. Everyone else just seemed to enjoy a day away from the classroom and had fun.

Regardless, some teachers can have a lasting effect on us throughout our lives. My first memory is that of Miss Howard. I remember her being oh-so-pretty, gentle and kind. Mr Tillman was one of my favourite teachers. One day while I was struggling to get the very heavy medicine balls from the leather-smelling porch cupboard, I found an unusual kneecap protector. Placing it over my knee, I inquired, how does this stay on? Mr Tillman quickly replied, "Just put it back with the cricket bats." I had no idea at the time why he, all of a sudden, looked flustered, and his face went very red.

Poor Mr Tillman. He was a great teacher, most times, usually a happy teacher, but his little chalk and duster throwing stress relief habit possibly may not be accepted if he were teaching today. We, as children, didn't think much of it, really; we just ducked.

Mr Hackett was an amazing headmaster. He was, as I recall, very strict, but he was interesting and knew how to give knowledge. He had a large family, and his daughter, Shelley, had the most beautiful singing voice. The headmaster's house was situated next to our playground. One time, when Mrs Hackett was ill, a chosen few were allowed to go over to the house during school hours and do cleaning for Mrs Hackett. What a privilege!

The cane and the use of the cane were still permitted when I was at school. Vivid memories of one of my friends, Gary, come to mind. Children didn't seem to have to do much wrong to get the cane, especially Gary. I'm sure one poor child was just singled out to make sure everyone else was kept on their toes. Unfortunately, this day, Gary was caned, as it was always done, in front of the whole class. I wanted so much to scream at Mr Hackett to stop. But of course, I had more fear of repercussions if I did so instead, I whispered, "Don't be mean. I hate you."

With that, Mr Hackett, who must have had a bionic ear, looked straight across at me and said, "Have you got something to say?"

Quickly brushing the welling tears from my eyes, "No, Mr Hackett," was my terrified reply. Oh, what a day can bring.

The very next day was one I will never forget. We were all doing our work when the door opened abruptly and in came Gary's mum – not a happy mum. We all watched, mouths ajar, as she proceeded to let Mr Hackett have it, both barrels blasting.

"How dare you cane my child when he has raging boils!" she yelled promptly, exposing the caned area for all to see. The discussion after that, I can't remember too clearly, as we were told to put our heads down and get on with our work, but I can remember clearly feeling an overwhelming sense of happiness and justice for our classmate and special friend. Yes, that protective and unconditional love of a mum!

## Fun and Friends

Nungarin was a very vibrant little town, as I remember it. During my happy school years, there always seemed to be something to look forward to. How very fortunate. I feel very humble and grateful that I was given such an amazing start to life. Most of the many children's functions were organised through the school, including an annual fancy dress ball. The good old Nungarin Hall was put to good use yet again, and much preparation was needed for this event. What could we dress up as? Would Mrs Tiller be kind enough to play the piano for us again? Who would we follow in the parade? Where would we stand? We spent hours marching from school up to the hall to rehearse our folk dancing so our parents would be proud.

With the costumes themselves, Mum and Dad never let us down, always producing fantastic and unusual outfits. Brian and I would quite often go as a pair. One year, we were dressed as a fisherman and his catch; Mum's sewing skills certainly came into use. I was dressed as a mermaid. My tail was sewn in such a way that once put inside of it, I couldn't move other than a small wriggle of my toes to make the tail look authentic. Brian was the fisherman with corked hat, and fishing rod over his shoulder. He pulled me around the hall whilst I lay on the sand-covered trolley, pretending to brush my hair. Dad had spent hours making the trolley, which fortunately was light enough for Brian to manage as I was no lightweight. Mmmm, was it just fortunate Dad was so clever?

Every year was just as exciting. We went as a page girl and page boy. Another year, this time, Mum's artistic skills also came to the fore as she hand-painted the costumes. Another time, I was dressed as a little Dutch girl; this was one of my favourite outfits, as Dad had meticulously hand-carved wooden clogs for me to wear, turned-up toes and all. I never forget them, as they were fully lined with (still smelling of sheeps' yolk) wool so they didn't rub my feet. I have only thoughts of love for my dad. Mum used yellow knitting wool to make my hair with thick, long plaits resting on a white frilly apron. Best of all, I was always allowed to wear makeup with lipstick. How good was that? There were so many wonderful costumes. Little Bo Peep was another one.

The fancy dress ball quite often fell during or near two school holidays. One year, our cousin Julie was holidaying with us, so Mum dressed her up in the Little Bo Peep costume. A few alterations were needed as Julie was such a petite little girl. Tears come to my eyes as I am able to clearly remember the joy on Julie's face when she saw herself in the mirror. Another year, Brian went as a gollywog, a name not seen as improper in the 1950s. Once again, nothing was wasted in our house. Brian's nugget-blackened wig was made from part of a sheep skin. Once again, teamwork by Mum and Dad ensured another very effective costume. Our years at school are not only for learning reading, writing and arithmetic, as we all know, but for learning life's lessons and where we fit as an individual to feel comfortable within ourselves. By far, these lessons for a young child are the most difficult, and of course, the many tears shed during this process are inevitable. Thankfully, most schoolyard squabbles are short-lived, and laughter takes its place. I had many best friends at school, Gail, Kay, Lyn, Pam, Kathy, Rhniara, Sandra and Robin, just to mention a few, most of which now have children, grandchildren and great-grandchildren of their own. I feel very fortunate that many of my school friends still keep in touch. Thus, a wonderful friendship remained to enjoy.

*Some of the wonderful fancy dress costumes were made by Mum and Dad during our primary school years. Brian, me and cousin Julie.*

With every schoolgirl squabble, the so-called best friend could quickly become another's best friend. However, this roundabout was, of course, just another valuable learning process, and with a quick response from a couple of protective sisters, most arguments just meant a swap of best friends for a while. During lunch, we sat under the peppercorn trees happily sharing our lunch and comparing whose sandwich was the most turned up at the edges because of the heat, but happily ate that same sandwich if it came from someone else's lunchbox.

As soon as the second play bell rang, we all raced down the back of the school ground to clamber into our much-loved tree-canopied, dirt-swept cubby house. Lots of girls' business went on here, and it goes without saying, 'No smelly boys in our cubby'. We knitted when knitting season came around, played knuckle bones, embroidered, giggled and planned who would sleep at whose' on the weekend, parents permitting. Stayovers were happy times and needed much thought. But that was not until the weekend, and this was lunchtime, and we needed to fit in more fun. So as soon as one person suggested we play on the swing or monkey bar, the single branch door of the cubby house would fly open and off we ran to fit a little more play in before lunch recess was over. Hand in hand, we wriggled our way along the rusty, wonky monkey bars and then pushed each other to great heights on the loose chain, splinter-riddled swing seat until our hastily consumed turned-up sandwich came close to reappearing in a slightly different manner.

Guy Fawkes night was celebrated on the fifth of November in the middle of the local football field. Always conditions applied. Everyone came from far and wide for this exciting night when kids could be kids, and more to the point, their dads could be kids too. By November, the memory of rain was long gone, and any small amount of green was a thing of the past. Therefore, the threat of fire was, once again, foremost on everyone's mind. Fortunately, this didn't stop every man and his dog from dragging sticks and wood to the centre of the footy field, piling them higher and higher until they resembled a distorted pyramid. Finally, somehow, a somewhat bedraggled, overstuffed scarecrow was precariously placed on the top of the wood pile, ensuring everything was now ready for the big night. Children began asking for chores to do, and with the fruits of their labour, enjoyed getting the best bang for their money, literally. All being well and with no strong easterly winds, the fire would, as it had been in the past, roar to a great height, lighting up not only the football field, but also the faces and hearts of the hundreds of men and women and children who came to have fun.

I was restricted to Tom Thumbs and Sparklers only (I have no idea why). Maybe it was for the best. This didn't stop me enjoying the fun when Brian and his friends let off their stockpile of Half-Penny and Penny Bombs, Sky Rockets and colourful Catherine Wheels. Children were running everywhere, screeching with delight as Tom Thumbs spat out sparks whilst bouncing between fast-moving feet. There were many "Ooh aahs" with eyes skyward as rockets exploded, releasing a myriad of colourful embers falling to the ground. The intense heat of the fire, the deafening noise of exploding firecrackers, accompanied by an even louder noise of every dog in the town barking, linger in my thoughts, but it will always be the gunpowder smell that is foremost in my mind.

Sadly, some children and even adults received burns and injuries during these otherwise happy events. Thus, during the 1980s, fireworks were banned from being used in most states in Australia. My friends and I were the lucky ones, not only enjoying many Guy Fawkes nights, but thanks to the careful watch of our parents, we avoided being hurt. I'm pleased to say that my favourite sparklers avoided the chop and are still available today to delight many, including my own grandchildren. Further down the track in my story, these simple little Sparklers, once again, bounce and spark and even explode across my wonderful Web of Life.

# Scripture at School

Whilst growing up in the country, going to church every week was not always possible, and of course, to have a priest, Minister, or pastor of the correct denomination was another issue. This was a time of very steadfast views about everything, including religion. Dad's family were of the Church of England faith. And Mum's family were raised as strict Methodists. Mum and Dad seemed to manage these differences well by maintaining their own faith but not regularly attending a church service on Sundays, which avoided confrontation. We did attend Sunday school when Mum was able to drive into Nungarin, or when we stayed over with friends who lived in the town, as then we could just walk to the hall where Sunday school was held. We did, however, attend church for special services, weddings, christenings, including our own Methodist christenings, funerals and, when in Perth, staying with Nanna Jess.

Nanna always dressed in her Sunday best, including hats and gloves, stockings and high heels with a crisp, clean handkerchief wedge prominently between the nobble-type clasp of a matching handbag. Scripture was held once a week at our school, and without exception, everyone had to attend. The school building comprised of three rooms only, and with the teacher occupying one room, the Roman Catholic service was held in the second room, and due to the number of children attending, the Church of England Service was held in the remaining room, leaving the smaller Methodist service to be held on the veranda. This served the purpose for quite some time.

However, due to the long distances the minister had to travel and his age, I'm sure, one day he stopped coming to our school. So we were placed with the Church of England pupils.

Oh, no, this would never do!

Fortunately, within a short time, a lady minister turned up, and Mum was a little happier for us to attend her service. To this day, I have no idea what denomination this lady was. All I know is that she was always kind and more than happy to hold her service in the tin lunch shed, putting up with the burnt orange peel smell drifting in on the back of an icy cold, easterly breeze. But most of all, it was from these warm, loving scripture lessons that I secured my interpretations of faith.

Up until then, I had always felt uneasy to the point of feeling afraid when anyone discussed religion or scriptures from the Bible. Maybe I went to the wrong sermons, I'm not sure, but even entering a church building with its definite smell of books and polished pews made me feel anxious, and the extended, mournful voice of the minister speaking of sin, wickedness, punishment, damnation and burning in hell didn't help, along with the ever-present picture firmly embedded in my mind of Jesus with the crown of thorns pressed into his head and blood running down his beaten body, only went to enhance my fears. The worst ever was a sermon about a poor man having to prove his faith by being prepared to sacrifice his son, a test of faith that to this day, pains me to the extreme.

How wonderful when the first hymn we sang in the lunch shed with our new lady minister was 'What A Friend We Have in Jesus.' Yes, uplifting and happy. I love this hymn so much, I asked Mum if she could paint these words on a large canvas so it could be hung on the shed wall for us all to read. Mum, with kindness, just added one more task to her many other jobs on the next scripture day.

I proudly presented this canvas, hook and all, thanks to Dad, to hang on the shed wall, and the minister spoke mostly of love and kindness and helping those less fortunate. Oh, my goodness, my fear started to disappear. Church and religion started to sound kind. She often spoke of missionaries in Africa and how they helped children and little babies who were sick and starving, all words which made my heart jump with joy, as I loved all babies – baby sheep, baby lambs, baby kittens and of course, dolls and especially real babies.

Children are very impressionable, especially when they are hearing things that feel safe and kind and happy. And I was no different. So when our minister said that if we want God to love us, we should tell him in prayer and we should go somewhere quiet, kneel and let him know that we believe that he will always be there for us, and yes, then we would always have a friend in Jesus.

During my book, due to the fact that some things are just too personal and/or hurtful to be spoken about, I will, from time to time, talk about a 'shhhh' secret. This should possibly be one such secret. However, it is only personal to me, and I've always been a bit of an open book. So not long after our scripture lesson, I did find a quiet place in Nanna Hattie's drawing room – a 'shhhh' secret until now.

This lady was only at our school for a short time, but her scriptures were always positive, and my love of the stories about Africa had a lasting effect. In fact, when I was asked what I wanted to be when I grew up, my answer was always a missionary. And throughout my life, the only two countries I wanted to visit were England to see where my dad was born and Africa. God does work in mysterious ways.

# Christmas at Sunnyside

Christmas at Sunnyside was truly amazing, not only for the day itself, but for many weeks of planning prior, needed to ensure the best celebrations of Christmas day could be had by all. It was an extremely busy time for everyone, with Dad still harvesting and Mum wanting the house to be just tickety boo for our many expected visitors, whilst at the same time helping Brian and me with our exams and also prepare for the end of year school concert.

The nativity play was always the highlight of the night, and none more so than the year I was chosen to play the part of Mary. In other years, I seemed to always be one of the three wise men with a striped tea towel shoved on my head. But to be Mary with the baby Jesus was so special, especially as this meant that I was promoted to wearing a sheet on my head and, best of all, allowed to use my favourite doll as baby Jesus.

December was, more times than not, still harvest time, and every year, it became a mad rush against the elements for Dad to finish, but somehow, he always seemed to make it in time to help Mum decorate and prepare for our wonderful family time.

The enclosed, louvred veranda, which went all the way around the front and one side of the house, was finally completed, giving Mum so much more room, especially during holidays when our aunties, uncles and cousins were coming to visit. Dad and Mum worked together, making beds, putting up extra stretchers, and, as with the plans of mice and men, working out who would sleep where, only to have their plans changed when all us kids decided to sleep outside on the pile of floor panels which had been stacked on the lawn ready to use in the new shed.

It was such fun sleeping under the stars with all of us sightseeing the saucepan, evening star, Southern Cross and seven sisters, even if we really couldn't see them at all. Mum loved decorating and insisted that more streamers be put up all the way around the veranda, as well as the normal abundance of streamers, tinsel, bells and mistletoe inside which glistened and tinkled for all to enjoy.

Importantly, the Christmas tree had been carefully chosen throughout the previous year as the tree of choice to stand proudly in the corner of our lounge room for the entire festive season. Great care was taken in covering the bucket in which it stood with red and green crepe paper, and then strategically and with loving care, the many shiny baubles and handmade decorations were tied onto the branches with cotton thread, finishing with another of Dad's masterpieces, the Star of Bethlehem, on the top.

Thanks to Mum, this very same but very fragile star is still part of our Christmas decorations.

These most delightful, precious memories will remain with me forever.

A very long table was erected on a different part of the verandah with wooden stools from outside and every chair in the house, even Mum's piano stool, completing the setting for Christmas lunch.

Christmas Day was very often 'one hundred and ten in the water bag', as extremely hot days were called. To this day, being one of my favourite expressions, therefore eating on the verandah made sense with the slightest chance of a breeze (although also hot) blowing through the louvres.

Of course, the main reason was simply that the kitchen was far too small and far too hot, with Mum cooking a traditional Christmas roast on the old wood-burning Metters stove.

Somehow, Dad always seemed to finish harvesting just in the nick of time, cheekily commenting that he had knocked off work to carry bricks but really enjoying every minute of it.

Preparing meals was a very big part of Mum's life, always ensuring Dad, the shearers, workers and Brian and I were all well fed for breakfast, morning tea, lunch, afternoon tea, tea and even supper.

Christmas day brought about the most important meal of the year.

From what I can remember, we did have a turkey roast one Christmas thanks to Dad's little barter arrangement with another farmer. However, roast chicken graced our Christmas table most years to the delight of everyone's taste buds. Unlike today, chicken was a special treat and were not killed very often, or at least until they became too old and could no longer lay eggs. Somehow, that always seemed to be at Christmas time. Mmm?

Darling Nanna Hattie would always help out with the overabundance of food, and on the day, Dad would drive down to Nan's to pick up the carefully prepared delights. It goes without saying, because I hardly left Dad's side, that I would go with him for this very important part of the proceedings.

This one time, Nanna must have over-catered a little, with Dad having all sorts of trouble getting the very many dishes of food into the car. Nanna's specialty was her trifle, which was decorated with two colours of jelly, mountains of whipped cream, and always sprinkled with coloured coconut. Dad carefully positioned this masterpiece on the floor of the car as I squeezed between the numerous salads that adorned the sloping back seat with a happy heart and smile. I remember Dad's words as clearly as though it were yesterday: "You'll have to sit with your feet up. Don't whatever you do, put your feet in the trifle."

With an added chuckle, Dad carefully closed the door and off we drove home. Although it was only a short distance from my Nanna's home to ours, for some reason it seemed to take an extra-long time that day, and my legs became somewhat tired from holding them above the trifle. Oh no! … "Dad!!!" You guessed it! Just as we turned into the driveway, my foot slipped into the top of Nanna's trifle. Dad, in his gentle, usual manner, simply asked Mum if she had any more whipped cream, scraped off the shoe-touched cream, and with Mum coming to the rescue, quick as a flash, all was as good as new. Dad quickly washed my shoe and the trifle saga was fixed. I did, however, have to put up with the whole embarrassing trip back from Nanna's being told as one of the Christmas jokes.

Mum always made plum pudding and hot custard. No one could have possibly had room left to eat plum pudding. But somehow everyone, especially us kids, said, "Yes, please" to pudding.

Mum, as it was a tradition when she was growing, always put threepence coins in the pudding. So, after declaring "Yes, we can definitely fit some pudding in," our biggest desire was to see how much pocket money we were going to find. Mum, being like all mums, made sure everyone ended up with the same amount, which was also very clever, as then we knew if anyone had swallowed one.

It was such a special Christmas if Nanna Jess and Pop were able to join us, with our adored Nanna Jess saying Grace before the happy clatter of serving spoons commenced; this was truly a glistening web time of my life.

Although the heat was enough to fry an egg on the bonnet of the car, we all laughed, pulled our bon-bon crackers, laughed at the stupid jokes inside, and waited happily for the breeze (no matter how gentle or hot) to blow through the louvres.

*Me and Brian with Father Christmas, mid 1950s*
*My outfit another of Mum's creations*

*Below: Cousins at Nanna Jess and Pop's home in Hotham Street, Inglewood, in the 1950s*

*Left to right: Darcy, Julie (Aunty Jane and Uncle Jum's children), Lynette (me), Stephanie (Aunty Rose and Uncle Ron's daughter), Brian, and Leigh (son of Aunt Rose and Uncle Ron.)*

# Summer Holidays

With the happy memories of a wonderful Christmas spent with our cousins still fresh in our dreams, more excitement was quickly upon us, as much preparation was already underway for our annual holiday at Palm Beach in Rockingham.

This delightful seaside holiday town was frequented and enjoyed, not only by us, but by many Wheat Belt farming families for their annual and extremely well-earned holidays. Mum, as always, had her old sewing machine working just as fast as it could go to ensure we all had many new outfits to wear, including one year excelling herself by making me a delightful pair of rouché bathers.

Dad was busy making sure all the sheep troughs were working, and enough water and feed were available for Uncle Monty to feed all the animals whilst we were away. It was quite a feat, packing the FX for the trip, everything but the kitchen sink was carefully and strategically placed in for ease of finding, plus to ensure balance on the suspension of the car and comfort for everyone during the journey. As we were very young, Dad always made a bed for Brian and me in the back of the car. He would place two butts of wheat on the back floor, one on each side of the tail shaft. Then all the bedding needed for our holiday would be piled on top, with four pillows for good measure. And presto, Uncle Lilo had his chook food, we all had blankets for our holiday flat, and Brian and I could sleep comfortably, that is, until I vomited everywhere except in the towel prepared for the occurrence.

We always left very early in the morning, before the rooster crowed, allowing time for a thermos coffee, coffee break, toilet breaks and a very regular clean-me-up after a car sickness break. With all of this in mind and the fact we always stopped at Clackline to change into clean clothes and have a sponge wash so we looked and, thanks to good old Johnson's baby powder, smelled good for Nanna Jess and Pop, the trip took at least five hours just to reach Nanna Jess and Pop's home, where we dropped off some lamb chops and a leg roast, enjoyed a bowl of Nanna's famous vegetable soup for lunch before heading off to the next suburb to give Uncle Lilo the wheat for his chooks. With a dozen eggs placed carefully in the little gap where the meat was, we finally headed south to Rockingham.

Beach shacks, caravan parks, and holiday rentals were all packed to the hilt with country people seeking rest and relief from a past year of overwork, extreme temperature changes and the swallowing of the odd Bush fly or two. It's hard to believe now, I know, but Rockingham and surrounding beaches boasted an abundance of fish back then, which gave a much-appreciated and enjoyed change of diet for these farmers-come-fishermen from the normal, being rabbit and hogget.

We holidayed at the Palm Beach Caravan Park each year until we were offered a self-contained side verandah flat on the corner of Park and Bell Streets, Palm Beach, where friends from Merredin, Mr and Mrs Yeoman and their children, holidayed in the other side flat.

These were truly wonderful holidays. We all swam every single moment we could with only a short walk to the most beautiful, clear, calm beaches with thousands of pretty shells to collect and sand castles to build. It was just too good to be true. I remember watching Dad cleaning his catch of fish on a piece of board wedged under the tank stand out the back of the flat before handing them over to Mum and the awaiting hot frying pan. Fresh fish, bread and butter and vinegar. What a treat, especially when followed by juicy, ripe red watermelon, unheard of in our house since the cows visited Mum's garden. We also loved the opportunity to go to the Speedway on a Friday night, held in Claremont Showgrounds; I can still recall fondly the smell of the mixture of methylbenzene, exhaust fumes, burnt rubber and wet mud. Safety Standards had a little bit to be desired in the 50s, with only a thin wire fence above a wood railing between the overcrowded race track and the excited spectators, creating, sadly, quite a few mishaps, including the time a flying tyre just missed Brian but did sadly hurt another man badly.

Rockingham boasted an amazing outdoor picture theatre in those days, situated on the corner of Parkin Street and Railway Terrace. It didn't seem to matter what film was showing; the outdoor theatre was always full of holidaymakers, who, I think, enjoyed the novelty of just sitting in the very comfortable striped canvas deck chairs staring upwards at the ever-twinkling stars more than watching the always flickering black and white cowboy film. These nights out, however, were a real treat, and I remember how we had to take a pillow to sit on just to be high enough to even see the screen, which probably didn't matter much as, after swimming and playing in the fresh sea air all day, we usually fell asleep soon after the cartoon. We were fortunate enough to experience more fun in those few weeks than some children ever experienced in all of their growing-up lives. I am and always have been very grateful I was blessed with wonderful parents who gave us so much on which to build our lives.

*Wonderful holidays at Palm Beach Rockingham in the early 1950s*

*Mum and Dad with Palm Beach Jetty in the background*

*Nanna Hattie, Me, Dad and Brian, just using the boat as a prop.*

*Me with my much treasured rouché bathers, and Brian*

*Me, Nanna, Hattie and Mum*

# Holidays at Nanna Jess's and Pop's

Although our annual holidays at Palm Beach were always filled with fun, happiness and family time, Mum, understandably, was very keen to spend as much time as possible visiting with her Mum and Dad when we were in Perth. Time permitting, we were able to stay a few days on our way home to Sunnyside, or we would visit during one of our shorter school holidays if farm commitment allowed Dad to drive us to Perth.

I have many very precious memories of time spent at Nanna Jess and Pop's home in Drummond Street, Inglewood, especially if we stayed during the summer months. Nanna Jess and Pop's home was on a corner block with a low brick fence and brick letterbox complemented by Agapanthus in a row along the side fence, and best of all, green lawn. Very few farm homes had lawn due to the lack of water, so to be able to run with bare feet on freshly mowed green grass was such a treat. My quirky sense of smell will never let me forget the amazing mixtures of perfumes – furniture polish, books, rose petals, hints of town gas leaking from the kitchen area, and best of all, the unforgettable smell of Nanna Jess's vegetable soup, all of which met us when we arrived, along with many warm hugs and kisses.

Brian and I would be so excited if it were suggested we sleep on the front verandah to avoid the heat inside. Yay, two freshly dusted camp stretchers would be placed carefully on the highly polished red concrete verandah with a pillow and blanket placed on each, and we were happy as little pigs in mud. There was no thought of danger. Why should there be? Most front doors were never locked anyway, due to the fact that crime was minimal, even in the city, with much faith and trust in your fellow man, prevailing the Australian way.

Oblivious to the adult conversation going on in the lounge room nearby, we would play our favourite game: Guess what car just drove around the bend? There were not many different types of motor cars during the 50s, mainly Holdens, Fords, Zephyrs and Morris and, as each motor had a particular note to it, along with the fact that the traffic was minimal, it was quite doable to distinguish their individual signature sounds – we actually became quite good at guessing which type of car was changing gears. Then we would quickly jump up to see if we were right. Being a girl back then was different and therefore, silly as it sounds, I was so proud of myself when I knew what a Holden car motor sounded like. We laughed and played until the Sandman had his way, and I don't think we moved until, more excitement for country kids, the milkman joined us briefly on Nanna's shiny red verandah with the clink-clink of the glass milk bottles. Things were so different in the city!

*A very special photo taken outside our home, Sunnyside. Mum, Jannie (Stephanie's best friend), Stephanie, Auntie Rose and Phillip in front.*

*Me, Steph, Sue, David and Phil.*

*Cousin Sue, just checking to make sure her dad, Uncle Don, was still behind that big men's bar door. Nungarin Hotel in the late 50s. This is one of those special photos. How cute.*

# Dark Clouds Gather

Sadly, always being able to skip happily over the tiny little threads of our lives isn't always possible. As we know, unforeseen storms can approach quickly, without warning, to shake the webs we stand on, making it difficult to regain a grip on life's happiness.

The school bus came to a stop at our top gate. Mr Harper handed Brian a tissue-wrapped loaf of bread, which Mum had ordered whilst in town the week before, and with an "… Afternoon, Mr Har-pa," by both of us, we headed off down the track to home. You've no idea how good that loaf of freshly baked (by Mr. Harper himself) bread smelt, especially on a cold day after a big day at school.

Many times, the lovely white middle of the loaf of bread protruded outside of the crust, not too far, but just enough to need trimming level with the crust. You guessed it, many times Mum received her loaf of bread with a concave in the end. I'm sure it was Brian's fault.

One day, on arriving home from school, I noticed Mum was ironing, but not just ironing. She was crying as she was ironing one of my light pink dresses. I raced to cuddle her and asked, "Why are you crying?"

Mum replied, "Because this dress smells like a baby."

I had no idea what this could possibly mean, but I knew Mum was very sad. When Dad came home, they talked a lot, but as I said, children weren't included in adult conversation. So it was only later, when I was told a little bit, that all the pieces came together, and I was able to understand Mum's heartache.

Mum was a 'sickly' child, as they would say. She was also a bleeder – another expression used when answers to medical issues weren't as advanced as they are now. When still in the Army, and just prior to Mum marrying Dad, she became very ill with peritonitis and almost died. In those days, they did not drain the wound, and her body became poisoned. Mum tells of how she was in hospital for three weeks, just lying in bed, so you can imagine how long it took her body to recover.

As you've read, Dad and Mum did have a beautiful wedding, and Mum gave birth to two healthy children. The doctor did say he was surprised that she was able to have children after what she had been through.

Mum's health seemed to be going okay, but unfortunately, the past did raise its ugly head one day, and Dad had to rush Mum to hospital for an emergency hysterectomy as she was bleeding uncontrollably. This was traumatic for them both, as it was a long drive to Merredin Hospital with Mum trying to stay elevated whilst enduring unbearable pain and fear. It took months to recover from this operation in the 1950s. We stayed with Nanna Hattie until Mum was well enough.

Mum's body was healing, but, sadly for Mum, her mental state suffered badly. Of course, as we know now, Mum was suffering from postnatal depression, which can be treated these days with positive results.

Mum was not the only poor woman who was told that she was 'just being stupid to be crying and upset' and to 'just stop being silly and get on with it'. Unfortunately, Mum's hormone levels were never going to right themselves, especially when the doctor just kept prescribing strong mind-changing drugs. This was a very sad time for Mum and Dad, with no answers and things getting worse. But the worst was yet to come.

The doctor explained to Dad that there was a new miracle cure for women like Mum. It breaks my heart to even be writing about this, but Mum and Dad suffered greatly because of this so-called Miracle Cure. Shock treatment was used extensively for all kinds of illnesses, and after talking through all the options to try to help Mum, Nanna Jess, and Dad with reservations, they agreed to go ahead with this new treatment.

Horrific! comes to mind. Of course, it had no effect other than to heighten Mum's failing nervous system. My mum is an amazing lady, and thanks to the unconditional love my darling dad had for his wife, they got through this terrible time in their life. Mum finally received help from a wonderful Jewish doctor who used hypnotherapy to help her, and he also encouraged her to play music. These and many other little encouragements were not instant cures, but over time, and later, with the help of new gentle medication, Mum and Dad were able to regain their grip on happiness again. The miracle was God's help and unconditional love. My heart goes out to all women who suffered from postnatal depression during that time.

# Later Years at Primary School

Nothing changed much for me during the last year or so at primary school, although my much-loved and ever-watchful security blanket, Brian, had moved on to Merredin High School, accompanied by many other older sisters and brothers, leaving most in our class feeling somewhat alone and a little insecure.

Not for long though; it took very little time for us to realise that we were now the big kids on the block, with responsibilities, so much so even our teachers seemed to speak to us differently. It felt really good in this new growing-up stage. Of course, no surprises here: I still came last out of the three of us, Lyn, Pam and me in our running races on sports day. Lyn, however, must have felt a bit sorry for me sometimes and threw a race or two for me to come second with Pam, as always, not even raising a sweat to finish so far in front it didn't matter.

All in all, I was bouncing from one strong fibre in my Web of Life to another with not much to worry about other than how quickly I could get to the swimming pool on a Friday after school.

We were so very fortunate, as the Army had built a beautiful swimming pool in the five BOD Army camp for their soldiers and families. Thank goodness for us hot kids, it was also made open for all to enjoy from the town and surrounding districts.

Friday was the day Mum came to town to do her weekly shopping, so instead of catching the school bus, I, along with most kids who could, or nearly could, swim, swam and swam and swallowed lots of chlorine water until our fingers and toes resembled white, shrivelled up prunes. Aunty Joan Matthews, a dear friend of Mum's, taught us all to swim. I'm not sure if Auntie Joan was a qualified swimming teacher or not, but back then, as long as you were willing to give your time and could do the job, you did it, and everyone was grateful.

Swimming, for me, was such a blessing. At last, I had found something that was not only the best thing to be doing during the hot summer months, but I was reasonably good at it, to the point where I didn't always come last in my swimming races. When we were growing up, we were always told it doesn't matter if you come last as long as you tried, and not everyone can win. But boy, it sure felt good when I won my first backstroke swimming race.

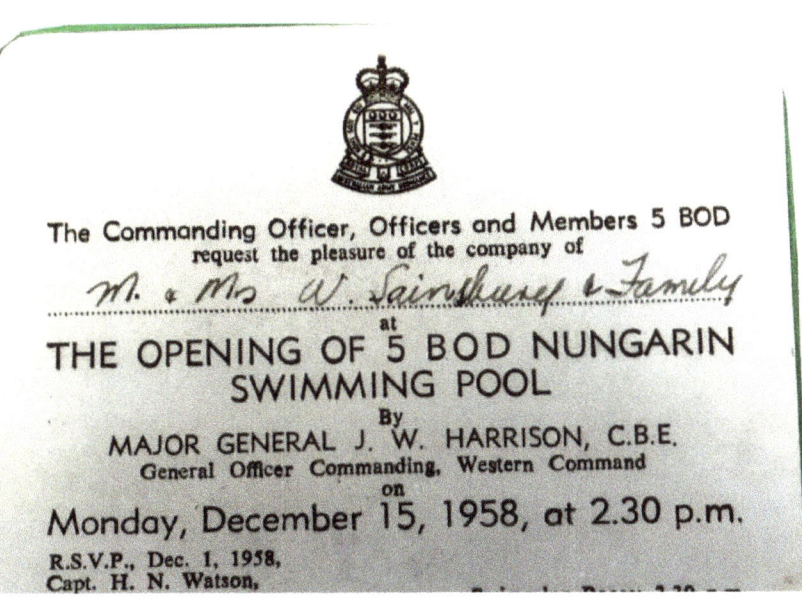

*The original invitation of the opening of Nungarin swimming pool.*

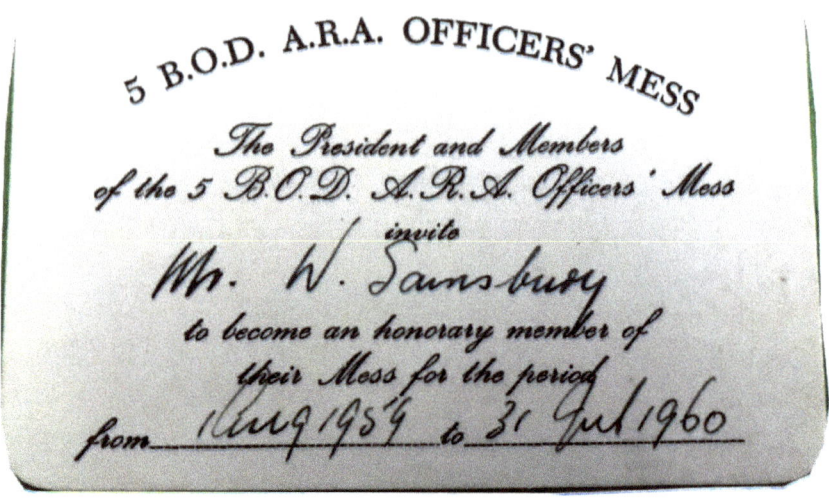

*The original ticket inviting Dad to become an honorary member of the Nungarin 5BOD Army Officers' Mess.*

*Nungarin Swimming Pool*
*Swimming lessons at Nungarin swimming pool, 1958*
*Left to right. Kay, Lyn, Aunt Joan (Mum's friend), Sandra, Lyn on the end. And sorry, I've forgotten the girl in front.*

# A Message in the Form of a Letter

It is now 5:30 am on the 10th of March, 2020, and a very real message from 1949 was given to me by the ones who are always with me to ensure that today is the day I recommence writing my book.

I haven't been drawn to finish my Web of Life for some years now, simply due to life's many totally consuming and exhausting, not to mention brain frying, issues which have made it difficult to find the peace of mind to relax and recall stored memories needed to complete my story. But yesterday, thanks to Mum coming across a handwritten poem she had written years ago, the real desire to continue writing my story, thus leaving my love of words for future generations to read became so strong that I immediately had to recommence building the tiny threads of my Web of Life.

I have included the poem Mum wrote so many years ago. Mum was a very talented lady, and had not long been discharged from the Army herself, so had a close affiliation with the Nungarin Army camp, which possibly prompted this letter. How wonderful that, thanks to her 'never throw anything out' attitude, I am able to show another talent of hers.

# Nungarin

Nungarin was once just a name on the map,
Friendly people, one big family, a sulky and trap,
but with coming of war, our dear folks all saw
its importance right there on the map.

Then all at once, in our quiet town,
the army came to settle down.
The people of this little place
really welcomed them in haste

Time went on and our new pals
made our men and, of course, their gals
members of the officers' mess
with lots of fun, as you would guess.

Next we saw, which seemed so strange,
bowling folks! My, what a change!
Men and women dressed the part.
Really enjoyed it from the start.

To assist us again the Army jumped in
with pictures each week. My, just the thing,
a pleasure for all where hubby would take
mama and kids, no fuss did they make.

Last but not least is the swimming pool.
Who doesn't enjoy it must be a fool.
The kids think they're made being able to swim.
They even tell Dad they're better than him.

Although our town would have normally grown,
we couldn't have done so on our own.
So here's saying thanks to 5 BOD
from all and Sundry, and this includes me.

                                                Peg Sainsbury

## Goodbye and Thank You

In the early 1960s, the Army Number Five Base Ordinance Depot (5BOD) departed Nungarin.

This was a sad time for the town, as approximately 1,200 army personnel lived at the camp, bolstering not only the school, but enabled the once struggling town to boom. Gradually, the soldiers and their families moved away until there were only a few officers and managing staff left to sell everything. Nothing was to be left. The site was to be as it was when they arrived some fourteen years prior – everything, including streets and streets of lovely, little different coloured houses, sheds and more sheds and tons of supplies, all of which were to go to auction. This auction was held in one of the largest building/hangar/depots ever built in WA.

What an auction! It went for days, and every man and his dog from all over the state attended with one thing in mind – to grab a bargain.

It was so exciting as the soldiers even built a tiered stand for everyone to sit on, just like a grandstand at the footy in Perth. There were jinkers and trucks all lined up to take away houses, sheds and heavy equipment, which were all sold one after the other. Farmers everywhere were buying these buildings to use as shearing quarters or new shearing sheds, or to replace many old Ti-tree hedge sheds with a new, already painted khaki timber, and, dare I say it, asbestos shed.

Dad, Uncle Monty, Keith and Brian were also very keen to purchase a new shed, as well as many different other preselected items that would make life easier on the farm. Oh, my goodness, the Army was big! The sheds were big, and all items that went under the hammer were big. Also, nothing was sold individually, crate upon crate of small items were sold one after the other. No time for consideration once the auction for the day commenced,

The Army auction attracted 1,000s of people, so Dad decided that we would get in on the action by taking our cocker spaniel dog's eight-week-old pups into the auction with us in the hopes of selling them. Presto, pups gone to good homes, and Tammy, our dog, was once again able to spend happy times riding on the tank of Dad's motorbike. Great job, Dad. As always.

I went every day I could to this amazing once-in-a-lifetime auction. But the most exciting part of this whole event was when we got home, all gathering on the veranda, opening up the many crates of purchases. Uncle Monty had bought a crate of, wait for it, toothbrushes. Even if, for some stretch of his imagination, he thought all our sheep were going to start cleaning their teeth, I'm sure hundreds of these little toothbrushes were never going to see inside a mouth.

A crate of heavy woollen khaki bomber jackets and another of khaki great coats stole the show, as these items were heavy, warm pieces of clothing, which improved the warmth and comfort of everyone during the freezing winter months, especially cold nights spent on the tractor.

Dad organised the truck and jinker soon after the auction to transport our new shed home. Much work was needed to be done to get this shell of a building home. Wires were stretched corner to corner and across the empty building to contain its movement whilst in transit. When the very large shed was strapped securely to the jinker, it looked safe and exciting. At this point, I asked Dad if I could ride inside the building on the way home.

"No, not this time," was his quick and firm response.

*Why not?* I thought. *Dad allows me to ride on the back of the truck and on the back of the ute, tractor bike, and in fact, Dad lets me do most things I ask to do, but not this time. Bugger*, I thought, but after a few more definite "No, not this time, chicken," I slid into the car to follow the truck home. When we arrived at the gate, the truck driver had stopped and was moving around inspecting the shed. He was concerned about the angle in which he had to turn with such a long building in tow.

I was instructed to get back into the car without question, and just as well. Within a few minutes, the truck driver moved only a few more feet forward, when suddenly the whole building collapsed to the left amongst a cloud of dust. Instantly, a very real lesson was embedded in me, and I've never forgotten this, realising how my dad's No's saved my life. 'No means no' for a very good reason.

Another one of Mum's little ditties that has remained hidden, but I think Mum was one very out-there woman of her time. Go, Mum!

### The Story of Hooley Dooley

Chinaman, named Hooley Dooley,
have Aussie wife and love her truly.
Years they long for little fellow,
but no want him skin be yellow.
Yo lo doctor, seek advice.
He no help. "'Tis nature's dice."
Watch TV, and while they sit,
find a way of having it.
On the job without delay,
sideways in the Chinese way.

Baby born to great delight
little fellow Ajax white
Doctor came and have a willy
"Why Chinese baby white as Lily?"
Up spoke Chinaman so proud.
Tell him TV show them how
Hoolly Dooley, me no fooly,
Me use Persil on my Tuli,
Lemon liquid in our baths,
Tickly bubbles around our ass,
Wifey, wifey, very canny,
Put Blue Omo on her fanny,
Colgate and a final rinse.
Give her ring of confidence.
No wonder where the yellow went.
Me brush balls with Pepsodent,
Instant Starch and Reckett's Blue.
Soon have baby number two.

*Mum and Dad ready for golf. Note Mum's tartan slacks. Tutt-tutt, ladies don't wear slacks to golf!*

*Brian showing his swing. Our FX Holden in the background with its new Burgundy and Cream paint job*

# High School, Life-changing Times

Transferring from the comforts of Nungarin Primary School, a very small country school in the 1950s which offered many security blankets to its students, including seven years of the same special friends with not many changes in teachers, to the enormity of Merredin Senior High School and boarding school catering for hundreds of children from all over the wheat belt, with dozens of teachers, along with being totally responsible for one's own actions, was life-changing, to say the least.

Most students boarded in Merredin. Even though it was only 32 miles from Nungarin, many families lived out of town on farms, and this proved too difficult for parents to drive children to and from Nungarin before and after school to be in time for the very early one and only school bus.

Brian had privately boarded whilst he was at Merredin High so Mum and Dad thought that this was a better option for me also. Mr and Mrs B were lovely people with one daughter, for the purpose of my book, Babs, still living at home, and although she was a couple of years older than me, I felt I wasn't completely alone. Mr B was the local baker, and every lunchtime, we enjoyed a variety of crusty delights, specially moulded from the leftover bits of dough. I can to this day remember the tantalising smell and amazing taste of his bread.

Other things I remember about boarding with Mr and Mrs B in Throssell Road, Merredin are: the house was a very neat and tidy, painted weatherboard and asbestos home within walking distance to the high school, with a back laneway and gate into a large yard boasting the most beautiful lilac tree. The back lane still showed remnants of why houses had a back lane back then, with many old dunnies – oops, sorry, Mum – lavatories still standing with their little wooden door flapping in the breeze as a reminder of how wonderful it was to have a pull chain toilet! I remember the largest purple coloured bougainvillea I have ever seen cascading into the lane not far from the backyard gate. My memory takes me back to going to church with Mrs B, but always hurrying home just in time to get to the swimming pool before it shut, in the hopes of seeing my boyfriend, even if only for a minute or two, and listening to Babs play the piano, with my favourite piece of music being Fire, Fire.

I remember being quite scared at night as my room was the sleepout at the back of the house, and security didn't exist in those days, with only a slip bolt keeping the back verandah secure. Winter was always freezing in my room as louvres were no barrier to the easterly, icy, cold winds. But the upturn of this was, of course, in summer, I had the best, coolest room in the house.

This was a time of the Edgar/Eric Cook murders, and sometimes my fears became too much, and I would sneak inside the house, rug and pillow in hand and find a piece of carpet near Bab's room and go back to my room as soon as it was light. Although I liked having my independence, I must say I loved going home on weekends, feeling relaxed, warm and loved.

On reflection, I must admit that I enjoyed high school very much. However, to be honest, and what must have been very obvious to all around me, I didn't use the opportunity of learning as much as I should have, allowing the very many distractions, and more to the point emotions of life, instead to take precedence. My grades were average, and I soaked up the parts of education that gave me pleasure, but my concentration levels for some subjects dwindled somewhat, with me choosing to roll Liptie lollies along the wooden floor to anyone who was also concentrating on something else at the time.

One of these moments was when I first saw the first S series Valiant two-door sports car in Merredin being driven down the road outside of our class window. Wow! I thought that car looked and sounded amazing.

French was another class where I had trouble concentrating, and I spent quite a few classes sitting outside the room, 3B, watching intently in case the headmaster walked by, at which time I would pretend I was going to the girls' room. I'm very sure this did not fool him for one minute. I liked English, Art, History and even Math, to a point.

Sadly, during this time, there was a definite mentality in society placing girls into a certain category with an expectation of not needing to be educated much, as a female's role was to get married and have children. They left school and got a job in areas such as nursing, teaching and secretarial duties. And even though these jobs could be careers, in the main, they were short-lived, making way for marriage and children and caring for a husband. Of course, having some of these skills was accepted as an advantage, so that when the kids were off your hands, you could go back to work, perhaps.

# Development into Life's Journey on my Web of Life

My belief is that no one, just no one, could have been given a better start in life than I was given. Of course, it would be very disappointing if others didn't feel the same about their lives. In my eyes, my parents were perfect with, perhaps, the only fault my parents did have was that of loving us too much. If you can call that a fault. We were truly blessed in every way, and loved unconditionally. We were able to enjoy a wonderful, large family with cousins to grow up with, and we were taken on holidays to the beach, brought up on a farm with fresh air to breathe, animals to love, mushrooms to pick, and sweet-smelling dirt to roll in.

I will never be able to express the love and gratitude I have for Mum and Dad for this start to life. I contribute my ability to love almost entirely to my upbringing by my adored parents, but also to the many people from many different walks of life that I spent time with throughout my young life. Love is the most important word in my Web of Life's journey. Love, as I see it, is the ultimate of our emotions. Love can be varied to suit each situation and can be deep and painful, so painful sometimes needing every fibre of our being to control, and love can also be as light as a feather, but just as genuine and meaningful. Love has a million faces, and I feel I have been blessed to have experienced more than my share of these entrenched and beautiful emotions. I have already spoken of the love I have for my Mum and Dad and brother. These are, of course, a special and deeply embedded sort of love like no other. The love a mother and father have for their children comes into this category and depth of love.

Totally different, I know, but I can honestly say I genuinely have a love for my dolls, my cats, dogs and even teddy bear. This real emotion, of course, is light love and extremely different. I have spoken often of my love of a calf's tongue licking my hand and the feeling of soft summer rain on my face, along with the indescribable wet hay smell filling my senses, along with that of sweet-smelling dirt topping the list of unusual things I love. These loves have always been very real to me, just a different level of emotion that I feel and that I have been very blessed to have experienced.

Throughout our lives, we all experience so many types of love, but the one love that engulfs our lives forever is that of a first love, a true love. This love remains with us for eternity and never varies in emotion. Some of us, like myself, have been truly enriched and are eternally grateful for this beautiful, stirring and unconditional emotion.

As a young teenager, living away from home for the first time, and with many changes occurring almost overnight, I was fortunate enough to be able to hold on to my emotions of love as a guideline to life's demands. The first year of high school was full of excitement with new friends, new teachers and different sporting activities, and most importantly, the experience of making decisions for ourselves. This, of course, was also a time of teenagers going through puberty with hormone levels reaching their peaks everywhere. As such, students were pairing off like love birds, with eyes glistening and spirits as high as kites. This was such a happy time with every student, adjusting their school uniform to bring in a little bit of fashion where possible, just like a bird fluffing its feathers to attract the opposite sex, sporting activities such as swimming, golf, tennis, football, better still, school socials enabled many young romances to blossom. Although we were young, our emotions were very real, and I was no different, with my heart pounding every time I came in contact with my first boyfriend. The attraction to him was immediate. I thought he was the most handsome, beautiful person, inside and out, and this true feeling grew more and more throughout our high school years. I remember with a tingle in my heart the many times we walked home from school hand in hand, chatting happily and experimenting sincere and gentle kisses lasting for hours, then meeting under the lilac tree until dark, after which spending hours on the phone until Mrs B eventually giving me the evil eye to finish the call.

I remember standing in the rain without a care in the world just to watch him play football and walking from one side of town all the way to the golf club lessons and to be with him. Because of our age, this emotion was sometimes referred to as puppy love, but was it? This is truly a shhhhh moment.

Not long after I commenced high school, Brian, my ever-protective brother, left school to work on the farm and help Dad and Keith; Uncle Monty was getting older, and it was a natural progression for Brian to take on farming as his career. I missed his support very much, and when I went home for the weekend, we enjoyed catching up and spending time together. Brian has always protected me and has had my back all my life. I am eternally grateful for our bond. Brian was going out with Mrs B's daughter at that time and would, on most weekends, drive into Merredin to take Babs to the one and only nighttime entertainment in town. The Drives, as it was referred to, was the whole package of entertainment, meeting, greeting, eating, drinking and parking and sometimes actually seeing a repeat film, usually only to catch up on what you had missed the time before.

It was a common place for young people to park their Sin Bins, as they were aptly called, in reverse, to the enormous screen and open the back door of the panel van, often revealing many teenagers climbing out from under mattresses, King Brown in hand, and saying that, although they almost died from suffocation, they had got through the gates without being noticed. Marijuana was around when I was a teenager, but illegally drinking the occasional King Brown, having puff on a Cool cigarette seemed to satisfy the boundary pushers.

Mini skirts and shifts were the fashion statement of the time, and although I lacked confidence in my looks because of my nose, I felt okay with my body and very happy to see just how short and tight a mini skirt could go. With Mum's sewing skills, I had many different shifts, but I do remember the many disagreements we went through about the length. I was very self-conscious about my nose, which didn't improve when one of the boys in my class said to his mate, "Gee, I'd like to have Sainsbury's nose full of gold." These nine words haunted me most of my life, and this tiny thread will be revisited later in my life.

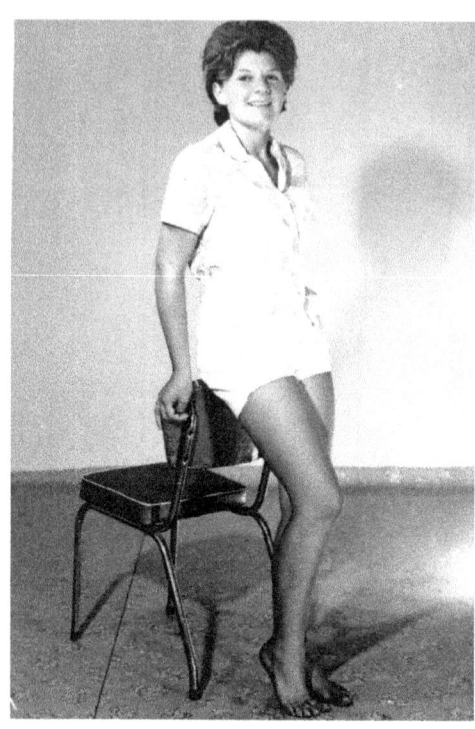

*This photo was taken when I was 15 years old. Rhonda Hughes and I went to a photographer in Merredin. We thought we were 'it' and a bit. Happy memories.*

*Me at age 16, taken outside our home with Percil the cat.*

# Wrong Decision Made

To this day, I still have jumbled thoughts in my mind with even more jumbled, confused reasons as to why I wanted to move to Perth instead of going on to fourth-year high school or go back on the farm to work, or find work locally. As the rest of the world could see, I had everything and a lot more going for me. Big moment here – yes, I actually had it all. Why then did I make the mistake of pushing my parents into allowing me to go to the city to work? Maybe I just thought the grass would be greener. Who knows. But what I do know is that out of the hundreds of mistakes I've made in my life, this was one of the worst I have ever made, resulting in a lifetime of consequences with many regrets as well as 1000s of personal heartache shhhh moments which have remained in my heart for a lifetime.

Fortunately, I was able to gain the strength to be stronger than my mistake, and with the knowledge that I would always have the support of my family, I simply relocated the precious memories of my short-lived teenage years to a special place within me, never forgotten, always a breath away. Another skip-a-beat shhhh moment. Happy threads of my Web of Life will be revisited further down the track.

# First marriage

I have anguished for years about being able to confidently write about my marriage to Jeff, so as to be truthful, as well as genuinely sincere, with an attempt to show how this part of my Web of Life didn't turn out as planned. And I feel confident when I say it possibly wasn't what Jeff wanted either. Sadly, our marriage did go awfully wrong, having an adverse effect not only on us as a couple, but also on our parents and families, but more sadly, the devastating lifelong effect it had on our two beautiful daughters, leaving me always with a deep, regretful heartache.

Most of all, in writing about our life as husband and wife, it is my innermost desire to possibly avoid hurt, blame, humiliation or anger toward anyone involved. As the saying goes, it takes two to tangle.

There can be no denying that during our 16 years of marriage, I, as well as my children, did suffer domestic violence at the hands of Jeff, either mentally or physically or both. Although I can't know for sure, and perhaps his pain was suffered in a different way altogether. I do, however, feel sure that Jeff would have suffered during this turbulent time also. Like every part of my Web of Life, I am only writing my memories and as we all know, everyone's memories of an event can be quite different. I will do my best to be as accurate as I can, keeping in mind people's feelings are very real.

We were exactly like thousands of other young adults, in our case, teenagers of the 50s and 60s who thought we knew it all, and young adults at that time were afforded much more freedom of speech and action than previous generations. We, therefore, like to push the boundaries just because we could. Sadly, in doing so, our actions had a devastating impact on many lives, especially our own, both then and in the years ahead.

Uncle Ron, Mum's brother-in-law, worked for the Perth railways in the clerical office, which was very helpful for me when I needed to change jobs back then – when it came to getting work, it wasn't what you knew, and it was who knew you.

My first job in Perth was at Ajax Furniture Company in Mount Lawley as a telephonist, which I enjoyed very much. The Exchange box was about two feet by two feet with about 40 little connecting switches which, when a phone call came through, I would answer it and ask who they would like to speak to, and then switch the incoming call over to the relevant number, much like a computer, I suppose, just all done by hand. Of course, I thought I was 'it' and a bit' putting on my best phone voice to impress my boss, as he had told me that if I did well on the phones, he would train me in sales. This appealed to me very much, as I always enjoyed talking to the customers. Talking was a big part of my upbringing. Sitting around the table with family at home was more like a busy marketplace with everyone talking at once, with the only quiet time being when someone took a sip of tea. Unfortunately, this was not to be at that time, as one day, I was asked to go with one of the older salesmen to clean up the storeroom, ready for stock take. I was always a willing worker, and thought it would be fun, but I was also very young and naive. I chatted happily away all the way to the upstairs storeroom, where, quite quickly I realised this man's intentions were not right. I was able to avoid a very bad situation, and quickly left the storeroom, and went back to work. Of course, nothing could have been or was said about the situation. After all, I was merely a silly young girl who was asking for it by wearing a short skirt, and Mr X was a happily married man and a great salesperson to boot, so, nothing more to be said.

After this incident, I asked Uncle Ron if there were any jobs coming up in the railways, and fortunately, there was a position in the office at the Midland workshops. So I jumped at the chance. It was very exciting, and I was given the job of 'already supplied' typist. The Midland workshops were situated right next to the Midland Railway Station, but the office was the last building at the end of dozens of giant red brick workshops. All of the staff who worked in the office had to walk past the never-ending gigantic doors opening into the work areas, with hundreds of blue-collared workers walking in and out. Fortunately for me, many of the girls I worked with were on the same train as I was, and were able to walk with me on my first day. We ducked in and out of the busy workers as we walked past what seemed to be a never-ending, diesel-smelling road with my new acquaintances laughing and chatting all the way, reassuring me not to worry and that it was perfectly normal to be wolf whistled and jeered at. "It happens every day. You'll get used to it. Men will be men."

Typing was something I enjoyed, and although we all learned touch typing at school, I struggled a bit at first with my speed, but everyone was kind, and some of the girls helped if I got behind with the daily orders.

One of the girls in the office lived in the same street in Bedford where I was boarding, and after a short time, we became good friends. B was a happy, confident girl, and taught me a lot. Boy, did she know a lot! B and her boyfriend had been together for quite some time, and when she talked about their many and varied escapades, it was like listening to an enthralling R-rated book, which I soaked up like a sponge, whilst oblivious to anything or anyone else on the train as we travelled home to Maylands station.

These never-ending snippets of B's love life became more than the general train ride home from work topic. Oh, my goodness, I had never heard of people doing anything in a phone box except making phone calls. This and many other chats can only be described as shhhh moments.

I was boarding in Rosebury Street in Bedford with a lady Nanna Jess knew from her church. Mrs Stewart was very nice, but of course, had her rules. I shared a room with a Uni student, Del, who was also a country girl. We managed okay in the one small room, but I'm sure my chatter was too much for her at times.

My pay from the railways was £16/5 shillings, and I paid Mrs Stewart £9/5 shillings board, leaving just enough for my train fare, personal items and a pair of stockings for the week.

It was whilst I was working at the railways that I met Jeff. There were a lot of older men and a few young men, but the first time I saw Jeff, I thought how good-looking he was. He had lovely dark skin and dark hair. Had a presence that I could not ignore. Of course, as girls do, I couldn't wait to tell B how I felt about Jeff.

During our train trip home from work that day, I excitedly gabbled on about how I thought Jeff was so good looking, and all the stuff girls say about the opposite sex at that age, only to have a stern response of "You don't want to go out with him. He's bad news." Of course, these comments just made me more intrigued to get to know him, and so within a few days, I was getting a ride home in Jeff's Zephyr 6, instead of taking the train. He was so proud of his car and took every opportunity to show off, which I considered very normal. I was all starry-eyed and thought he was wonderful.

Things progressed quickly, and it wasn't very long before he took me home to meet his mum and dad, which I was very happy to do, as, since moving to Perth to live, I missed my family very much. I remember the first time we said hello and just how warm and welcoming his mum was, and I can honestly say, as far as her love and kindness towards me, nothing ever changed. The whole time I knew her I remember her as a lovely mother-in-law. Like most mums, perhaps the one debatable fault she did have was that she loved her children too much. My first impression of Jeff's dad was that of a happy, carefree, friendly man, always making light of a situation. And actually, that didn't change during the whole time I knew him either. He was always kind, loving and respectful to me, but the carefree part of his character did cause Mum a hell of a lot of heartache and pain during the time I knew them. Jeff's sister-in-law was at the house with her two children that day, which I loved, as she was beautiful to me and made me feel like I was in a family home. Jeff had three brothers, he being the second eldest.

Jeff and I started dating regularly, which involved many family functions, and I became more and more smitten with him. Very quickly, love and lust got entwined, and we threw caution to the wind and just followed our selfish emotions. We loved each other.

There are many things I remember as being the worst things to happen in the 60s to a family. One was drinking under the age of 21 years which, of course, did occur regularly, having sex prior to being married, which did also happen more times than people like to admit, however, the worst and the one thing that caused unimaginable shame to many families was that of a girl falling pregnant prior to marriage.

This caused more family shame, forced abortions, forced giving up of babies, illegal adoptions, and in some extreme cases, suicides, than any other wrongdoing in the 60s. There was no easy way of obtaining precautionary aids, as it was illegal for doctors to prescribe the pill to anyone unmarried. Detailed and informative sex education in schools was not even heard of then. So, other than the responsibility of parents to give a birds-and-bees talk to their children, we all, in the main, gained our knowledge in those areas by talking to our peers.

I was just a month off seventeen when I felt pregnant. I was overjoyed. The thought of having a baby of my own filled my heart with happiness, and to this day, I can remember the euphoria I felt within. No one will ever be able to take that feeling away from me. It is locked in my heart for eternity.

It is not for me to say how Jeff felt, only he himself can remember that. However, I remember only acceptance of the situation we both found ourselves in from him after the initial sheer joy I felt, which sadly was very short-lived. My life became very real, and most of the following weeks remain in my memory as a blur of heartache and pain, not only for me, but for my darling mum, dad and brother and all my adored family. My selfishness had broken their hearts, the pain I felt was indescribable, but knowing their pain was incomprehensible and left me in a bubble-engulfed state, trying to work out how to right the wrong. The answer did not come easily. My Web of Life was at breaking point with the wind and rain dragging the little threads out from under me, leaving me hanging on, trying to pull myself up to find at least one secure thread from which to be able to rebuild.

But this was not to be, as this particular blow was only intensifying, and I was going to have to hang on with every inch of my might to be able to right my wrong.

Mum and Dad's reactions were perfectly normal, as having a 17-year-old daughter pregnant prior to marriage was not what they had planned, and after being the most loving parents ever, they were in an utter turmoil as to where they had gone wrong, which, of course, they hadn't gone wrong. I most certainly had by stepping over the boundaries.

Although this news gave Mum and Dad immense pain, they didn't for one second take into consideration the ongoing criticism that they themselves would now and in the future have to endure from their peers. They only had, as had always been the case, my future well-being in their minds.

It makes me feel sick to this day thinking about the options given to all those in my situation at the time, I almost couldn't hear what was being said. It was as if my ears were rejecting the words with every inch of my being screaming inwardly. No one is going to take our baby away. It was time to fight with all our might to keep this gift of life that had been bestowed on us. It goes without saying that we didn't for one minute consider any negatives of the situation or even a flicker of a thought, as we were too young and selfish, and although we had been disrespectful to our families and ourselves, for both of us, the gift of life outweighed all.

A visit to the doctor to make sure everything was as it should be was possibly the first indication to me that Jeff had some inner personal issues with things that I, because of my upbringing, considered perfectly normal and totally acceptable. I had never needed to go to a doctor in Perth, so Mum suggested we go to a doctor that she had been to because his surgery was close by in Bedford, and he was considered to be a very good doctor. By this time, I was starting to have morning sickness, and was just pleased to be going to a doctor, any doctor, for a check-up to make sure all was okay, and, most importantly, find out when our baby was due. This almost immediately started conflict between Jeff and myself. He was enraged that I had gone to a 'male' doctor. I honestly didn't even know that there was such a thing as a female doctor, and certainly, where I had lived in the country, we were all just grateful to have a doctor, even if the drive to get there took an hour.

Jeff was relentless with his objection to me seeing a male doctor, and another side of his personality became very evident very quickly when he told me I was nothing but a s--- and he would not allow me to go again. This reaction was so upsetting and something I had never known before. So, of course, I hid it from everyone as I wanted to believe it was just him loving me and trying to protect me.

This was an extremely painful time with more tears and angry words than I care to remember. However, with much soul searching and possibly too much unconditional love for their only daughter and still carrying fear in their hearts, we received Mum and Dad's blessing to have our baby, but as was expected in those days, a very quick wedding was to be planned. Mum and Dad were very wise and watchful over me, and I remember them saying, "Are you happy?"

"Yes," was my reply.

# The Wedding

How many mixed emotions can go into planning what is supposed to be the happiest time of your life? Dad and Mum, trying to put all negative thoughts behind them and wanting their only daughter to have a beautiful wedding day, commenced planning as quickly as possible to give us the best wedding they could. Remembering even back then, weddings put everyone under a lot of pressure, both with the planning aspects and financially. This gave me so much heartache and guilt to see my most precious parents going through this stress, but, being the beautiful parents they were and still are, they reassured me that they just wanted us to be happy.

Jeff's family were wonderfully supportive, and Jeff somehow presented me with a beautiful engagement ring, and with sincerity in his words, told me he loved me, giving me the reassurance of why I loved him.

Happiness turned to sadness almost immediately when we visited the Minister to ask if he would marry us. His borderline nasty rejection of us due to his, of course, correct assumption of our circumstances, was so upsetting that I was in tears within minutes of arriving at his office, plus the dusty smell of his wall-to-wall old brown books made me (already suffering bad morning sickness) want to vomit. Somehow, he agreed to seeing us again and to performing our marriage ceremony. I have to say my thoughts of that man were not very nice, and to this day, haven't changed.

Happiness, however, did show its face again when choosing that ever so important wedding dress. My chosen bridesmaids, my cousin Stephanie, and B, my friend, and I had lots of fun laughing about having to be mindful that when choosing my dress, provisions needed to be made for a slight outward adjustment if required.

It went without saying that I would be married at the Methodist Church in Mount Lawley, the same church that Mum and Dad and Auntie Rose and Uncle Ron – in fact, where all of our family – had been married. I would also wear the same beautiful gold brooch that came from Scotland and worn proudly by Nanna Jess and every generation of girls thereafter, with the promise of good fortune.

My memory is very clear of the day we had to have a rehearsal of how the service would run and which vow out of three choices would we choose, all being pre written from ancient times, and with that ever so important love, honour and OBEY sentence always front and center of the wife's promise to God with no personal, sincere written words written by the bride or groom included at all.

I wasn't feeling well at all when we arrived at the church, but as soon as we entered the church, I felt not only like vomiting, but also I felt an uneasiness, which to this day remains with me when entering some church buildings. If the church is a shed or old, rundown wooden building, I'm okay, but the very big, brick, overpowering buildings just frightened me. The minister's approach to us didn't help either, as he was still the same unpleasant person, and became more so when I said quietly that I did not want to say the word OBEY in my vows. At this stage, I had to run outside and vomited uncontrollably behind the first tree I could find. Once again, we somehow came to an agreement on something, and to be honest, I had to put the pressure on Jeff to finalise things, as I was not thinking clearly at all.

It must have been increasingly difficult for Jeff to feel good about anything, as I had left work because of my morning sickness, which I'm sure was heightened by nerves and sheer guilt, plus with everyone organising things around us so quickly, we didn't seem to have time to get our thoughts together or even be together.

Sadly, there was nothing that could be done to help with my continual morning sickness. The devastating effects of taking Thalidomide whilst pregnant during the 50s and 60s put fear in all pregnant women, and even taking an aspirin was out of the question. I remember drinking lemon health saline and eating ginger lollies to try to make the horrible nauseous feeling go away.

The most difficult thing to organise for the wedding was the guest list and seating arrangements as protocol always played a big part, even though most times these protocols were simply an unnecessary part of every function in the era, this caused havoc, to say the least, and had most of us in tears with more upsets than was needed. But somehow, once again, we got there, and the day was finally organised.

Regardless of all that had gone on, I felt like a princess on our wedding day, and was so happy to walk down the aisle to Jeff looking very handsome and knowing that we would be living together and having our baby. I thought nothing on earth could be better than this.

I somehow managed to get through the service without being sick, and even lasted through the reception. Our honeymoon was not so smooth sailing as we had booked accommodation in the Southwest, and the driving didn't help me with feeling ill – not exactly ideal honeymoon circumstances for either of us. Surely, things could only get better from here. Sadly, no. Finding somewhere to live with only Jeff's wage to support us was never going to be easy, and with the then added need to be close to public transport, this became another hurdle to cross.

One option offered to us was to share a house with an elderly lady in Mount Lawley. But because of my protected country upbringing, I felt very uncomfortable with the option of living in an inner suburban share house, especially when the old lady offering this to us told me that the bedroom we would be sleeping in was previously her daughter's bed, and that her daughter had recently died of a broken heart.

"Yes," she said, "they say you can't die of a broken heart. But my daughter did, no doubt about that."

I felt like I couldn't breathe in that very dark, gas-smelling Death House, no matter how nice this lady was.

Jeff had done the right thing and sold his much-loved Zephyr car to help with the wedding, so we needed to find accommodation near Midland to enable him to get to work. Jeff's family were all looking for a suitable home for us, showing kindness and support. Dad and Mum were helping us look also, but, unbeknown to us, they were trying to find a house for us to buy, not rent. Dad was a very frugal and wise man, and could not see the benefit for us to rent if we could possibly afford to buy. So, with a much-appreciated helping hand in the form of a deposit from Mum and Dad, Jeff and I went to see a house they had found in Midvale that was within our reach, financially. How very fortunate we were. This house was so perfect. It had a shed, front and back verandahs, a fully stocked wood pile, chook pen, big yard and a lavatory down the back. It even had a tin roof so we could hear the rain, just like Sunnyside. What else could any young couple starting out need. Tears of joy at last. It felt like home. Everyone was happy for us. The gifts came from everywhere to help us make our home complete.

# Married Life Begins

Life was so good. Happily married, with both of our families supporting us as much as they could, living in our own home and planning for the arrival and sheer joy of our baby. What could possibly go wrong? Sadly, many things.

Of course, the most obvious problem was that we were both very young, and although I was always going to be happy being a housewife and mother, Jeff, as I see it now from more mature eyes, was far too young and certainly was not ready to endure the restrictions and pressure of marriage and a child. We had a lot of issues to sort out, just the realism that we really had nothing in common was difficult enough with totally different upbringings and perspectives about life itself.

There was an old saying: 'you can take the girl/boy away from the country, but you'll never take the country away from the girl/boy.' How very true this is, as to this day, I always feel more at ease when I'm somewhere in the wheat belt, as just breathing the air makes me feel secure with a sense of belonging. Jeff, on the other hand, was born in the city and had just found his young adult freedom with a job, car and mates to do what boys of that age did. How very sad for him to all of a sudden have his wings clipped with overwhelming responsibilities and no free money for smokes or a beer to boot.

I did feel very sorry for him that he had to sell his car. But not very long after we moved into our home, his dear dad found an old Prefect car that we were able to afford. I loved that car. It used one dollar's worth of petrol and one dollar's worth of oil each week. How good was that? We were able to visit his family in Inglewood and Morley without costing too much.

It was about at this point in the early part of our life together, that Jeff's almost unnatural jealousy and quite often nasty personality started to appear during one of our chats. Jeff revealed that he had not long broken up with a special girlfriend prior to us becoming engaged. He then asked me about my past relationships, which, as he had just revealed all, and I believed it was very important to be truthful at all times, I told him willingly that I too had had a special someone in my past. My life of hell began.

Many times, after enjoying a day with his parents, brothers and their families, I would hate the thought of going home as, by this time in our marriage, his anger was never far from appearing, especially if he had been drinking.

Jeff was always the life of the party, laughing, joking and drinking, but his mood would change almost instantly after a certain amount of drink. When we arrived home, no matter what I did or said, he would be angry, quite often, ending in physical abuse, and always verbal and mental abuse.

Jeff did work around the yard on weekends, and between us, we built a barbecue. However, because I didn't work and earn money, he was very demanding of me to keep the house and yard immaculate, which I didn't mind at all. However, if for any reason, the lawn hadn't been mowed, or some little thing was not quite up to scratch or wasn't done, I would cop abuse and be made to feel guilty and worthless to the point of convincing myself that God was punishing me for my sin of having sex before marriage. In fact, for the rest of my marriage to Jeff, this is what I firmly believed, and many times I asked for forgiveness and help to stop the fear and pain I was experiencing.

It is difficult to imagine. I know for those that have not been caught up in this roller coaster of domestic violence, and many, many ask, "Why didn't you just leave?" I also know that the thousands of other people who have also been victims do understand there are a million different reasons why these relationships fail, and even more reasons why people remain. But, like I've always said, these are only my memories and interpretations of events.

No matter what was transpiring, I was blessed with the joy of being pregnant, and I would often just hold my tummy and feel an overwhelming emotion of warmth and happiness. No matter what else had or was happening, nothing could take this feeling of unconditional love for my unborn baby away. Sheer happiness filled my heart, and I have my beautiful daughter to thank for that, Terrie, my precious firstborn. I loved you then. I love you now. And I will always love you.

I loved my home and wanted to be the best wife ever. Mum's wise advice was for me to make sure you always look nice and put makeup on before your husband gets home from work, and never let yourself go, even if you don't feel well. Remember, a little bit of powder and a little bit of paint … makes a girl what she ain't.

Another common expression was how to keep a man happy was through his stomach. I tried very hard to keep Jeff happy and felt confident that I was a reasonable cook, as I spent many hours learning from my Nanna and Mum on the farm. Unhappiness sneaks up on you. Each time there is a nasty word or a push or slap, you go to bed and think that it was your fault and that tomorrow will get better. Sadly, it quite often doesn't get better.

With the upcoming birth of our first baby drawing nearer, I was filled with so many mixed emotions – no different to most first-time mums, I'm sure – pushing aside the knowledge of the pain I was about to endure with only happy thoughts of what will our baby be, boy or girl, and what will our baby look like? Will it have hair? And many other fuzzy thoughts. Unfortunately, I also had to contend with the added pressure of Jeff relentless and overbearing jealous nature, which sadly engulfed my thoughts with nothing but anxiety and even fear. How was I going to be able to give birth to our baby, respecting all of Jeff's vicious and verbalised unnatural demands, whilst trying to relax for the well-being of our baby during labour? Jeff did not want anyone to see me, not even the nuns, even though he must have known his demands were unrealistic.

He continued with these demands: the doctor better not look or touch you. I had to be completely covered at all times. And in Jeff's words, I was already nothing but a fucking slut for having a male doctor. I also had to make sure the screen was pulled across so no other male doctors walking past could see me.

Things were just starting to change with regard to fathers being permitted to attend the birth of their child, and Jeff wanted so much to be one of the first, but sadly, St Anne's was very set in its ways, and Jeff had to wait to be called in as soon as the baby and mother were considered without risk. It would have been wonderful if he were with me during the birth, and perhaps it may have helped him feel more secure and see things in a different light.

Our beautiful daughter, Terrie Lynette, was handed to me. Tears of sheer joy welled in my eyes as I thanked God. No other feeling could ever compare. I was a mother, and unconditional love for a lifetime began at that instant.

Many of the other mothers in my room at the hospital were so amazed at my young age that they kindly felt the need to help me with all the new experience of being a first-time mum, I couldn't stop looking at our tiny little miracle, finding the need to unwrap and wrap her back up again just to see how beautiful she was.

Sadly, this happy, euphoric feeling came crushing down when Jeff said to me, "She's not mine. She's got slanty eyes."

He was oh-so young and a first-time dad, and did not realise that her squashed head and face would change very quickly, and her eyes were just perfect. And in fact, to this day, his daughter looks very much like him.

Breastfeeding became another major upsetting issue, as if it wasn't hard enough adapting to all involved with trying to give your newborn the best start in life health-wise, but to have the added pressure of being made to feel like you were doing something bad and even wrong didn't help in any way. The nuns were very matter of fact, and after a day of me failing to be able to feed my daughter, a very officious nun insisted showing me how to get the baby to latch by grabbing my nipple and pushing the baby to accept whilst all the while, the only thing I was worried about was trying to cover myself up and be discreet so as to please Jeff and avoid him showing anger. Oh, my goodness. I didn't realise that I could feel so tired.

# Married Life with First Child

The September of 1966 was a very cold, wet month. Of course, I remember it well as I spent hours and hours trying to dry nappies and baby blankets, the so-called plastic nappy cover pants of the day protected almost nothing, and therefore with every nappy change came the need to also change the sheet and blanket, and almost always the little singlet. Thank goodness for the slow combustion wood stove in the kitchen, as I was able to open the fire door and get our clothes dry when the weather was wild and windy. But nothing could take away the happiness I felt in my heart every time I looked at our beautiful baby girl. We were both very proud.

During the first few months of becoming parents, our marriage showed some form of normality, and I even felt from time to time that I could relax and be happy. But sadly, Jeff's jealousy and insecurities would, out of the blue, raise its ugly head, making me realise that the feeling some form of contentment, self-worth, and even happiness I may have been developing was nothing but a fleeting, heartfelt wish.

We did, I'm sure, have many happy times, but most of these times were when we were spending time with his family. Although I wasn't able to see my family very much, when we were able, it always proved to be a time of negativity, arguments, and the very many tears I shed could have filled a river, as the love and need to keep close to my family was being taken away from me with Jeff's every demand of me to change the way I felt towards my own wonderful dad, mum and brother. This could not happen.

*Terrie on my shoulders, six months old, Cope Street, Midvale.*

*Terrie copying her dad. Not appropriate now, but seen as cute in the 1960s*

*Terrie Lynette Anderson*

*Our first house Cope Street, Midvale.*

*Terrie and Nicole standing in front of our second house.*

*Our house Read Street, Bassendean*

# Baby Number Two

Fortunately for me, we spent almost every weekend with Jeff's brother and his young family. This was, for the most part, a time where I could relax, as my sister-in-law was, and still is, a wonderful sister-in-law, always happy and welcoming. The brothers would spend hours working on, talking about, looking at 'cars', or, should I say, Street Rods. They had two young children at that stage, and to this day, I remember and admire how relaxed their house felt. Nothing ever seemed to ruffle my sister-in-law, with cats, dogs, kids and people in and out all day. She always kept up with it all and had time for another cuppa. We spent hours chatting, feeding everyone and, most importantly, keeping the beers up to an ever-increasing number of Hot Rod fanatics who congregated in the oversized garage.

Terrie, our beautiful firstborn, was only 13 months of age when I felt pregnant with her sister, but in that brief time, she had given me more love, sheer joy and fulfilment than I could ever have imagined. Unbeknown to this darling little girl, she was the very reason I wished with all my heart to make our marriage, thus our life, happy and stable, so both she and her sister could experience a 'childhood of dreams', as I had been blessed to have been given by my wonderful parents. Sadly for Jeff, me, and especially our daughters, this proved to be a wish which struggled against all odds in its quest to be granted.

A very precious Nicole Marie was born at Swan Districts Hospital on the 6th of August, 1968, weighing 6 pounds, 11 ounces.

This was a much more relaxed birth for me in comparison to the stress I had experienced during the birth of Terrie. Jeff was not at the hospital. Therefore, I wasn't continually suffering from anxiety, worrying if a male doctor walked by or not. It was, however, a more difficult birth, as Dr Langley had to use forceps to bring Nicole into the world. Jeff was away when Nicole was born, as he had joined the Air Force cadet program in the hopes of finding a suitable career that would benefit us as a family.

Not long after Nicole was born, Jeff was granted a discharge from the Air Force on compassionate grounds and returned home. I was so happy for him to return home to see his gorgeous little girl Terrie and to meet our precious new little girl, Nicole. These feelings of excitement were very quickly turned into total disbelief, sadness and tears. Jeff did make a genuine and affectionate fuss of Terrie, which was so special. However, when it came time to meet his new daughter, all happiness quickly faded, and things changed forever. I found myself having to encourage him to move to the bassinet to even meet his beautiful new baby girl.

Jeff took one look into the bassinet, turned his back and stated in a tone of voice that, to this day, I have never recovered from, "She's not mine, you slut! She's too ugly!"

My wish for happiness for us as a family was, from that moment on, shattered.

Jeff would not have anything at all to do with Nicole for some time, but thanks to my sister-in-law's skills, and after many weeks of negotiating and encouraging, she was able to convince Jeff that how he was behaving was wrong. After a very long time – in fact, I think it was when Nicole started to say 'Dad' – that Jeff accepted his daughter Nicole. I remember at one stage I was so distraught with the fact that he would not bond or even pick her up that I ran down the street crying, saying, "If you don't love her, I'll take her away."

God only knows what I thought that would do anyway.

Thanks to my sister-in-law, things got better.

Life continued, with me devoting myself to our children, our home and trying so hard to be the wife he wanted. Jeff started bodybuilding as a hobby and achieved great heights. He came third in the Mr Perth bodybuilding competition, which was a great achievement. During these years in my marriage to Jeff, I managed to stay happy with the joy my beautiful children gave me, avoiding confrontation as much as possible with Jeff to protect our girls from witnessing me being abused in any way. Jeff was only young, and I understood that he needed to go out with his mates for some relaxation after working. But unfortunately, when he relaxed, he also drank; he would often come home very angry, and no matter what I said or did, it was not right. And many times he would attack me, either physically, but always mentally.

Sadly, from this early age in their lives, our children either heard and/or witnessed these attacks. I was always grateful if the girls were asleep, but obviously, many times they did wake up, and when I saw the fear in the eyes of our two little angels sneaking down the passage to make sure I was all right, I felt so ashamed. I felt I had let them down, and I knew I was not being the mother I wanted to be. Jeff went through stages. When he was drunk, first he was happy, then he was angry, then he was violent. But if I was fortunate, he would then get sleepy and passive. The worst thing was that after the abuse, Jeff would, many times, insist on going to bed for sex, and he could not understand why I was not able to respond as he wanted, which, of course, made him angry again. In the morning, all was normal in his eyes, and we all had to carry on as though nothing had occurred.

I had disgraced my family by being another statistic of the 60s, falling pregnant and having to get married. Therefore, the last thing I wanted to do was to be a divorce statistic. Also, my beautiful family were all well respected in the small town where they lived, and I certainly didn't want to bring any more embarrassment into their lives than I already had done.

There was no safety net for victims of abuse in the 60s, and I was also afraid that my children would be taken from me if I chose to leave Jeff. This was my biggest fear. Even though Jeff did not show love for me, I thought I was doing the right thing by not taking the children away from their father. Was this right? I know now that this was also another of my many mistakes, accumulating within as a heartache that never goes away.

Even with all these fears within me, when things became very bad, I did try to leave. One time, I tried to make a game for the children. We grabbed a few things and started off in Jeff's car to go to Mum and Dad's farm. Back then, with me being a slow driver, it was going to take four hours, but because I had to keep filling the radiator up with water and be very careful not to get burned by releasing the radiator cap too soon, it took much longer. But we finally arrived, and, as I knew, we were welcomed into loving arms.

Jeff arrived the next day on his motorbike and appeared remorseful and cried; he promised my dad that he would never hurt me again; he asked for another chance and promised faithfully to do the right thing. It was at this point that Dad told him, in no uncertain terms, that 'if you ever hurt my daughter again, I will not be afraid to go to jail for what I will do to you.'

The next morning, with Jeff under oath to my darling dad, and against all my family's wishes, I got into the car with Jeff and our children to go back to our home in Midvale. Sadly, before we had even driven five miles, Jeff was verbally threatening me that if I ever tried to leave him again, he would kill me. He continued abusing me and pulling my hair out by the roots as he was driving along. This was a nightmare trip back to Midland, as I wasn't even permitted to see to the children, as they were just told to shut up and go to sleep. From this time on, I knew I could never, ever disclose anything Jeff did to me to my parents, as I was not about to allow my darling dad to go to jail for my mistakes, and the thought of what would happen to my children if I was killed was more than I could bear.

Instead, I did all I could to give as much happiness to our daughters as possible, and to just accept the way things were and always try to make the best of a bad thing, burying my own personality and needs where possible to keep the peace.

Jeff would often go to bodybuilding competitions with his mates, and they would take their wives or girlfriends, but he never asked me to go with him. Sadly, by this stage in our marriage, I don't think Jeff felt love for me. In fact, his words to me often were, 'you're nothing but an ugly, fat nosed cunt.'

Many, many terrible things go on in abusive marriages and only those thousands of others who have fallen victim to becoming an abused person know how someone can successfully manipulate and control you to a point of no return.

I am to this day, however, so grateful that deep down, I did know, because of my upbringing, that the way I was existing was not right. But at that time, I thought God was punishing me for having sex before marriage. I heard many times about people being punished for doing wrong and going against the teachings of the Bible. So I spent many nights praying and asking for forgiveness. I would often say, "Please, dear God, I have been punished enough. Please make it stop."

Although I was ashamed, I sometimes really needed to talk to someone about my situation; perhaps I just needed a friend. Unfortunately, even when I felt I was confiding in a trustworthy person, I felt like I was, yet again, being abused in a different way. I know I possibly wasn't', but certainly felt criticised verbally by some of these friends or family. They would help, they thought, by saying things like, "It can't be too bad, or you would just leave him," or "It's your own fault … you should just leave", or "No man would ever do that to me".

As with all experiences in life, only those who have experienced the same truly know how it can be. Leaving sounds so easy to those who have not been in the same situation. Marriage, as we all know, involves thousands of tiny threads, including brothers, sisters, nieces, nephews, mothers-in-law, fathers-in-law, grandparents, friends, work, colleagues and a myriad of connections, which are all part of leaving. Not as easy as said.

Throughout our 16-year marriage, thousands of things happened, and of course, far too many to mention. But the next few little snippets I write are some of the sorts of things that I remember happening during my first marriage.

*Gaslighting! Yeah!* Finally, after all these years, there is a word for what Jeff did to me. So many times, Jeff always managed to turn a situation around where he was wrong into me either being the reason why he was wrong or somehow me just being wrong. A good example was how there were many nights during our marriage when Jeff would go out and come home late. This was common, and he always said he was drinking with his mates. As time went by, he started going out with his bodybuilding mates, and the times he arrived home became later and later. It goes without saying that even the naivest wife would feel the need to question these actions. One particular night, I heard Jeff arrive home at three-ish in the morning. Unlike other times, this time I crept down to the bathroom to observe him showering, not in a normal manner, but like he was very dirty indeed. When I questioned him as to why he needed to shower at that time of the night, and was it because he had been with another woman, he, as I know now, proceeded to gaslight me. He proceeded to yell and swear at me. With his anger turning into rage, he told me that I must be having an affair to think such things, and that I was nothing but a slut, because I was having an affair, and before very long, he was physically attacking me for being a slut and having an affair!

So many times he used this technique. Unbelievably, only now there is a name for this process. It's many years later now, I know, and possibly I'm being very childish, but golly, I feel so happy that I was not imagining this thing that he was doing to me.

Jeff was always the life of the party. Happy go lucky, charming, an all-round good bloke, as it would appear to everyone at a function. Sadly, I would call it, the 'ten-drink-turn', when Jeff would change his move from this happy life of the party person to an angry man. It may not have been so, but it certainly appeared that, after a certain amount of alcohol, he changed for the worse. Depending on the circumstances, an argument would develop, which quite often resulted in a physical altercation with a friend or brother or someone. Unfortunately, going home with this angry man was usually unpleasant. Sometimes, however, the girls and I were able to create a little fun if Jeff fell asleep in the car. We knew from past experiences not to leave him in the car and waking him up was almost impossible. So instead, we all huffed and puffed and dragged him out of the car and up the front steps, down the slippery lino passage, laughing as quietly as possible if we 'accidentally' hit his head going around the bedroom corner. We had no way of lifting him onto the bed, so we just put a pillow under his head and a rug on top, then we snuggled up in bed together, feeling a little smug that we had got away with being just a little naughty.

On a bad night, things could be different. One night, coming home from his brothers, where he had been drinking for many hours, we had reached a dark road. I was very nervous, as he had put Terrie on his knee to drive, and I had to be very careful with my words, as I knew he was very close to becoming very angry. Sadly, and I honestly can't remember what I said, but it was obviously just enough to make him turn. Within a split second, he stopped the car and yelled at me to get out: "Get out and walk, you ugly, fat-nosed cunt!" I did as he demanded and walked along the very dark road for what seemed like an eternity, with nothing in my mind but wanting to comfort my beautiful little girls. Suddenly, Jeff started driving the car towards me and yelled out, "I'm going to kill you." Then he started to laugh, stopped the car and said, "Get in, you stupid bitch." These sorts of mind games squashed my spirit further and further.

Both of my beautiful daughters tried to protect me, each in different ways. Terrie was always defensive, and even spoke back to Jeff, as little as she was, but this was, I knew, very dangerous, and so I always tried to avoid situations where this precious little angel felt the need to protect her mum and sister. How very, very sad. My heart aches to this day when I think about it.

Nicole, on the other hand, was the protector, and was always making sure I had done everything possible to avoid Jeff getting angry in the first place. She would say, "Mum, have you made Dad's chips? Mum, have you got Dad's dinner ready? Mum, have you raked the carpet? Mum, did you buy

Dad's drink?" and so on and so on. Bless her little heart, she tried so hard to make sure nothing would upset him when he came home, but sadly, most times to little avail.

One very sad memory I have is that of a very big argument occurring late one night, resulting in Jeff pushing me and Terrie (after she tried to defend me) outside the front door;, he locked us out in the cold – literally very cold as it was a winter's night.

Of course, I was not only extremely upset, but also embarrassed in case the neighbours had heard the abuse. I huddled up with my little Terrie on the floor of the carport between the car tyre and sliding side door where we were out of the breeze as much as possible, and hopefully no one could see us We were very cold and scared. It was quite some time later when I heard a tiny little voice.

*Psst! Psst!* Darling little Nicole had waited for Jeff to go to sleep, and bless her little heart, had opened the sliding door and pushed some blankets and pillows out to us to keep us warm. Can I ever get over these heart-wrenching memories?

No.

Early next morning, I went to the front door and it was open. When I questioned Jeff, he just laughed and said, "I never locked the door, you stupid fucking bitch."

So many horrible mind games.

One of Jeff's favourite displays of being a very unpleasant person was coming home from the pub and yelling for his dinner. Most times, I had it ready, but as his favourite food was steak and chips, which could not be prepared ahead of time. I had to quickly fry the chips after I heard the car turning the corner. It's still, to this day, a common joke as to how quickly I can peel potatoes. My little green peeler would peel those pretties quicker than lightning sometimes. However, whatever I prepared was not good enough, so he would proceed to throw his meal up the wall and around the room. Sometimes, just to make things more difficult, he would then demand a roast, which somehow I was expected to have ready. Now, if we were lucky, he would either go out again or go to bed. When I think about it now, it is hard to believe that the girls and I often turned this horrific event into a joke and laughed, always quietly, about it as we cleaned the flattened chips, dripping tomato sauce, fruit and custard from between the featured brick wall and off the carpet.

Jeff was a perfectionist in everything, from his personal hygiene, his home and his garden, and particularly his cars. This is not a bad thing, but it can be extremely difficult for everyone to keep up with these expectations. We had a beautiful house in Forrestfield. In fact, I loved our first house in Midvale and the one in Bassendean, but sadly, I longed for a home, not just a house. And there is a vast difference, as we all know.

The girls were getting older, and I was working at the local Coles supermarket, so we were able to purchase a new carpet for the girls' bedrooms. It was the time of shag pile carpets, and Jeff loved his home looking the best it could. How wonderful, you would think. But somehow, even the pleasure of new carpet became just another nightmare for Jeff's three possessions. I referred to Lyn, Terrie and Nicole to put up with. He very kindly bought the girls a plastic garden rake, which was to make sure there was not one footprint to be seen on their carpets. Naturally, sometimes, the girls would have walked through the doorway without raking, only to be yelled at and told that they were nothing but ungrateful little bitches.

We had a very large frontage corner block in Forrestfield, and he insisted that we clip the edges every week. He was kind, and brought us a rechargeable set of hand shears to do this job, which even with the help of the shears, due to the enormity of the length of hedging, this was a mammoth task.

The girls were given the task of cleaning the mag wheels on his car with a toothbrush, and we were all required to wash and polish the car to a point of stupidity. I knew I kept a clean and tidy house, but having things just for show, as they say, can become a very sad way to live. It was whilst we lived in Forrestfield that Jeff told me that if I ever left him, he would carve me up with a knife. I had no reason to doubt this, as he purposefully reiterated his intentions by holding our carving knife above my head and thrusting it into the lounge right beside my leg. Although I did hide the cut in the cover of the foam lounge, I always left the knife cut in the foam underneath as evidence. How silly. What difference would it have made if I was dead.

It's funny how, in amongst many very hurtful situations where some dreadful things are either said or done, it is often a very small, even insignificant in comparison, act which becomes so devastating that it can actually influence major decisions and outcomes.

We were driving past Guildford Grammar School one day on our way to his parents' house in Inglewood with the girls, who were young at the time; I had put some toys in a bag for them to play with. Unfortunately, a dispute between the girls occurred about a very special pink plastic rabbit. I honestly can't remember why it occurred, but I do remember, like it was yesterday, the girls crying as Jeff deliberately smashed it on the floor of the car. That pink plastic rabbit with black glasses was very special, as it had been given to me by my darling Nanna Hattie, and as I have explained, Nanna was someone who, through my childhood, gave me more love and life's teachings than anyone else, except my parents.

Of course, in that instant, it was not fear or upset, but hate that set into my heart. This may seem an overreaction about a small toy, but sadly, I was still mourning the sad loss of my much-loved and adored Nanna Hattie. We hear so often that everyone manages death differently, which I do believe. In fact, I would talk to Nanna every night in my prayers, knowing that she would now see my anguish, and I always felt comforted keeping her with me in my heart forever, my soulmate.

There was another time when fear instantly turned to hate, and yet again, some would laugh at the insignificance of the issue, resulting in such resentment and sheer hate. My love of animals is very real, and cats to this day are very special to me. My pet cat at that time was not only a wonderful part of our family, but he was so intuitive that he could, I'm sure, know when I was sad, so much so that he would follow me everywhere, even when I was working in the garden, laying down beside me every time I moved, giving me a special kind of support enough to lift my spirits. Cats show much love and warmth. Jeff knew how much I loved our cat. Mind Games again. One afternoon when we turned into the driveway, I noticed the cat asleep in the carport, and I said, "Please be careful. The cat's asleep." With that, Jeff sped up and laughed, and said, "Hopefully I will run over it." My heart was in my mouth, but thankfully, the cat moved in time. Too many hurtful mind-games result in pain and defeat.

*Terrie and Nicole, and Jason Skeggs, taken whilst holidaying in Denmark with friends, Alan and Helen*

*Terrie and Nicole*

## Family Life Continues

Sad but true, dysfunctional marriages not only affect the husband and wife and children, but these unpleasant ripples of a struggling marriage flow on, affecting a complete network of family and friends, who naturally, after many years of involvement, become aware of the situation, which then puts greater pressure on the already strained victim to cover up and hide the bruises (play on words).

One instance that comes to mind was during the early part of my marriage when Jeff had a friend over for a drink. Nothing unusual, and most times I would just do my own thing. This often included preparing snacks for them while they chatted and had a beer. I cannot remember why Jeff became terribly angry with me, but quite possibly, I had voiced my disagreement with them purchasing more beer or something to that effect. Unfortunately, Jeff's anger would usually result in him physically assaulting me. However, this time, as his friend was sitting at the table, he must have realised that it would not be right to hit his wife in front of a mate. So instead, and as he always had to make his point clear, he pushed me and said, "Go and stand in the corner, you ugly, fat-nosed cunt."

Instantly, I felt so demoralised and humiliated that I was unable to do anything else but go and stand in the corner.

As if the situation wasn't bad enough, I looked around foolishly, waiting for him to try and make a joke about it or something, only to be told to face the corner. "Nobody wants to see your ugly face." I couldn't help but notice the look on his friend's face. He was obviously in shock and embarrassed. Also, I am ashamed to admit that this did happen to me.

As I said, sometimes the littlest things hurt the most. My dear mum-in-law had taught me how to knit in a basketweave pattern. This pattern is easy for those who knit a lot and are clever. However, for me, who was just learning, it was very difficult, and I had to concentrate. Therefore, as a little pink jumper I was knitting for Terrie grew into shape with only a few errors, I became so proud and happy that our little girl would soon be able to wear a jumper that her mum had made. This little bit of happiness and pleasure I had created for myself was also taken away from me. One morning after an argument the night before, I went into the kitchen and noticed my knitting was not where I had left it. I searched for quite some time before a very bad feeling came over me, and I was right. I opened the door of our combustion stove only to see the burnt remains of the little pink jumper and the knitting needles lying on the burnt-out coals. I was so upset I couldn't stop crying.

Considering that through this marriage, there were many worse things that had happened and many more shhhh moments not able to even be mentioned, it seems silly to be crying over a jumper. Perhaps it was just a release of many things that were out of my control in our marriage.

Finding work for me whilst the children were young was difficult as Jeff's jealousy of me even talking to men almost narrowed employment opportunities to zilch. He told me I was useless and lazy because I didn't go to work. But every time I mentioned a position that I could apply for, he would get into a rage and accuse me of wanting to fuck the boss. However, the anger within and need for me to help with the income did eventually get the better of him, so reluctantly, he allowed me to apply for a few positions at night or when a neighbour's daughter could look after our girls. The interview itself for a position as a kitchen hand at the Midland Drive-in Picture theatre was stressful enough, let alone working there.

Of course, the boss was male, and I was required to go into his office for my interview. God only knows why he even offered me the position as I was so nervous, I was almost in tears.

However, I was to commence work that week.

Walking back to the car to tell Jeff that I had secured the position was so scary, and my heart was in my mouth knowing the reception I would receive. I was not wrong, and no matter how I answered his questions, I ended up being called a slut, and nastiness occurred.

The position was in the kitchen and entailed handling boxes of frozen fish and toasting under commercial toasters, as well as using strong chemicals for cleaning. In those days, occupational health and safety did not exist, and unfortunately, this job led me to suffering dermatitis of the hands, which still reoccurs. I worked with my head down and spoke only to serve customers when required, and only to my boss when he asked me a question. But sadly, every time I finished work, the nastiness would start all the way home and into the night.

What made it worse was that Jeff would drop me off at work and then drive straight back to the Woodbridge Hotel and drink all night with his mates and leave our beautiful little girls in the car in the car park. This was very upsetting for me, and I felt like I was failing as a mother again.

The Achilles Heel was when, one night, Jeff was already in a filthy mood prior to taking me to work, and to prove his point, he drove like a maniac from Bassendean through Guildford, all the while calling me for everything whilst exceeding the speed limit and driving dangerously. I tried to console the children and just prayed for a cop to pull him over but to no avail. That night, I gave my resignation. I also tried working at a C-Class hospital, as they were known, doing night shift so I could be home for our girls before Jeff went to work in the mornings.

Mum-in-law secured the position for me, as she was a cook at the facility. Jeff only permitted me to work there if I only worked with women patients. Bless her, my mother-in-law told him, "Yes, I will make sure Lyn will only work with the women patients." It is extremely difficult working as a nurse and not answering a call for help just because it is a male patient. My nerves were always on end, as I knew how Jeff would react if he found out what my duties really were.

I also worked at the local fruit and vegetable market in Midland, where most staff were female, which made my life at work a little less stressful. I did have to serve male customers, however, but it was so busy I just kept my head down and worked. Most times, Jeff would pick me up from work, and all the ladies I worked with would make a fuss of him and praise his physique as he was also into bodybuilding, and always wore muscle shirts to show off his pumped-up arms. He just loved the attention.

The ladies would make a fuss of Terrie and Nicole also, and it would appear that we were one big happy family. How very wrong appearances can be.

I remember clearly one day after work, Jeff did not arrive to take me home, and, as it was raining, many other staff members asked me if they could drive me home. And every time they asked, I made some excuse as to why I was okay to walk. It was only about three kilometres, but unfortunately, I had done quite a large shop during my lunchtime, and I had to carry many heavy bags of groceries all the way home, with a lot of rests and changing of hands and bag positions. I finally reached the house in the next street where our children were being looked after.

The Bradys were a large family, and their eldest daughter looked after our girls for pocket money. When I arrived, they all came out and asked me in for a cup of tea, but once again, I knew I would be in big trouble if I went inside as Mr Brady was home, so I made another excuse, and sat outside for a long time until Jeff finally arrived after being at the pub, and you guessed it, in a very bad mood. We all quickly got in the car, and before we had reached the corner, he asked, "Who the hell gave you a lift?" When I stated that I had walked home, he became even more mad, calling me a fucking liar and screaming, "You couldn't have carried all that shopping." And with that, he hit me across the face with his arm. And for once, in a long time, knowing that I would come off second best, I hit him back as hard as I could. Of course, that was not the end of it, and I once again suffered, knowing I had let my children down.

Of course, we did have some happy times during the 16-year marriage.

Sixteen years is a long time, and yes, we did have some happy times, thanks to the warmth and love from our beautiful little daughters and encouraging love from our wonderful families. One of the happy times I remember was when Jeff helped me sew and make a sit-on horse for Nicole, who, from an early age, just loved horses. Jeff did make such an effort, and he made it with love for his daughter. We even cut off the head of my broom so that we could use the handle to support the neck of the horse. It was times like this that I could see that Jeff did have another side, and I cherished these moments. I still have a photo of Nicole's happy little face when we gave her this special gift.

*Nicole Marie Anderson*

*Nicole on the handmade horse with sister Terrie.*
*Reid Street, Bassendean.*

I remember also one Christmas when Terrie and Nicole were young, the joy I felt seeing their little eyes light up when they received their big new dolls, along with an array of clothes for each doll, which Father Christmas had lovingly sewn just in time.

Erecting a much-longed-for ten-foot above-ground pool was an incredibly happy day for the girls. Jeff worked as quickly as he could assembling the pool, considering our girls and their best friend Nicole from next door were out of bed at the crack of dawn in their bathers with surfboards at the ready for their first swim. Fortunately, and much later that day, half full became deep enough for an excited and happy test run. We enjoyed many happy times with Jeff's brothers and their wives and children on the weekends, including one time when my father-in-law bought an old, quite large wooden boat. The excitement was out of control when all the kids were told we were going in Pop's new boat.

We all arrived at the river with kids, dogs, food, drinks and sunscreen, amid screeches of happiness, ready for this great adventure. Oh, my goodness, when we eventually saw this boat, which we had heard so much about, we couldn't stop laughing, as there it was in all its glory, half-submerged on the muddy bank of the Swan River. Jeff's dad had forgotten to mention that we needed to somehow float the boat before we could even think about tonking down the river.

After a few minutes of coming to grips with the situation, no one seemed to mind, as the brothers knew their dad very well, and nothing was ever too much of a surprise with some of the things he did. Needless to say, that day, and after Pop gave warning to his grandchildren not to swim in the river because of bull sharks, the cousins spent their time amusing themselves eating the food and getting dirty, whilst us girls sat under a tree chatting. Jeff, his dad, and brothers arranged to hire a pump to refloat our transport for the next day, hopefully. There was an early replay the next day, with the same excitement, except with a little touch of anticipation added, to see if the boat had stayed afloat during the night, or not. Yes, it was afloat, but unfortunately, it had taken in enough water to need a quick pump out prior to seven adults and eight children climbing on board for the long-awaited ride in Pop's amazing new boat.

Off we went, inhaling a strong smell of fuel all the way, and with everyone quietly nervous, a quick Jetty stop was made for supplies from the Mayland's pub, then back on board to return from whence we came before the boat sank. To this day, I think the world of my sisters-in-law from my first marriage; they gave me love and support and protection, and that bond remains, even though many years have passed and much has changed in all our lives. We still sometimes touch base with each other, and the warmth is still between us. I will always have fond memories.

My mother-in-law was a very special lady, and nothing was too much trouble. We could all turn up together at meal times unannounced, and within a fleeting moment, she had managed to make a pound of mince feed fourteen or more. Her dessert specialty was shortbread apple pie, which was almost devoured prior to it even coming out of the oven.

My mother-in-law had a beautiful garden and a big backyard. In those days, burning rubbish in one's backyard was a normal practice, and just loved a big fire. Hmm, maybe that's where my grandsons got their pyromaniac tendencies. Only joking, of course. However, many memories are suddenly flashing into my mind, like the day Cody built a massive fire in a hollowed-out black boy with flames and sparks billowing high in the sky, and the time Jake, Cody and Luke made tennis balls into giant firecrackers by using the scrapings from the outside of sparklers, then packing the powder into tennis balls, and presto, a massive accident was going somewhere to happen.

Oh, yes ... don't think I've forgotten the big bang at the caravan park that you all knew nothing about. Actually, the more I think about it, the more I think about it, my mother-in-law's weekend burn-offs may have had a bit to do with a few things that occurred. Who knows? All I do know is that nothing made the grandkids happier than helping Nanna burn off. Yay. There wasn't a stick left anywhere as the kids fueled the fire with anything and everything.

My poor mother-in-law certainly had her time cut out watching who was throwing what into the fire. This particular evening, we were all sitting out the back watching what was going on, with Mum happily raking the edges in as the fire had come to its end. All the grandkids were just running around, lapping up being kids, when all of a sudden, from the middle of the almost extinguished fire, there was a big explosion with black ash filling the air, bringing everyone to a silent halt. Within seconds, and after ensuring no one was hurt, uncontrollable laughter erupted when Jeff's mum, covered in black ash, eyes wide open, rake still in hand, turned and said, "I probably shouldn't have left that empty hairspray can in there."

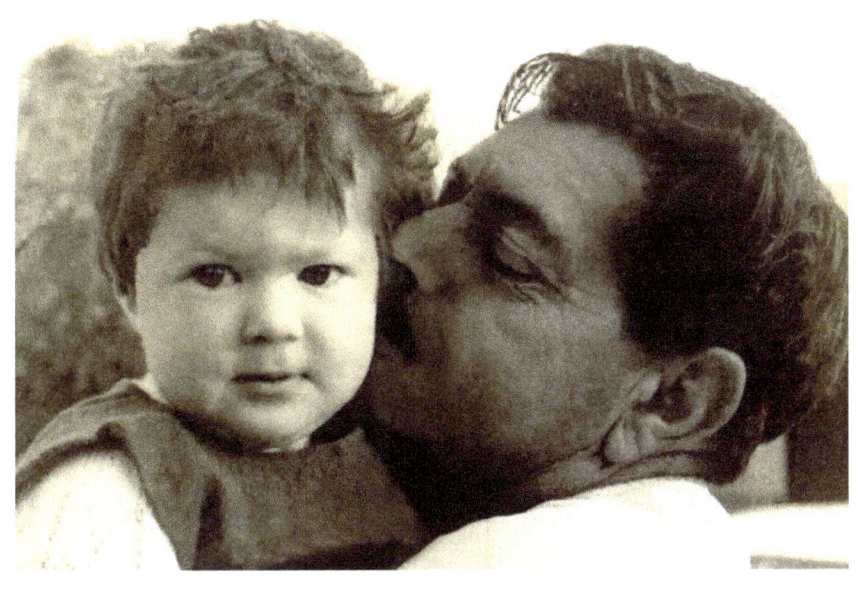

*A beautiful photo of Terrie with her Pop, my dad.
Every picture tells a story.*

# Holiday Happiness at the Farm

Mum and Dad were unable to see their adored grandchildren as much as they desired, mainly due to the livestock commitments at Sunnyside farm, but when they did visit us, my heart was filled with joy, accompanied by an indescribable feeling of being unconditionally loved, bundled together with such a warm feeling of security and safety. There is no doubt in my mind that Terrie and Nicole felt this total love and safety also. When it was school holidays, Mum and Dad would arrive at our house with a car full of much-appreciated gifts, including meat packed ready for the freezer, copious, lovingly sewn outfits of clothing for Terrie and Nicole, a butt of wheat for our feather legged bantams, plus a couple of spare wheat bags to use as mats at the back door when the ground was wet and muddy.

These visits filled me with memories of home.

Sunnyside Farm was and always will be my home. Although I moved back to Perth to work as a teenager, Mum and Dad and Brian always had my back, helping in any way possible to ensure that my life was comfortable and, above all, happy. Many times, Dad would hand me an envelope with money in it, which had been split three ways between Brian, Mum and myself, as it had always been done, from the money was made selling the off-cuts of wool after shearing. Thank you is just not enough to express the gratitude I felt back then and to this day for all the support I received from my family.

School holidays were a time when Mum and Dad could spend some precious time with our girls, and although I missed them so much, I also knew just how beneficial the time at Sunnyside was for our beautiful girls. In fact, the time Terrie and Nicole spent on the farm with Mum and Dad did, I now know, have an enormous impact on them for the rest of their lives. It was here with my mum, dad and brother that Terrie and Nicole's little torn souls had time to mend, and where they were able to see another side of family life.

Yes, there were still arguments and disagreements in my family, but the hatred, bitterness and physical attacks were not part of my upbringing, and my girls were able to see clearly the differences, thank goodness. As I have done throughout my life, they were able to base their lives on the memories of these happy times at Sunnyside Farm. My mum and dad gave my children their childhood back, playing in puddles, riding on the tractor, picking mushrooms, playing in the freshly plaid paddocks, learning how to ride the Vespa, climbing rocks, catching tadpoles, feeding the baby lambs, learning how to play golf, lighting the fire, cooking, feeding the cows, collecting the Mallee roots, toasting toast on an open fire, enjoying the feel of a calf licking their hands, looking at the stars on the dark night, listening to their Pop whistle as he worked. Unconditional love.

## Too Many Storms

No matter how many times I tried to rebuild all the tiny, little broken threads in my Web of Life during this marriage, there came a time when the threads became too bare, and I knew that it was time for me to find the strongest thread and stand firm, allowing what was left of the tiny, little broken marriage threads to fall from my life.

This decision did not come easily. As everyone who has suffered the humiliation, pain and mental torture of domestic violence knows, the hardest thing is to regain enough confidence to rebuild, including finding yourself again. This sounds silly, I know, but after a marriage where you've been totally controlled in every aspect of your life, you actually 'feel' like a nothing person.

During the latter part of my marriage to Jeff, I was working at Coles in Forrestfield, which was within walking distance of our house. I loved my position as a Check-out Controller, and work was my happy place. I had a wonderful relationship with all the girls, and we spent our lunch hours chatting, as girls do. As far as they knew, I was happily married with a nice house and two beautiful daughters. Obviously, for many reasons, they never heard anything to the contra from me. I did, however, listen very closely to the many situations like mine that were occurring in other marriages.

Throughout my marriage, I suspected Jeff of being unfaithful, but every time I broached the subject, I would end up being either abused or gaslighted to the point of being the perpetrator. Many of the behavioural patterns that I had noticed in Jeff were mentioned repeatedly by other women in these conversations, which made me realise that it was not my imagination.

Jeff was on holidays, and at that time, I was still working. Many little changes in his behaviour made me suspicious to the point of setting a little trap to catch him in the act of having an affair. This was a huge risk for me, and I was scared beyond words. That night as I turned all the lights out and checked all the doors before we went to bed, I deliberately unlocked the side sliding door, which led into the dining room and adjoining lounge room. The following morning, everything was as normal. The kids went off to school, and I kissed Jeff goodbye and shut the front door behind me and commenced walking down the road to work, but, as I reached next door's driveway, I quickly and quietly snuck back, crawled inside through the side sliding door and hid behind the bar in the lounge room. As luck would have it, within a minute or two, Jeff went to the phone nook and made his call. I remember this call very clearly.

Jeff said, "Hi, darling. I'm sorry I didn't ring sooner. It took a while to get rid of her this morning." He did say more, but that was all I had to hear. The look on his face when I walked out from behind the bar was so rewarding in itself. I had waited such a long time to catch him in the act, and I had finally succeeded.

I remember being completely out of control for quite a while, screaming, crying, yelling, hitting out at him, and for the first time, he did nothing, but try to calm me down. Somehow, the turbulence turned to talking, which was something we never did as the norm in our house. Usually, Jeff said how it was, and we his possessions, just listened and obeyed.

What I'm about to tell you next is difficult for me, even now, to comprehend in any way, shape or form, but it is what happened.

Jeff told me that his girlfriend was a lovely person and that I would like her, and he wanted to take me with him to meet her. Oh, my goodness, I did want to meet her, *but not to be friends*. My mind was like a washing machine. I honestly couldn't put two thoughts together. Jeff drove me to her house, and this woman greeted me like a friend. It was just too much for me to process, so when I was offered a drink, I accepted and kept drinking until I vomited repeatedly whilst hanging in this strange woman's toilet who had been having an affair with my husband.

Could it get any worse?

Yes, of course, it could, as in amongst all of this, I was repeatedly saying that we needed to be home for the girls when they arrived home from school. What I didn't realise was that Jeff had already driven home and brought them back to witness their mum crying uncontrollably whilst throwing up in a stranger's toilet. My poor children ran to me with horrified looks on their faces, as they were totally confused, scared and just didn't know what was happening. His girlfriend firmly told me that she didn't want to lose Jeff and suggested openly that we should share him. My thoughts when we left that house were of disbelief and hatred. Of course, I was going to end the marriage. I had every reason and more to leave, but as always, Jeff was very convincing that he was sorry and would leave his girlfriend and never, ever do it again. Blah, blah, blah.

Why did I let him convince me to stay, you ask?

Only God knows.

I can say that perhaps it was the millions of things that would come into the equation of a 16-year marriage breakup, or just the endless longing I had inside me to never be a divorce statistic, or even just me being stupid, holding on to my dreams of Jeff finally being able to give me love and to have a loving father for my children, or maybe I was just completely exhausted, both physically and mentally, and could not face the unknown. Who knows? But it goes without saying that I went back to work the next day with a smile on my face, encasing myself in the warmth of my friends, whilst all the while knowing deep down, I had made another, maybe the biggest, mistake in my life.

Leopards cannot change their spots is a phrase I have used so many times since then in my life, and for very good reason. Although I did not leave Jeff after this affair, I was never able to recover to the point of acceptance. From that time on, my mind relentlessly went over and over everything that had occurred during our marriage, night and day, never letting up. I was hiding just how very far from being normal our marriage was, I quietly bided my time from then on, knowing I would not have to wait long and, lo and behold, my prediction was right, which in turn added to the small amount of confidence I was slowly building within myself.

About a year and a half later, I knew Jeff was having another affair. As luck had it, by this time, Terrie had taken up a hairdressing apprenticeship in Perth and was staying with her auntie and uncle to make it easier to travel by bus to work. Nicole was staying with Mum and Dad in Rockingham during the school holidays. Therefore, I didn't have to consider the girls, leaving me free to do what had to be done. For some time, I had been noticing Jeff displaying the same behavioural patterns as a year prior to this time, but this time, I was prepared and focused and was no longer afraid of becoming a divorce statistic.

One afternoon, Jeff was being ever so nice and said, "We'll go to the Drive-ins. You cook the chicken to take and I'll be back in time. I'm just popping down to see my mate. I waited a short time, turned off the oven and drove to where he said he was going. His car was not there, so I knocked on the front door, only to be greeted by a very red-faced, flustered friend of his. "Where is Jeff?" I demanded.

His friend had trouble answering me, but the first thing he did say was, "Don't worry about it. Just go home. He'll be home soon."

Not good enough for me by this stage, and I remember screaming at the top of my voice, "Where is he?"

After this person came to grips with seeing a very different wife of Jeff's bringing some unwanted attention to his door, he quietly said, "He might be at the local pub." This was going to be my next point of call anyway, but it just confirmed what I already suspected.

If I wasn't already fired up enough before, I certainly was when I walked purposefully into the bar of that pub, immediately seeing Jeff and his girlfriend sitting happily together having a drink with not a care in the world. Not for long! I am actually very proud of myself. I didn't raise my voice or make a scene that anyone else would have noticed. I did, instead, just walk up behind them both and look her in the eye and said, "Thank you. Thank you from the bottom of my heart. You have done me such a favour. He is all yours. Good luck." Then I turned to Jeff and said, "Goodbye. I am leaving you. You will never hurt me again. We are over." And with that said, I dropped my wedding ring into his glass of beer and left.

Oh, what a feeling! I love that saying!

He followed me out to the car park, and we exchanged a few words, not that I heard much of what was said, but I do remember seeing him trying to stop me, but I just kept driving. I arrived at Mum and Dad's home in Rockingham, and said,

"I've left Jeff. Could I please have a cigarette?"

I remember Mum saying, "But you don't smoke," and Dad's follow-up words, "But she wants one now."

Nicky put her arms around me and said, "Have you really left, Mum? You're not going back, promise. You've really left."

I said very calmly, "Yes, I have left for good."

I then rang Terrie and told her, and after an immediate response, almost the same as her sister's, she said, "Are you sure, Mum? If you are, I'm coming home."

The unbreakable bond between us three girls, Terrie, Nicole and myself was, from that time on, sealed with unconditional love for eternity. One for all, all for one.

*Nicole's 16th birthday.*

*Nicole with a rose.*
*Ssshh heartfelt thoughts.*

*My beautiful daughters. My love for you is unconditional.*

*United for life. Terrie Lyn, Nicole,*

# Love, Laughter and Happiness

Not long after I left Jeff, I heard that his girlfriend had moved into the house with him, and for this, I felt nothing but happiness. Another unusual reaction, you might think, but I felt that if he was happy, he might leave me alone to get on with my life also. Thankfully, this was the case. The girls and I had moved into the local caravan park, where for the first time we could relax, enjoying the moment, making plans for our new future together as us, three girls, bonded as one forever. Staying at the caravan park was like a holiday for us. Close to the bus, work, school and with a swimming pool as well, we were living the life. Most importantly, I could afford the rent on the wage I was earning. I am immensely proud to say that even though I left with only $240 and a tax return, which paid the bond on the caravan, I managed to support the three of us with the help of board money, which Terrie paid willingly.

Remember, there was no single mother's supporting benefit in those days, and no child support rules, either. Women were on their own.

All good. I was happy.

I was more fortunate than many women in my position back in the 60s, as I always had the unconditional love and support from my dad, mum and wonderful brother, for which I, to this day, remain eternally grateful.

I don't think I even took a day off work, but when I did return to work, I certainly remember feeling lighter of heart, almost like the cat that swallowed the canary as I put my bag in my locker, and greeted my friends, just like any other day. I loved my job and the friendship of all the girls at 365 – all Coles supermarkets were numbered when I was working as Check-out Controller at Forrestfield Coles. I didn't mention to anyone that I had separated from my husband for quite some time, but when I did tell the girls that I was now living at the caravan park and separated, they hugged and cuddled me, voicing nothing but words of support for which I felt truly blessed.

Communication with any of the male staff remained very formal. Years of being abused and called nothing but a slut or worse, if Jeff ever saw me speaking to a male, forced me to have an inbuilt ability to show no emotion or even facial expression when at work if any of the male staff had to discuss work issues with me. Only those who have experienced a similar situation will understand when I say, from that day I left Jeff, every minute, every hour of every day of my life became saturated with sheer happiness, enlightened with a sense of freedom of thought, freedom of speech, and most of all the power to use my long-lost ability to live. Tiny little things insignificant to others gave so much joy – turning the TV knob, even if it made a noise – this was one thing that the girls and I always laughed about. And actually, to this day, Terrie remembers how we exaggerated the knob turning for months later – making up my mind to go out or go shopping without having to justify why I needed to go and how long I'd be away and how much money I could spend, – and for once, being able to go somewhere without having to hear the never-ending accusations and being questioned as to whether I was going to meet someone. The amount of pressure that had been lifted from my heart and soul was overwhelming, to say the least.

I'll never forget the first time I decided to drive into Perth to buy a new pair of bathers. Driving into the city on my own was never allowed, for what reason I'm not sure, but possibly just another way of keeping me under his control. So you can only imagine the sheer joy it gave me to actually drive into the city, park in an undercover park, and most of all, choose a pair of bathers of my choice. This was a very happy day. I even remember laughing uncontrollably in the change-room when trying on a pair of bathers. I unconsciously bent over to see if my cleavage would show, which, in the past, was the most important condition for me to be able to wear bathers, when all of a sudden, I burst out in uncontrollable laughter. It must have been the devil coming out in me when I realised that it was my choice to wear the bathers, even if they were slightly revealing. I'm sure the lady assisting me wondered why I was laughing, but I wasn't embarrassed. I was happy as I purchased my new revealing bathers with much joy in my heart. Snuggling up together on the lounge, even putting our feet up, was such a special time for us, three girls – just being able to relax was an unbelievable feeling.

Not long after we three girls had started our new life together, I was driving to work and noticed a lovely unit for rent just opposite the high school. Living in the caravan was wonderful, but having a toilet and laundry and even our own bedrooms would, I knew, be so much better, if it was at all possible.

The confidence to be able to make decisions for myself was becoming bigger than Ben Hur by then. So the next day, I made an appointment to look through the unit in Berkshire Road, Forrestfield. Thank goodness, renting a home back then wasn't as difficult as it is now. The real estate agent was extremely helpful, and with the return of the bond from the caravan park and help from the bank in the form of a small loan to cover the rent in advance, I was able to secure a very comfortable home for us. I did have some furniture, but thanks to the always kind generosity of my wonderful dad and mum, who made a quick trip down to the local second-hand dealers, all our simple needs were taken care of.

We were as happy as pigs in mud.

I just loved the Laminex table they bought as it was very similar to the one at Sunnyside. And, of course, anything that reminded me of Sunnyside brightened my day. Naturally, this newfound freedom we had all discovered after years of being totally controlled as though we were possessions, was bound to have some consequences. The girls were teenagers. Need I say more. Combine this with a new and so exciting boundary-stretching desire, coupled with the fact that I was working full-time and studying three nights a week, and you've soon inherited a few developing issues to address. I was so pleased that the unit was over the road from the school, but so were the girls and all of their friends.

On returning home from work, I would often be greeted by wall-to-ceiling teenagers all waiting, in turn, to give me the biggest hug as I tripped over their bags and shoes piled high inside the front door. Endeavoring to make myself be heard over the ear-piercing music and sheer loud voices of a house full of excitable teenagers on the loose was the next task. Almost every time I arrived home, I felt sure that, in a very short time, I had adopted half of the Forrestfield Senior High School.

I loved this chaos, but it goes without saying, adjustments had to be made with not only this situation, but with many other newfound freedom occurrences we were faced with during this adjusting time as us three girls. It was just so wonderful to be able to enjoy my daughters to the fullest, and even more wonderful for them to want to be part of the enjoyment.

My daughters treated me like their sister. This may seem wrong to some, however, the girls only ever saw me being treated exactly like they were treated. Thus, I never, for one moment, felt they were disrespecting me as their mother. They loved, respected and adored me as their mother and both of my beautiful daughters gave of themselves to protect and love me unconditionally, so much so I have never felt that I have thanked them enough for devoting their young lives, in fact, their entire lives, to ensuring I experienced every happiness possible. I love, adore and thank you, my beautiful daughters.

One amazing time we spent was going to the Royal Show. I had never driven to Claremont before, let alone with seven screaming teenagers crammed in my HR Holden making so much noise that I couldn't hear myself think. I did, of course, try to explain that no way everyone could fit into the HR. But, of course, I was proven wrong when every sweat-smelling teenager reassured me that they could still breathe and were in! The uncontrollable high-pitched screams and laughter reached an all-time high every time the poor car bottomed out on the smallest of bumps. Looking back, this was totally irresponsible, I know, but did we have fun! Perhaps I shouldn't even mention getting back into the car with all the show bags, teddies and fairy floss. No, I won't mention that, but I will just say sticky, along with even more sweat odour. Nice.

## Newfound Happiness

Every day was a new challenge, as now I realised it was me and me alone making decisions that would not only affect me but also have a huge influence on two teenage girls who were by that stage, soaking up life with gusto. I knew I must endeavour to be the best role model possible for my beautiful daughters. I was building new and exciting threads in my Web of Life. My money was a little tight on my wage, but we didn't go without a good meal, and all the bills were paid, and thanks to my reliable HR, who knew that she had to run on the smell of an oily rag for a few days before payday, we were happy little chappies.

Going to work was like meeting my friends for a coffee. I enjoyed working, and it always gave me pleasure if I could turn a sad, angry-faced customer into a happy, smiley customer, just by giving them the time of day and a kind word. Being able to relax more at work also helped, so much so that I became competent enough to enjoy a joke or two with some of the male staff members, although things were still very formal and every staff member was referred to as Mr, Mrs, or Miss. My girls, as I call them, called me Mrs.

We had so much fun at 353.

Once we dressed up as shopping bags – remember shopping was put into brown paper bags back then. We made big bags with our Cole's logo on the front and our heads poking out of the top, surrounded by cardboard shopping items. Standing at the front of the check-outs we sang, "We're happy little check-out chicks, we hail from 353, we all enjoy our customers and hope this you can see ..."

I've forgotten the rest, but it was to the old Vegemite tune. No one minded making a fool of themselves to make the customers laugh.

In the 80s, check-out chicks, as they were referred to without offence taken by anyone, entered a competition to find the fastest and most accurate check-out operator in, not only each supermarket, but in WA. Registering items was done by hand, with the operator pulling each item past her, reading and pricing it, then ringing it up on the manual cash register and sliding it into the packing area in one smooth action. This was done with amazing speed. Many a can of baked beans would go hurtling over the back end of the check-out, sliding to a dented halt well into the mall. But, of course, the girls would be judged on accuracy as well as speed.

Mary was our entrant, and often after work, we would put her through her paces, cheering her on in the hopes that our supermarket would be the winner.

*Happy little check-out chicks*

Sadly, I can't remember all the girls' names, but Kay, who was also my neighbour at Alamanda Way, Forrestfield, is fifth from the left, and I'm last. PS. Afro hairstyle was in fashion.

With my newfound or resurrected confidence, I also organised an inter-supermarket Sports Day. This was held at Tomato Lake, and, from what I can remember, six supermarkets competed in either a relay, sack, egg and spoon, or wheelbarrow race, and everyone made some effort to have a good day. The girls at work kept me busy, and it was wonderful to relax with my friends at work. I do remember having a few shhhh moments during this time.

One afternoon, whilst finishing work, which included closing off the registers not in use, Mr Writer, the supermarket manager, approached me, inquiring about the roster for the next day. This was a standard end-of-day procedure. However, then, in a very different manner, he asked caringly, "Are you going okay, Mrs A?"

My immediate answer was "Yes, really well, thank you."

We continued our conversation for a short time before he headed back to the office. Within a few minutes, my thoughts were working in overdrive. I felt somewhat flustered, confused, anxious and certainly slightly scared, as I realised that Mr Writer was talking to me as a friend, not as a work colleague. This could not be happening. Why would anyone want to talk to me like that? My insecure thoughts quickly went back, "You're nothing but an ugly, fat-nosed c...," convincing myself that the conversation that had occurred with Mr Writer was surely only my imagination. I shook myself, tried to regain some composure, completed my duties, while all the time trying to ignore my scrambling thought flashes, then hurried to the safety of my home, trying ever so hard to process these long, hidden emotions.

For me, working at 353 was never the same from that day on, and I could not have been happier. Mr Writer made it clear how he felt, and we started seeing each other, always under the cover of darkness, as the saying goes, to avoid one of us being transferred to another supermarket. Back then, it was company policy to not permit couples to work together. At this point, I would just like to say that no one goes into marriage with the intent of becoming a divorce statistic. Obviously, I can only speak on behalf of myself. I stayed in my broken marriage for 16 years, always praying for things to get better, but sadly, they never did. Becoming another statistic made me feel like a failure in every way, and I am surmising that most people who divorce feel the same. There is so much pain and suffering for not only the couple that go their own ways, but their children, family and friends also. Sadly, many people have become very blasé about divorce. However, the decision to divorce can have devastating outcomes. Children, no matter what age, suffer the most, and this silent pain and suffering can and does often carry on long after their parents have separated.

I saw this pain, not only in my own children, but the heartache and pain Max's children suffered to this day makes my heart heavy. I will never be able to thank both my children and Max's children for enduring so much pain and suffering while at the same time supporting Max and me in our endeavour to find true love and happiness.

And we sure did.

## Snippets of Memories

As I mentioned before, it was always kept quiet if a staff member was in a relationship with another staff member within the same supermarket. It was not permitted, being seen as inappropriate. It goes without saying that most times everyone knew anyway. It was coming up to the annual Christmas party for the staff and management being held at the local venue in Forrestfield. Most of the girls attended every year, but unfortunately, I was never able to attend before this year. When they asked, out of politeness, if I would be going, as they had always done in past years, they also cheekily asked if I was going to bring a boyfriend. When I replied, "Yes," they all became very excited and said, "Really? We don't believe you have a boyfriend." I, once again, said, "Yes," and they all looked extremely surprised, and I could tell not one of them believed me, as in the whole time I had worked with them, I had hardly ever even spoken to a male.

The night of the Christmas get-together, Max and I were a little late, and when we walked in, no one took any notice. They were just glad we had finally arrived so the long-awaited finger food could be brought around to help soak up the copious amounts of alcohol being consumed. I joined the girls who were already showing signs of their drinking skills, and within seconds of me arriving, one of them said, "I thought you said you were going to bring your boyfriend. We knew you wouldn't."

I replied quietly, "I did."

Less than a minute later, the penny dropped, and all the girls were screaming with excitement, hugging us and saying how happy they were for both of us. I may have forgotten some of their names, but the sincere warmth I felt from these wonderful friends will remain special to me always. Needless to say, within a very short time, I was transferred to another Coles supermarket.

## Second Marriage: Life Begins Again

Without a doubt, Max was truly God's blessing sent to me, not only to show the true meaning of love, but to give me the strength, support, encouragement, and, with his unwavering total devotion, the strength to become my true self again. Max gave me life and laughter beyond my expectation, but most of all, with his unconditional love, he gave me my freedom. This much-welcomed gift of freedom encouraged me to embrace life and relive all that was good and true, including the values that had been lovingly instilled in me as a child by Mum and Dad.

Although circumstances during my first marriage sometimes prevented me from using these life skills, I always treasured them, carrying them in my heart as protection, which gave me the strong foundation needed to rebuild a happy future for my beautiful, deserving daughters. The enormity of joining two families who didn't know each other from a bar of soap could and, in many similar cases, would have been impossible. However, because of the compassion and unselfishness of our combined five children, along with support from their husbands, wives, partners, Max and I were able to strengthen our love and together build the most wonderful, strong, loving and bonded family, which we planned would last a lifetime.

It goes without saying that we encountered many hiccups along the way. However, because our love was so strong, together we were able to handle the world just as well! Our wedding was unforgettably beautiful, with copious overwhelming wishes for our future happiness showered upon us by our families and friends. My darling dad and mum were there to see their prayers answered as Max and I held hands, declaring our deep, emotional love and happiness. Our children all helped organise the day and honoured us by not only all being in our bridal party, but by showing acceptance of our union.

*Wedding of Maxwell John Writer and Lynette Margaret Anderson.*

*I just love this photo. Happy memories.*

*Left to right. Annemarie, Ceri, Terrie, Nicole, Lyn, Max, Greg, Paul and Michael*

## Our Life Together

How difficult can it be to build a Web of Life? We all know the answer. It takes all the strength we can muster to build and rebuild those tiny, little threads of life over and over again, as storms continually occur throughout our lives. We must never allow ourselves to slip under the weight of the heavy, wind-blown raindrops, even if we feel we can hang on no longer. Max and I had a united love, and that strong shared love gave me all the strength I needed to keep building tiny threads after tiny threads of our ever-challenging and ever-enlarging Web of Life.

Our honeymoon was amazing. I had never travelled out of WA. Max's family lived in New South Wales, and were unable to attend our wedding, so it only made sense for us to travel to Sydney and Young, to include them in our celebrations, and for me to meet Max's dad, brother and sisters and extended family. How wonderful. It felt like we had known each other for years, as I was made to feel so welcome, we had much in common, and, when we arrived in the country town of Young, I felt like I could have been in Nungarin. The big difference, of course, was that Young was the cherry capital of Australia, and Nungarin was well … Nungarin was my wheat/sheep capital of the world. The truth is that the country town, any country town, atmosphere, is second to none, and to this day brings joy to my heart.

Max's sister Shirley and her husband, Colin, went out of their way to make sure we saw and did everything possible whilst we were there with them. We play cards at night, wetting our whistles with a little drink or two, and talking nonstop until the wee hours of the morning, all the time, laughing at Colin's clever, dry humor until we could laugh no more. Although I pride myself for having the Sainsbury's gift of the gab, I'm telling you, Shirl could give anyone a run for their money, and I just loved it. We had an immediate bond, and this bond remains today. Love you, Shirl.

## More Snippets and Memories

To put years of memories into words isn't quite as easy as I first thought, so I will just write snippets of events that come to mind and that occurred during this very hectic time in our lives. Jeff had sold the house in Alamanda Way, and there was a small amount of money as a result of the sale, to be equally shared between Jeff and myself. Thank goodness for Mum and Dad, who had insisted that our house be in both names. I received this quite unexpected windfall from the bank while still living at the unit in Berkshire Road.

I remember Max asking what I was doing on a particular afternoon.

My reply was, "I'm going to Belmont shopping centre to buy some sheepskin seat covers for my car. I won't be too long."

Whilst driving along Berkshire Road, I noticed a sign saying, Unit for Sale. With my newfound relaxed disposition, I thought, *I'm not under any pressure. Why not? I'd like to just have a look and get an idea of prices around Forrestfield.*

The unit was the last in the street, with bush and trees alongside, which I thought was really nice. I entered the lounge area through a fern-covered courtyard, which immediately gave a welcoming feeling. The unit was very appealing, with three bedrooms, separate lounge-kitchen, and surprisingly, a good-sized backyard.

Out of interest, I asked the price.

The real estate salesman very confidently explained that I would be able to purchase the unit quite easily with a small deposit, plus the fact that my income was sufficient, and best of all, the repayments would be no more than the rent I was paying. Within 20 minutes, I had made an offer subject to financial approval from my bank. All good. No need to overthink or procrastinate. I already knew the advantages of owning your own home, and besides, I was on an adrenaline rush of making my own decisions. I sat in the car for a moment to think about what had just transpired, only to feel an overwhelming sense of joy and excitement. No time to go to Belmont now – I had just bought a home, and the sky is the limit. When I spoke to Max, he asked if I had managed to buy the seat covers, and I replied, "No, I bought a home instead." Love and laughter.

Soon after we were married, Terrie moved out to live in a caravan park with a group of friends. I knew the parents of one of the girls who shared the costs with Terrie. What else went on is possibly better left in Terrie's past as the beginning of building her own Web of Life.

When I visited the caravan as a mother would do, there seemed to be wall-to-wall teenagers all discovering freedom with not a care in the world, and the one thing I remember clearly was that obviously none of them used deodorant.

The caravan park was close by, and although the situation was not ideal, I could only have faith that she would be okay. Terrie's strength and capability had been put to the test many times in her early life, and the sister-mother-related bond we shared was very strong, therefore I had no fear that Terrie would turn to me if she felt the need.

In hindsight, I now feel that it was at this very early stage in her life when my darling daughter Terrie began her inherited life of walkabout, which to this day remains. Removalist's phone number always at the ready.

Nicole and Greg were living home with us. As I've mentioned, blended families can have a few hiccups. Greg was Max's youngest, and Nicole was my youngest. Sometimes, they didn't see eye to eye, to say the least.

Our unit was small and Nick's bedroom was off the kitchen, and Greg's was off the lounge room. One evening, after finishing our dinner, Max and I settled down in the lounge to watch TV when I noticed what I thought was a horrible large poster stuck on the door of Greg's bedroom. I loved the simple but colour-coordinated decor in the lounge room, and this poster did not look good, so I immediately removed the poster only to see why it was there. I must say the hole in the bedroom door did a lot less to enhance the decor. The one with the red fist was given a week to fix the damage. Oh, my goodness, that large, grey blob of putty jammed into the hole did even less to improve things.

The painting at the top of the next page is very meaningful to me. I painted this for Elizabeth for her 80th birthday. It was taken from a photo that I noticed on the wall at Elizabeth's home in Albany.

For some reason, I was attracted to it, and especially when I was told it meant so much to Elizabeth, as it was the home she grew up in as a child. That was enough for me, as I knew how much Sunnyside meant to me. Bill helped me get a copy of the little photo, and I just loved painting these happy memories for Elizabeth.

I painted the Boab tree for Marika, one of her favourite native trees.

*Some of the many paintings, thanks to Max encouraging me to revisit what was important to me.*

## Kindness, Always

Max was one of the kindest men imaginable. During the entire time we were married, his total devotion, love, kindness and understanding, and compassion never wavered. He encouraged me to do and be the person I wanted to be, no matter what that was. Max helped me achieve my dreams of a marriage full to the brim with trust, truth, togetherness and so very importantly, sensual fulfilment.

Art was something that I loved, and Max encouraged me to get involved with that passion of mine. He praised every painting I did, good or bad, but most of all, he gave me as much time as needed, always. After we moved to Rockingham, I joined the Dorothy Lily Council for Art Rockingham and exhibited many pieces of my art. Most pieces showed clearly that I was an amateur, but in Max's eyes, he always saw them as the best. Rose coloured glasses are amazing.

I did, however, win People's Choice one year, thanks to Max encouraging everyone he spoke with to vote for my painting, I'm sure!.

Golf was something that I grew up with. So once again, Max, who also liked to play golf, made sure I was back at it, and paid for me to join Hartfield Golf Club as a Business Girl, as it was known, because I was working full-time and could only play Saturdays. This was so exciting for me. But in those days, everyone who joined a golf club was required to present for an interview to see if they were a desirable person suitable to join a golf club. This was all new to me, as I was from the country, and things were mighty different at Merredin or Nungarin golf clubs. The members at these clubs were just pleased to have a new member, bolstering their much-needed numbers of players. Of course, you were required to have a drink or two after finishing your game to help with the funding of the club. And it goes without saying, that it was a great advantage as a lady member if you could bake a mean cake or two for afternoon tea. Wanting to impress the panel of ladies who interviewed me at Hartfield, I wore my newest clothes and arrived early. This interview was another one of those times where one day, much later in my life, circumstances would have me revisit this tiny thread in my web of life.

Joy was one of the ladies asking me all sorts of questions as I sat shaking in my boots, wondering if I really wanted to play golf again. After what seemed like hours of questioning, I was told I was allowed to join, but Business Girls had to hit off at 7.30 sharp and were under no circumstances allowed to hold up the members (men). Although we pretend things have changed these days in golf clubs, I'm sure there are a few men from the old school who still think that 'that rule' should have remained.

Relieved that the interview was over, I quickly headed for the door, only to be stopped by one of the ladies who quietly said, in a condescending manner, "By the way, jeans are not suitable attire and are not permitted in the clubhouse." That was the straw that broke the camel's back. After apologising, I almost ran to my car, holding back tears of sheer hurt and embarrassment. What I thought were my best clothes were not good enough.

After more encouragement from Max, I reluctantly turned up the next Saturday at 7am to play. The ladies I played with, possibly trying to be helpful, alerted me to everything I was doing wrong, thus having me in tears within the first few holes.

The next week, and with more encouragement needed, I turned up again to play Business Girls at Hartfield. Everything takes time and perseverance in life to survive, but to this day, I have the utmost compassion for every new player as they too, I know, encounter *help* when learning to play golf, and more to the point, endeavoring to join a golf club.

This experience occurred to me approximately 50 years ago, but I revisited this tiny thread in my Web of Life when I joined Rockingham Golf Club in 1998. Joy had moved from Hartfield to Rockingham to live, where, as an avid golfer, she joined RGC. After years of not being in touch, we laughed about the past and enjoyed numerous happy games of golf together. Joy played golf into her 90s. When you love golf, anything is possible.

Thanks to Max, I have now been a member of RGC for 26 years, and have gained fulfilment in my life with the wonderful friends I have made at golf, especially with the ladies, who are, without a doubt, some of my dearest friends in life.

Max loved life itself. Among his many interests, he played tennis. I had played or had tried to play tennis at high school, and was happy to try again. We enjoyed many happy times playing on a local, hired tennis court with Paul and Ceri, along with as many as possible of our 'we'll get there if we can' remaining Brady Bunch. I'll never forget Ceri's boomerang, moving low, deadly serve. Nothing much had improved with my tennis, but we had so much fun that it didn't matter at all.

Max liked to have a bet on the horses, dogs, football, in fact, anything that moved, but he was wise enough to be in control, and never betting the kitchen sink. This was such fun for me. And once again, small bets just gave me the feeling of being free to have control of my actions.

Playing Two-up on ANZAC Day was such a buzz. Max included me in everything and proudly introduced me to his friends as 'my Lyn'. His friends were just wonderful to me, and although it wasn't kosher for any of the girls to join in the once-a-year Two-up when Max said I was going to have a spin, no one objected. Yay.

I didn't overstay my welcome, and was very happy to leave with more money in my pocket than I had started with. I also was happy to give Max his freedom, and never objected to him doing his own thing. I know that our way of allowing each other to do their own thing was the reason we worked so well together.

Having five grown-up children between us ensured that there was never a dull moment in our already busy working life, what with getting the youngest few into the workforce, assisting with buying cars, driving lessons, noticing the arrival of a few grey hairs because of the driving lessons, the coming and the going of girlfriends, boyfriends, the mopping up of buckets of tears because of the coming and going of the girlfriends and boyfriends, parties, too many of the wrong type of parties, organising birthdays, engagements, weddings, and the arrival of our many much-loved grandchildren. Max and I were flying high with life and all it could throw at us.

We did have a lot thrown at us.

One day, we arrived home from work to find Terrie and Nicole laughing and joking around as they were jamming the last few of their entire belongings, plus some of our belongings, into Terrie's new car, which was previously an ambulance. Only Terrie would want this heavy monstrosity as her car of choice. But she was so proud of her almost painted white, cream, grey, ex-sick, not sick anymore, people carrier. The back of the van was now packed to the hilt with a small area free of any packages. This, I found out later, was for Prince, the dog. Yes, they thought of everything.

Our first reaction was, of course, not quite as well thought out as perhaps it should have been, but events went something like this. What the hell are you doing? Where are you going? Where are you going to live? Where are you going to work? No. Nicole, you are definitely not going. You're just too young. You are not taking Prince. No, no, no, no.

Yes, you guessed it. Bad parent.

The next morning, we were loading up the trailer with everything that wouldn't fit into the ambulance and heading off to Nungarin. The girls, with the dog, had left earlier for the almost four-hour drive. Terrie had organised for them to move into an empty farmhouse, only five kilometres as the crow flies from Brian and Gail's home. The old house they had arranged to move into belonged to the parents of one of the girls I went to primary school with, and was over the road from Nanna Hattie's old home, or where the home once stood on Lavington Farm. Of course, this made it seem better somehow, thinking back, how on earth could this be better? Always tiptoeing over webs of the past.

We arrived at the very run-down, dilapidated old house to find the girls running around excitedly because the farmhouse had an old Metters stove in the kitchen, just like the one that their Nanna had in her kitchen at Sunnyside. Although it took a lot for us to even see the Metters stove because of the mountains of mouse droppings and wire-like spider webs, along with ten years of dust, we managed to put a somewhat strained effort into showing excitement for them.

Prince, the dog couldn't have been happier. Max and I both had work the next day, so, after unpacking the trailer and trying to make some sense of how the girls would even be able to clear enough dust from the house to sleep, we reluctantly drove slowly off up the driveway amid waves and calls from the girls of "We love you. We'll be okay. Bye. Love you.

Thanks."

I knew I wouldn't sleep that night, even if they did.

Credit where credit is due, those girls managed to clean up the house, make it livable, thanks to Uncle Brian's help from time to time, find work, and although they had many hiccups, they made it work.

# Busy Times

Whilst working as Check-out Controller at Victoria Park, I was asked if I would consider moving into the role of Personnel Management, which would involve working from Coles-Myer Head Office situated in Canning Vale. At this stage in my life, and with thanks to my supportive husband and children, why not? The sky was the limit.

Coles-Myer was extremely professional in their training and follow-up. I attended many training courses, including a trip to Melbourne for a Train the Trainer course. The fact that I was already attending TAFE, studying Personnel Management was of great benefit. Therefore, without hesitation, I embraced this amazing opportunity. When offered one of the positions in State Personnel, my home life became busier by the minute.

Max's eldest son, Michael, had driven up north to meet Annemarie, who lived on an outback station with her parents and siblings. He and Annemarie had been corresponding as pen pals for some time, and as love goes, they both arrived home with happy plans for their future. Paul, Max's second son, and Ceri, his fiancée, were busily planning their wedding. Terrie and Nicole had just shifted again, this time to a farmhouse east of Nungarin. They were both working and kicking up their heels to the fullest. We were both working, visiting Nungarin as often as we could, socialising with friends, playing golf and tennis, watching hockey matches, going to meetings, studying and, time permitting, enjoying as much intimate time together as possible, forever in honeymoon mode.

Brian and Gail were also extremely busy with married life, children, and busy farming life. I found myself often revisiting the tiny threads of my Web of Life including the time I found out my brother Brian was going to marry one of my best friends from primary school. How wonderful we were already friends, but then became my special sister-in-law.

Dad and Mum had been contemplating retiring from the farm for some time, but it took a health warning for Dad to finally agree to leave the farm. But it goes without saying he didn't leave without a condition that he would help out during the busy seasons. Brian knew he had to agree to this to ensure that Dad, for the sake of his health, would stop overworking.

Eventually, semi-retirement occurred, and Dad and Mum moved into a brand-new home in Safety Bay. I was thrilled, as I would be able to see Mum and Dad more often. Dad had suffered from undiagnosed rheumatic fever as a child, which sadly caused an enlarged heart in his later years of life. More sadly, there was no cure, but with care and rest, Dad could hopefully slow down the progress, allowing him and Mum time to play golf, go fishing and enjoy friends and family being able to visit them in their lovely new home. Max allowed me to love and care for my family as a daughter, sister and mother should and the ties between us as a family once again became strong.

# Dad and Mum's Retirement

Retiring is one of those words that can confuse and or even upset many people who have known nothing else other than working. From an early age, Dad worked and prided himself on always giving 100% to every task he put his hand to. When he and Mum married, they both worked extremely hard to achieve great results, and this showed. Together with Brian's added hard work in later years, Sunnyside was a working farm to be proud of.

Moving to a quarter-acre block in Safety Bay was a big adjustment, but as their home was a new build, there was plenty to do to keep them occupied. Before very long, floor coverings were in. New furniture was slotted into place. Lawn was planted, and enjoying the fruits of their labour could begin. The Rockingham Golf Club was, of course, one of the first clubs they joined when arriving in Rockingham. They also became members of the Yacht Club, Probus Club, bought a little fishing boat and settled into a well-earned retirement. Should I say semi-retirement, as Dad needed to go back to help. Letting go is not easy, understandably.

# Dark Clouds

I was at work, happily going about my duties when I was called to the office. A phone call had come through from the Fremantle Hospital. Dad was ill after suffering a stroke.

My immediate reaction was of numbness and the overwhelming need to get to the hospital to give Mum support and pray that Dad would recover. I'm not sure if I even saw another car or a set of lights as I was on autopilot, with nothing on my mind except getting to that hospital as quickly as possible. As predicted, Mum was distraught, and Dad was still being assessed and treated in Emergency. I'm normally a very soft person, but when I need to be strong for someone else's benefit, a strength from within seems to engulf me, allowing me to be constructive in my thoughts and able to console others in their time of need.

I called Brian, and before I had walked back to the room, he was on his way to help. Our lives can change in the blink of an eye. Thank goodness we don't know when. Sadly, Dad and Mum's lives did change, but their love shone through, which allowed them to adjust and conquer the setbacks as they occurred. Mum also gained strength from somewhere. Every day for months, come rain or shine, she caught a bus from Rockingham to Fremantle to be by her husband's side, caring for his every need whilst he slowly but surely recovered enough to return home.

My beautiful dad did suffer some mobility disabilities, but was more fortunate than many, and Dad, being Dad, kept his spirits high and never complained. However, suffering a stroke can be more debilitating than just the physical aspects, as the emotional, nervous system is affected also. This was the hardest to see, especially when you know the person you love so much is suffering inwardly and discreetly. It is simply amazing just how strong we can be when adversities strike. I went to visit Dad and Mum after Dad arrived home from hospital, only to find Mum walking around and around the backyard. When I inquired as to why, Mum replied, "No need to say anything to anyone, but I've stopped drinking, as dad needs me now, and I must be able to drive him if required." Mum has never had a drink since. Unconditional love and strength. Love you, Mum.

# Time to Move

The uncontrollable need to be close to Dad and Mum in their time of need became greater with each visit, noticing how comforting it was for Mum to have family helping her. Max always supported me, and within days, the unit Max and I had called home in Forrestfield was sold, and soon after, we moved into Craig Mews in Safety Bay, walking distance to Mum and Dad's home. It was, of course, a long way to drive to work for both of us, but a small price to pay. Max had begun work as Supermarket Manager with Stammers supermarket in Fremantle by this time, which was less distance for him to drive. Max felt appreciated for the first time in a long time, and before long, we felt part of an amazing family. The staff were well-trained, and every Friday night, they would be sure to remind Max to buy flowers and chocolates for 'his Lyn', as he affectionately referred to me. We attended Christmas parties and some family celebrations with the family and work colleagues. It was a breath of fresh air to work for such giving people. I can't believe that a little later in my book, I will again revisit this tiny web.

Different home for Max and me, but same chaos.

Michael and Annemarie married and gave us our firstborn, beautiful grandson, Benjamine. Terrie and Brett married and gave us our second beautiful grandson, Jayke. Paul and Ceri married. Ceri became ill with food poisoning when they were on holidays, or not. The so-called food poisoning was a beautiful baby girl called Rhiannon.

These first of many grandchildren were very close in age, and my love for babies heightened with every little hug I received from these precious gifts. Many Saturday nights we would willingly be minding all of them. I had cots and prams everywhere with all different baby formulas in different baby bags, feeding bottles, all different shapes and sizes lined up on the kitchen bench, and nappies by the dozens. And noise, lots of noise. We just loved it.

In the morning, Max would wake up and say, the kids are all good. I didn't hear a thing. I, on the other hand, had spent all night running from cot to cot checking that they were all still breathing. Loved having them, loved giving them back.

Wedding photos and baby photos began appearing on the walls. Prince, the dog, came home to live with us, so did Sam, the budgie. Max and I had started riding our push bikes for exercise and to take time out from our busy lives.

One morning, Max was pumping up the bike tyres as I finished reading the Sunday Times. Yes, yes, yes! With excitement, I ran outside to let Max know that I had found a ragdoll kitten for sale within our price range. I did have to say, also, there was a little problem. The kittens were in Bridgetown. With his gentle smile, Max simply replied, "Oh, well, suppose I'll put the bikes away and go and get some petrol in the car."

My wonderful and caring husband drove all the way to Bridgetown, waited patiently while I pondered forever trying to decide which one of these adorable little kittens I would choose. Eventually, the new addition into our mad house struggled up around my neck and we headed off home.

Beau cat was adorable and floppy (one of the Ragdoll's characteristics) and *very* spoiled. His name came from a famous Trotter from WA – Beau Heed. This horse was amazing, and fortunately, Max had placed a bet on him during a local meet in which Beau Heed won easily. This had enabled us to purchase our new and precious cat. Thank you, Beau Heed. Welcome Beau, the cat.

Dad was slowly adjusting to things being a little different in his life, but he missed the farm very much that Brian could see his need to visit Sunnyside.

*A proud moment for us all with the first five generation photo in our family. Jayke (proud dad), Terrie, me, Mum and baby Deegan.*

*Cool cats, Nanna and Grandma*

## Don't Tell Mum

Brian and Gail enjoyed life and laughter. Dad missed the farm life and took every opportunity offered to go back to Sunnyside. Mum was, unfortunately, never able to control her nervous nature so every time Dad was going to the farm, Mum would give strict instructions to Brian to look after Dad and not let him do anything dangerous, or even remotely dangerous.

"Of course, I will look after him, and I won't let him do anything dangerous," would be Brian's promise, fingers crossed behind his back without a doubt. Although not quite as mobile as he would like to have been after his stroke, Dad's interest in anything new on the farm never changed, and where at all possible, he wanted to be in on the action. Brian was so excited when he had finally bought a new high-tech tractor and drove Dad down to the shed to get his opinion on the new purchase.

The tractor was huge and the cab was so high that Dad could not even see inside, let alone get inside to check it out. With Mum's words still ringing in his ears, I'm sure, but with Dad's pleading eyes looking at him, Brian convinced himself that it would not be dangerous to put Dad in the bucket of the front-end loader and hoist him up level with the door of the cab. And presto, one little pull from the driver's side, and Dad was inside the cab grinning like a Cheshire Cat. No, definitely, no danger. All good as gold.

Another time I recall was when Max and I were visiting the girls in Nungarin. We called into Brian's and Gail's to see the girls and Dad because they were staying with Brian and Gail at that time. We all ended up driving to the top paddock to wait for Brian to take a break from ploughing to have lunch. Gail had prepared a yummy lunch, as always. We sat with Dad on the freshly ploughed dirt, one of my favourite things on earth to do, chatting and eating lunch. Dad was sitting on his fold-up chair without a care in the world, enjoying his sandwich, lapping up the beautiful fresh air and sunshine when I noticed the back of his chair slowly moving. I let out a "Watch out!" but before I could reach him, the chair sunk into the soft dirt, with Dad doing an almost perfect backward somersault, legs overhead, landing legs pointing skyward, still seated in his chair. Instant fright and fear by all gave way quickly to uncontrollable laughter when we were reassured by Dad that "I'm fine, but could do with some help here. Someone, help me up, please."

After helping Dad back to the upright position and dusting off the sand, another sandwich was handed to Dad, and he quietly said, "Don't think we better tell Mum about that one."

'Absolutely not' was the consensus of all.

# Our Life in the Fast Lane

It was filled to overflowing with love, work, study, children, with all their issues, more love, family, sport, kids sport, boyfriends, girlfriends, misbehaviour, lots of misbehaviour. Tattoos, odd-looking plants in the palm garden, family barbecues, more barbecues, unacceptable noise from teenagers' bedrooms, family birthdays and more birthdays. Bike racing, more tattoos, more bike racing, accidents, visits to Nungarin, crazy toga parties. Go Kart Racing, more mud flying, go kart racing, car buying, more car buying, more family get togethers, sickness, love, breathtaking intimacy, lots of intimacy. Holidays, house moves, engagements, weddings, babies, more babies. And sadly, a touch of living on the edge more than occasionally, but most of all, ever-growing happiness, laughter and never-ending love engulfed our crazy lives.

# Holiday Snippets

As I mentioned, Max and I enjoyed life to the fullest, and went on as many little holidays, breaks, long weekends as possible. One of these was spent at the caravan park in Lancelin. We were only going for a short break, and Nicole and her friend Julie decided that they would come with us. They were very happy to pitch a tent and do little or nothing except sunbake and dip their toes in the water. One day, Max and I were doing much of the same, just resting in our fold-up chairs when the girls took off to go to the beach, which was only a short walk over the sandhills. On returning, they both were very happy, and more to the point, they had that added look about them, much like the cat that had swallowed the canary look, so I immediately asked, "What are you girls up to?"

With that, they couldn't wait to tell us. "We found a Nudist beach. You and Dad should go and check it out."

Max and I never shied away from a bit of excitement so we finished our drinks, and amongst the many cheeky grins and even more cheeky comments from Nicky and Julie, we headed off to find this special beach where we too could swim in our altogether. You guessed it. Of course, there was no Nudist beach. Nicky and Julie were just young and carefree and had taken their bathers off when there was no one around, and thought nothing of it. We, on the other hand, thought better of it, had a laugh at our own expense, and arm in arm, walked back over the sandhill to a greeting of laughter and more cheeky comments.

# Snippets of Memories

Our home in Safety Bay was a home, and everyone was welcome. We always wanted our children to feel free enough to come and go as they wished. They all had keys, so we were also free to get on with what pleased us, as long as when we got home, there was still enough milk left in the fridge for a cuppa. Nothing else mattered. Today, everyone seems to need large games or theatre rooms in their home with a purpose-built complete outside kitchen, but our warm, happy home boasted only a fly screen-enclosed tin patio with a basic barbecue out the back. These two areas were always scattered with ride-on toys, leftover half-deflated balloons. But there was hardly a weekend that went by when we didn't have family and or friends celebrating something in our patio area. We played in pool competitions, dart competitions, card competitions, with everyone being patient with children doing their own kid things in between. When the hunger twangs hit, the pool table was quickly converted into a massive dining table by simply putting a large wooden lid on the top, followed by a tablecloth, bowls of previously prepared salads, and last but not least, Max's perfectly cooked every time barbecue steak and sausages. Everyone ate, drank and enjoyed family life.

Nicky was back home and working and wanted so much to buy a mini-Harley, as she called it. I was worried about her riding a motorbike, but Max reassured me by saying, "Don't worry. She's got to get a license first, and they're very strict on young people getting bike licences." Of course, these were just words that were simply a kind of way of saying 'there's not a lot we can do about it, so let's not worry.'

Sadly for Nick, she did fail her first two attempts, and was very disappointed, not only for failing to get her bike licence but because it was expensive paying for lessons and tests.

One Sunday afternoon, Max and I were doing some gardening when we heard a great-sounding motorbike pull into our driveway. This slight, young girl dressed in black with an open-faced helmet stepped off this black bike – yes, it did look like a small Harley – and with a beaming smile, Nicky walked over and said, "What do you think of my bike?"

So as not to burst her bubble, I said, "I like it. I love the throaty sound it makes. But when did you get your license?"

The answer was, "I got my license this morning."

Max looked at me and put his arm around Nicky and said, "I'm happy for you."

We both knew that licensing premises weren't open on Sundays. With many positive words of support, we ensured Nicky did get her license. After quite a few wet days of riding to work and having to take a change of clothes each day and the fact that wearing a helmet doesn't lend itself to a great hairdo, the bike was soon traded for a car. Yay.

*Nicole Marie proudly showing off her mini-Harley motorbike outside our home in Safety Bay. Not sure how she even reached the handlebars, but achieving any goal in life is commendable and is wonderful for Nicky to be so proud of herself.*

*Shhhh moments forever in my heart.*

# The Darkest of Clouds, Never Forgotten

It was a sunny day in February, and we were enjoying one of our usual busy days at home.

The phone rang.

As I picked up the phone, I could hear Mum trying to get her breath so as to be able to speak.

"Are you okay, Mum?" I asked quickly.

"No, no, no," Mum sobbed out. "I think Daddy has died."

There are just no words to describe my reaction to these words – heart-wrenching pain like being stabbed with a hot knife, fuzziness, numbness, disbelief, unable to breathe or get words out, followed by uncontrollable sobbing mixed with all sorts of emotion, and heartfelt pain for Mum, knowing she was on her own, I managed to get the words out. "I'm coming, Mum, I'm coming. Love you, Mum. I'll be there in one minute."

Nicky and Simon were at home when the call came, and within seconds of me putting down the phone, we were in the car. I think it would have only taken us three minutes to get to Dad and Mum's home, and I remember running over the front lawn in bare feet, feeling the prickles in my feet but unable to notice the pain.

Mum had called the ambulance and was saying, "Why won't they hurry? Where are they?" as she cried uncontrollably. We hugged so tightly. My thoughts were 'not Dad, my hero in life, my protector, and our families' rock throughout our lives. This is too much pain.'

Mum had found the strength to phone my darling brother. Dad was Brian's world, and to this day, I don't think there are many times Brian isn't solving problems or working in the shed where his thoughts don't reach out to Dad. Affectionately, I ran into where Dad was in his chair, and although in my confused mind, I knew he had passed, I thought there just might be a chance of a miracle, and he might wake up if I gently breathed air into his lungs. I gave mouth-to-mouth until the ambulance got there, and then I was asked to leave the room. Poor Mum was hysterical by this time, and she could hear them trying to restart his heart. We were all praying for that miracle, but God had another plan and a better place where a much-adored husband, dad, granddad and the most beautiful man that ever drew breath could rest eternally. Locked in our hearts forever, Dad. XXXX

It is an understatement to say Mum's life changed forever.

When our darling dad said goodnight for the last time, not only did the world change for our mum, but the world changed for so many in more ways than imaginable. Terrie and Nicole lost the one man in their lives that they felt completely secure with, the one man with the strength of character who would always speak the truth and show kindness, empathy, understanding and never waver in his goodness and guidance. Both Brian and I knew exactly how our children suffered, as well as everyone, family, friends and acquaintances. Bill was loved, and to this day, he is still spoken about with admiration and affection.

It was an extremely hot day in February when we said our goodbyes at the old Rockingham cemetery. I have been to many funerals, and I've always found that there is one person in attendance, other than the obvious, that tugs at your heartstrings, so much so that years later, when reflecting on this saddest of days, that person comes to mind. For me, at Dad's funeral, I have never forgotten the pain on Uncle Jack's face.

Dad's best mate could not hide the enormity of his own cancer-induced pain, but his face also showed the sincere, overwhelming pain he was feeling with the loss of a comrade and mate for life, sincere and respectful memories. Dad left an amazing legacy for us all, and there is never a time when we don't benefit in some way, shape or form, from Dad's teachings.

## More Blessings and More of Life's Storms

Nicole and Simon married and gave us our third-born, beautiful grandson, Luke Peter. Once again, the old cane pram was wheeled out for what had become a tradition by then, to take a photo of the newest addition to our family, in the 1940s Australian cane pram.

I have photos of myself as a baby in one of these amazing prams. They are so well sprung and cleverly designed with open-weaved cane, allowing the breeze to filter through, perfect for the Australian heat. As I was referred to later in my Web of Life, I have always been a little 'queer-odd', and for some reason, I just had to buy a cane pram, very similar to my original one, to have as a collector's item. It gave me a lot of joy to walk around the streets of Safety Bay with one of my grandchildren sleeping comfortably in the old cane pram, and to have people inquisitively stopping to look at the pram, not at the new addition to our growing family.

Although these following photos are from much later in my story, it shows the continued tradition of the cane pram.

*Grandchildren in compulsory 'photo-shoot' in cane pram, at the same age as the one I had as a baby. Sorry, kids, but it is nice and comfortable.*

*Above: Bohdi*
*Below: Ash*

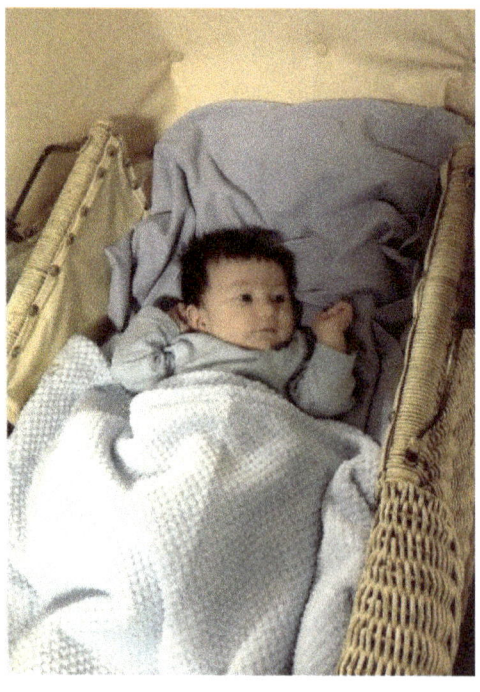

*Bodhi in the pram, Deegan standing*

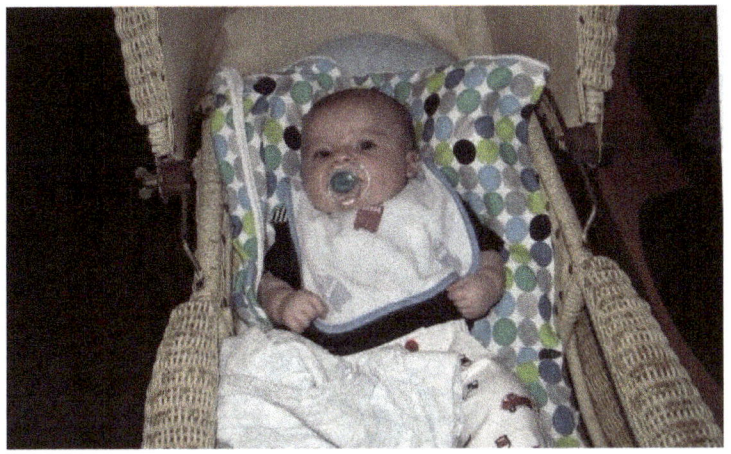

*Amy*

Cody James was Terrie and Brett's second beautiful son and our much-loved grandson – plenty of space for another tin of formula on the kitchen bench.

The most important thing I've learned since writing about my Web of Life is that, at this stage, our children were very quickly building their own Webs of Life, and because of this, they were also experiencing dark clouds and heavy storms in their own lives. It goes without saying that when our children suffer in any way, no matter their age, we as parents also suffer. Therefore, where possible, we endeavour to comfort and protect their webs of life from being destroyed. Of course, we, in the main, can just support comfort and sadly, sometimes pick up the pieces, but always be within reach if they call for help.

As I mentioned when talking about my own first marriage and divorce, we all start out in marriage with the same desire to marry and be happy with the one we love for life. Unfortunately, circumstances can change, and quite often, through no fault of our own, what we thought was perfect can be blown away by unforeseen, interfering storms, that come so quickly and without warning, destroying everything in their path.

It is not for me to go into detail about our children's Webs of Life. I am very happy for them to tell their own stories. Goodness knows, they've all got plenty to write about, but I will mention a few snippets here and there.

There are no words truer than 'the children suffer the most' in any marriage breakdown. For grandparents, the pain is not being able to take away this undeserving, incomprehensible fear and pain, which clearly shows in the eyes of these beautiful children.

The one thing I have always tried to achieve in my life is to always be there, unwavering in my compassion, constructiveness and unbiased support for all my family. I have never wavered in this desire, and although I know only too well this desire is unrealistic at times, 'Never give up' is my motto.

New baby photos were strategically placed on the family room wall, but sadly, the wedding photo wall appeared to have decreased slightly in numbers. Not to worry. More wedding photos on the way.

Some may not appreciate our slightly blasé sense of humour, but with so many storms and moments throughout this time in our lives, stupidity and laughter seem to say it all with no need to go into detail.

Terrie, as young as she was, had experienced unexpected and traumatic storms in her Web of Life, being battered in all directions, making it almost impossible to keep her grip. But she adored her babies and knew that they needed her strength in life. I will never be able to tell my daughter how much I admire her strength. With all she has endured throughout her life, there wouldn't be many webs stronger.

Terrie and Brett went their own ways, and eventually, after years of sorting out, came to an amicable arrangement with their children. There are so many shhhh moments here, but this is not my story to tell, and some things in life are best left unsaid.

Terrie married Sass (Mark) and, after they both decided that they were happy and wouldn't have a child of their own, lo and behold, a beautiful baby girl was on the way. Sophie Marie, our much-adored granddaughter, arrived, completing Terrie's family of three children.

Paul and Ceri went holidaying with their lovely little Rosebud girl, but Ceri became ill with another virus. This time, the virus turned out to be another much-adored grandchild, Amelia. I think I know why they didn't go holidaying much more after that, when their children were still little.

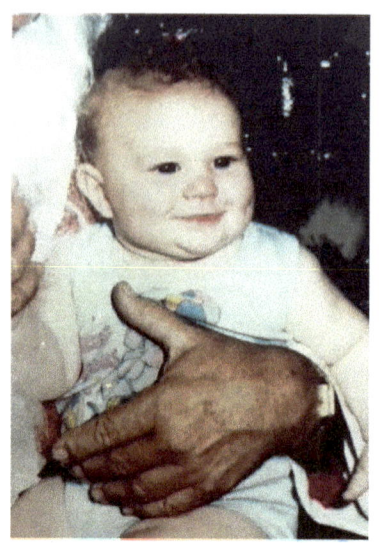 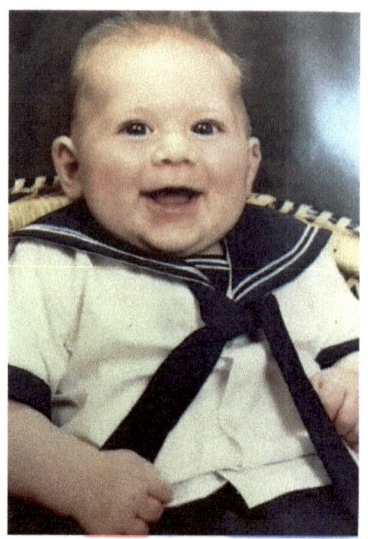

*Treasured baby photos*

*Above Left to Right: Jayke William, Luke Peter Whistler*

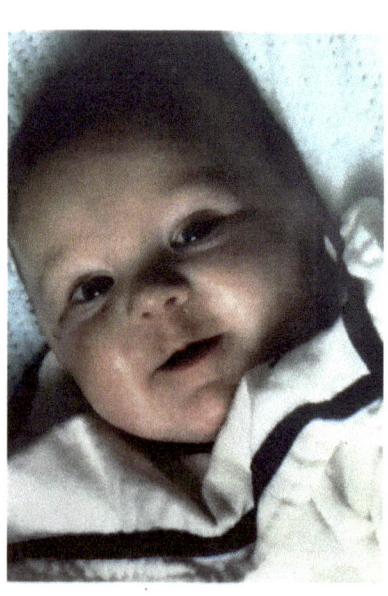 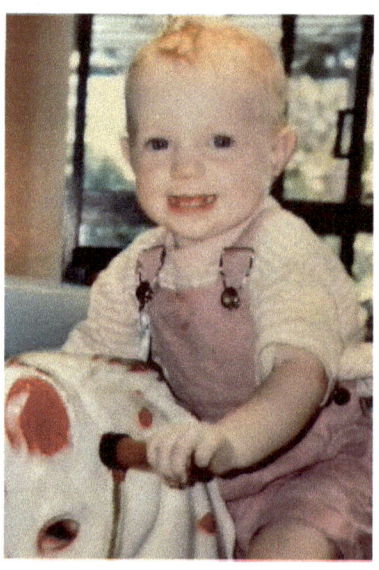

*Above Left to Right:*

*Cody James, Sophie Marie*

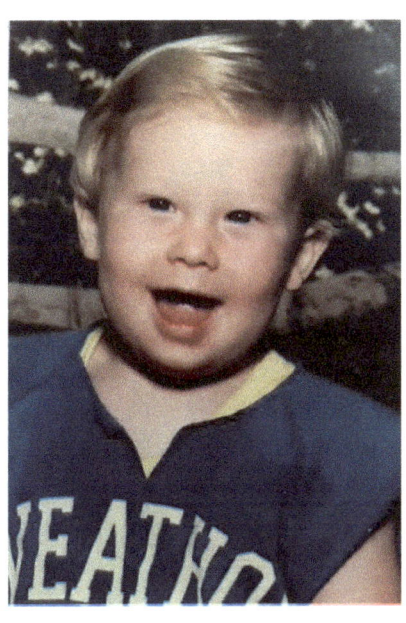

*Treasured Photos*
*Above: Benjamin*
*Below: Left to Right: Rhiannon and Amelia*

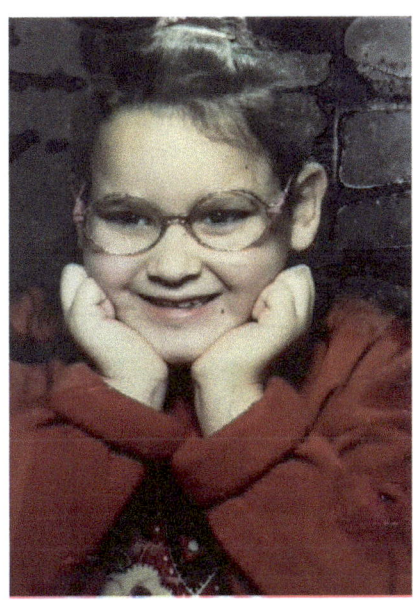

## Battering Storms Ahead

Max and I were working full time, and I was driving to Canning Vale and Max to Fremantle each day for our work. We also fitted in as much of life as we possibly could, playing golf, socialising, supporting Mum, babysitting, entertaining, going to the races, weekends away, and most of all, loving each other.

Max had gone to work on a Saturday, and as he always did, he rang me for what I thought was just his normal chat, but this time, he told me that something strange was happening to him.

When I asked, "How do you mean strange?" he replied, "My hand won't work."

This sent shivers down my spine as I knew from past experience with Dad that it sounded like signs of a stroke. Without hesitation, I suggested a visit to the doctor, but of course, Max said he would see how it goes. Unfortunately, we all know how it could go.

When he arrived home, all was good, and in his words, it must have just been a cramp. Tragically, within a few days, I received a phone call to say Max was in hospital and had suffered a stroke. My heart is aching as I'm writing this, as nothing prepares us for this sort of phone call, and we usually don't respond or act responsibly when we do receive a call like this. I was no different. I jumped in the car and drove to the hospital without even seeing another car, or stoplight, or anything at all. But I do remember I had nothing in my mind except the urgency to get to the man I adored. *Hurry. Hurry.*

*Why is it taking so long? Please, dear God, get me to the hospital.*

Max was not well, and I was told he would need to remain in hospital to have an angiogram to find out if there were any more blockages. Sadly, at this stage, I could only assume they were doing all they could to help, which I'm sure they were, but the added risks were not explained to me with clarity, and naturally, when forms were put in front of you with a convoluted explanation, your mind only hears and sees what you want to hear. 'This will help your husband recover.'

'Max is tired and needs rest,' is what I was told. So I reluctantly went home.

Early the next morning, I received a phone call saying that an angiogram had been performed, and unfortunately, Max had suffered another stroke. They called it a completion stroke. This time, I remember nothing of how I got to the hospital, but I remember, like yesterday, the pain I felt for my beautiful husband. He wasn't able to speak or move his left arm or leg. In fact, he was motionless, except for tears uncontrollably rolling down his distorted face. My tears joined his as I put on my bravest body language, reassuring him with every word that together we could overcome this challenge in our lives.

Max's children arrived very quickly to comfort their dad and, as always, support me at this time. My children were there in a flash, always supporting, encouraging and with positive comfort in times like this. We had yet again met another crossroad in our journey to happiness. This time, we all needed clear thoughts, heaps of energy, and perseverance to achieve even the smallest gain in Max's recovery.

The horror of being told you would be sent to Shenton Park Rehabilitation Centre is enough to set you back a mile. But Max took it on the chin, and although his emotions showed differently, he indicated that he knew it had to be done. He was very frightened and never wanted to let me go. I travelled from Canning Vale to Shenton Park every night after work and spent every weekend day with my beautiful husband. How extremely determined can one man be? This man worked every therapy session like he was training for a marathon, never stopping until he dropped. I attended as many sessions as I was able with him, supporting, encouraging and wiping away the thousands of tears shed during this painful time in Max's life.

The gains were slow and few and far between, but I remember the first time Max was able to move his thumb. It was as though he had run a mile. We were crying and hugging, and the nursing staff were showering Max with accolades and more encouragement. Slowly, slowly, he was able to gain movement, and some muscles resumed their normal function.

It was twelve weeks before my darling came home to what was supposed to be a quiet reception. We all tried very hard to be subdued in our welcome home, but we were all so overjoyed that a small, quiet welcoming party was never going to be possible. His family loved him.

Max was a fighter, and he slowly improved and was determined to let nothing, not even this, stand in his way of a happy life.

It took some time and a lot of rebuilding before my Web of Life felt secure enough to move from thread to thread again without fear of falling.

# Rebuilding With Love

After any major setback in our lives, often a few gentle and worthwhile adjustments need to be made so that life can resume being lived to the fullest, exactly how it was meant to be.

It's just a matter of realising that the fibres in our Web of Life, which we had previously been building, may now need to change direction. Sometimes, at first, we find it difficult to give up the work we were doing on one fibre and start again on the new, perhaps slightly more delicate fibre, but this is often the only way we can achieve a way forward that includes fulfilment for all.

Max never gave up on anything, and he carried on as normally as he could, within his power.

He had worked since he was a trolley boy in Coles Supermarket in Young in New South Wales, working his way up the ranks, as was done until he became a supermarket manager. Coles had a policy of moving their managers around all over the countryside for the betterment of the company, as they saw fit, without any consideration for the families that were uprooting and being put under extreme pressure in the process – the kids had hardly put their books in their desks of a new school when they were moved again. Needless to say, this was an enormous pressure on marriages throughout the company. Although New South Wales was their home, Max and his family were never moved back to New South Wales once he was sent to a Perth supermarket. Coles were quite ruthless to their managers, but they were known as the company to look up to, and their staff were respected throughout the other outlets. Max was also what they referred to as a 25-year member, which was recognised, and rightly so, as a great achievement.

As I mentioned before, Max had found his happy place of work. The family-owned and run Stammer Supermarket was known, respected and admired throughout as being a wonderful place to work, as well as being a fair and equitable business.

It was an extremely sad day when Max retired from his duties at Stammers; he was showered with well wishes and accolades by all of the staff. But even if his desire was to continue working, some things cannot be rushed.

It didn't take long for me to realise that I wanted to spend more time at home with the man I loved, and if I could somehow alleviate the three hours a day travel time, which would be a good start, but perhaps I could do more. I subsequently allowed my mind to extend to a bigger plan.

As I mentioned before, I was blessed with the newfound courage and nothing seemed to be out of reach, especially with the continuous support from Max. I resigned from my position as a Personnel Manager for Coles-Myer, and by doing so, I was able to access my small superannuation package, which was accessible after completing ten years' service. Although it was a small amount, it enabled me to purchase some stock, rent a small shop in Hokin Street, Warnbro, and fulfil a dream.

Trendy Tots was a dream come true. My love of babies had prompted me to open the shop selling all babies' needs, including prams, cots, clothes, etc. This shop was the answer to all of our prayers. It was within walking distance of our home. We would be able to work together, and best of all, our family could be part of this venture. Max worked every day getting our happy place ready to open. Mum was able to help with sewing curtaining, and designing the posters and advertisements for the local newspaper. How exciting! Before very long, Trendy Tots was open for business.

What a happy shop. Our customers felt welcomed, and quite often, they were greeted with one or two of our grandbabies lined up in their capsule behind the counter, always dressed in Trendy Tot clothing. Great advertising.

Love, laughter and happiness, once again, filled our lives.

It was at this time that I met a special friend who is and always will remain to be one of my most dear friends in life. Lorraine and her husband Les had opened a ladies' clothing shop next door to Trendy Tots. They had thought this was going to solve a few of their issues in life. Also, the idea was that Lorraine would get the shop going, and then her daughter, while studying, would run the shop – the plans of mice and men, as the saying goes. Lorraine and I would often take our chairs out into the sun and have a chat. We bonded immediately, both from country backgrounds, both with two children about the same ages. And best of all, both loved to chat. In fact, sorry to tell tales, Lorraine, but later in my story, Max nicknamed Lorraine Av-a-Chat-Rainy-Days. These are, without a doubt, words of endearment, as we both love this special lady, and I still do to this day – the 'Rainy Days' comes from her own grandchildren trying to pronounce Nana Lorraine – Nanna Rain, which sometimes became Nana Rainy Days.

Lorraine and I still have a giggle today about Lorraine being slightly disillusioned that her children would never do silly or wrong things. I'm sure every parent would like to think that they taught their children better than the next, but often things become out of parents' control.

We both went to work in our little shops every day, helping each other, especially with our weight-watching efforts. Come to think of it, thirty or more years later, we still walk every week, trying to keep fit, but more importantly, we built a lifetime friendship. Thank you for the amazing friendship, my friend, Rainy Days. XX.

Trendy Tots was never going to make millions during the recession of the 80s, but it was perfect for what we wanted, and gave a small wage. I was so happy. Another big part of life we learnt in a heartbeat is that happiness can disappear as quickly as it arrives. Max and I were going to have a night away, and Nicole and Simon said they would be happy to open the shop for me in the morning, as we intended to be back home the next day.

The next morning, we were contacted to say that our shop had been broken into during the night, and we were needed as the police were waiting to speak to us. How many times in our life can our heart absorb these blows?

We arrived at the shop to find Nicole and Simon in a terrible state, not knowing how to make things appear better. When we arrived, the shop and car park looked like a bomb had gone off. It had been a very stormy, wet night, and the perpetrators had backed up a truck, smashed the large window, and dragged all the items from the shop, dropping many of the items on the way to the truck. I picked up handmade christening gowns, baby booties and clothing of all descriptions off the rain-drenched car park.

Very little left. Words are not enough.

After the police questioned me for some time, and realised that I had not robbed myself for the insurance money, because I was only insured for cash, they left, as they put it, 'to deal with some big, important jobs'.

The painful clean up could only go on for a short time, as I had to find work to keep paying the rent for a shop that was no longer. We were in a depression, and to borrow more money — if the bank would lend it to me under the circumstances — was not an option, and the owners of the shop would not let me out of the lease agreement, even on compassionate grounds.

Therefore, the only option was to get a payout lease figure from the owner and get a loan and a job quickly.

This took me a long time to recover from, but I was able to work two jobs, sometimes three, to keep the money coming in, and Max contributed always. I worked as a short-order cook at the Penguin Island Cafe. Then in the evening, I changed my apron and worked in the deli on Parkin Street, Palm Beach, finishing at 9 pm. I managed to get a job as a representative for Master Foods, which was full-time, and allowed me to work one job. It took three years to pay off the loan, and what a relief when we paid the last payment.

By then, Lorraine was working for her sister in the deli on the corner of Fifty Road and Old Mandurah Road, Baldivis, and told me her sister needed more staff and would I be interested in working with Lorraine and not full time? Sounded wonderful. And before long, my tiny fibres of life were being woven in another direction. Maybe this was what they mean when they say variety is the spice of life.

As with every job I have done in my life, I always found ways of enjoying and learning from each experience. For example, whilst working at this deli, I had the privilege of meeting Mr Tommy Smirk. He was once the owner of most of the land where the Baldivis Shopping Centre now stands and where most of the surrounding houses are built.

He would drive up to the front of the deli once a week in his old, past-its-used-by-date ute and walk through the door wearing mended jeans, worn shirt and a hessian half apron tied with binder twine over his clothes. He would then purchase a newspaper, packet of biscuits, a loaf of bread and carton of milk. He was, at the time, a very wealthy man, as he had sold so much of his land to developers. But this polite, quiet man just went about his business as he had always done, and when asked if he was going to buy a new car, he simply replied, "No, but I might put a new motor in the old girl." I worked with Lorraine for some time, until another opportunity was offered to me.

*A photo original business card designed for Trendy Tots*

*Me in front of all handcrafted signage and crafts*

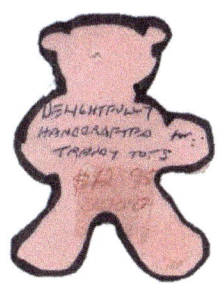

*My teddy price tags*

*Happy photo of Maxwell John Writer and Lynette Margaret Writer*

Max never gave up on himself in any way. After his stroke, as well as doing all the household duties, while I was at work, he took up woodwork. He worked using one arm/hand, and although I was extremely scared every time he used the band saw or jigsaw, I tried not to show the fear I felt by encouraging and praising his wonderful creations. He also played golf with one arm and played to a 27 handicap. Such a positive, wonderful man.

The next photo would have been the most talked-about happy photos ever. The family always laughed at my cut-and-paste abilities.

It was something I became very proficient at due to necessity. If there was a breakup in a relationship, I would just cut out that person from the photo and replace it with someone else. Simple. Couldn't waste a good photo. No clever phones back then.

This beautiful picture needed a 'cut and paste' for a nicer reason. Max was a wonderful pop, and I thought he would like ALL of his grandchildren around him. Spot the added extras. It wasn't Greg or Susie's fault that their beautiful children arrived after this photo was taken, and I just knew in my heart that Max wanted all his grandchildren together in this photo, so presto, there they are.

*Left to right, me and Max, Sophie, Cody, Rhiannon, Amelia, Ben, Jayke, Luke, 'Amy', 'Max' and 'Lisa'. That worked.*

*Max's work.*

*Some of these pieces still have pride of place in his children's homes.*

*Bookcases made by Max. Unbelievable! Some of these are still in our homes today.*

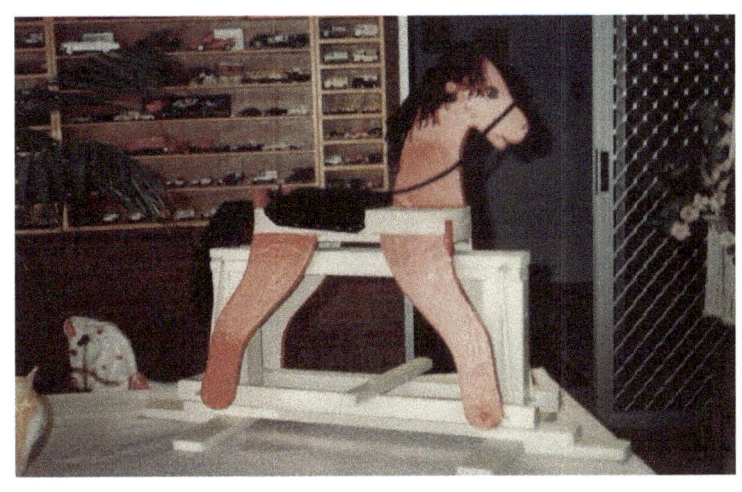

*More of Max's work*

*Wonderful photo of cousins' reunion (Mum's side of the family). This was a truly happy day spent at Brian and Gail's in South Guildford*

**Left to right: David Taylor, Lyn Writer, Brian Sainsbury, Leigh Martin, Stephanie Martin, Darcy Taylor, Julie Broome (nee Taylor), Peg Sainsbury, Ron Martin, Rose Martin, Jane Taylor, (sorry, forgotten her married name), Shirley Taylor, Sue Mack (nee Taylor), Annette Painter (nee Taylor), Philip Martin.**

Very happy memories, remembering Sunnyside childhood.

# Second Marriage, Happy Holidays

During our wonderful life together, Max and I went on many unforgettable and truly soul-enriching holidays, but none more memorable than that of our family holiday to Broome with Brian and Gail, Colin and Shirl and Lorna. Still to this day, thoughts of this holiday fill me with such a happy fuzz, always bringing a smile to my face.

Planning our Broome holiday was not an easy feat, but thank goodness, at that time in my life, I was so incredibly happy that nothing ever fazed me, and I thrived on proving that anything was possible.

Max and I had just purchased one of Brian's Tarod off-road camper vans (sister's rates, of course, XX) and we couldn't wait to plan a holiday together with Brian and Gail. One thing led to another, and before long, the holiday became bigger than Ben Hur and a family reunion of a lifetime.

Fortunately, Brian was a seasoned caravanner, but more to the point, an extremely well-prepared ex-farmer with an on-board toolbox, which I'm sure was the envy of *Ultratune* themselves. With the added ability that Brian could turn his hand to anything at any time, I was extremely confident that all would go well as we set off on the first leg of our trip. He and Gail loved holidaying and had travelled off the beaten track successfully many times. Max and myself, on the other hand, had little or no experience, but just wanted to take every opportunity possible to enjoy the beauty of WA's gorges, Pearl farms along our coastline, outback mining towns, and for me, revisiting some tiny threads of my Web of Life, as I walked, sat and ran my hands through the delightful, sweet smelling rich red dirt.

Brian's and Gail's never ending skills would be put to the test, not only with the almost 5,000 kilometre road trip we had in mind, but with the fact that I had asked Max's sister Shirley and brother-in-law, Colin from Young in New South Wales, as well as his sister Lorna from Queensland to meet us in Broome so we could all see the sights and then visit as many places as possible on our way back from Broome to Perth, where they would then holiday with us.

This would have been perfect, except that I didn't take into consideration that Colin had just had a hip replacement and was still using a walking stick to support himself, and of course, I also forgot to mention that Shirl is legally blind. Amazingly, though, her imagination can turn the brown shadow that she accepts as vision into a world of sight and colour, the power of the mind, how fantastic it can be. Oh yes, another little thing I forgot to mention is that Lorna suffered from chronic asthma. The bus trip from Queensland that Lorna took to meet us in Broome was over 4,000 kilometres, and consequently played havoc with her asthma, so much so that when we picked her up from the bus station, we had to take her straight to Broome hospital, where she remained for the next three days. Shirley and Colin arrived at Broome airport from Canberra, also showing signs of discomfort, but after a few cold WA beers, Colin was right as rain, and darling Shirl's positive spirit ensured that under no circumstances she'd be kept down.

Roebuck Bay Caravan Park was just amazing, and sitting in our deck chairs watching the enormity of the tide changes in the bay was fascinating, to say the least. We had so much fun, including the little bet or two on the crab races at the local pub, fishing off the jetty and laughing at each other, while our well-baited hooks, lines and sinkers hung aimlessly above the water as the tide went out. As you can imagine, Max and I and Brian and Gail were always ensuring that our guests were well catered for and safe at all times. Keeping Shirl from falling off the jetty and Colin from getting his walking stick stuck in the gaps in the jetty was one thing, but getting Shirl to the ablution block and safely back was another. This memory still prompts a mention every time we relive our unforgettable, happy time together. It was peak time, and everyone seemed to want to shower at the same time. So this particular day, I walked Shirl to the shower, made sure she was okay, and independent Shirl decided that she could find her way back from the shower without help. Gail was hanging washing, and happened to see Shirl with her toiletry bag and towel, and kindly thought she would help by taking her arm and escorting her. The only problem was that Gail thought she was going to the showers, not coming back. After their round trip to and from the ablution block again, they both wandered into our camp needing a sit-down and a drink.

We spent many happy hours in the Broome Pearl shop and Shirl buying copious pieces of jewellery for her daughter-in-laws and grandchildren. Max spoiled me, of course, and we all spent the rest of our time in Broome, lapping up the amazing weather, visiting the breathtaking sites of Cable Beach, weekend markets and local pubs.

One day, we did venture out to a local water hole known as a great fishing spot, but with more than a few reservations. Word was around of a sighting of a big croc at that same water hole, possibly the locals' way of keeping 'all the bloody drifters' away from their fishing spots.

But of course, for us, it just increased the impending excitement for the day ahead. As it was just a short, day trip, we decided we would all go in the one vehicle. Great decision. Gail and I were chosen to squeeze in the back with all of the eskies, fishing rods, complete with hook lines and sinkers ready to go, and more smelly bait than was needed for a fishing trawler. There was plenty of room, as long as we didn't mind our knees around our ears and the odd hook or two swinging precariously close to our heads. With all of that said, and the never-ending comments from everyone else sitting comfortably in the seats about how we would smell just perfect to attract the crocodile.

When we arrived, Gail and I were laughing so uncontrollably we almost wet our knickers as we dodged another hook in the face, when Brian's four-wheel drive bumped lazily over every rock in the road, amongst more laughter from all. Gail and I fell out of the back trying to regain circulation in our legs so we could race to the nearest bush for a well-needed tinkle.

Without realising it, we also had to wait for the tide to come in to even recognise the water hole's existence. It wasn't difficult filling in time, as it was very hot and humid and the eskies were full. It seemed no time at all after we saw the first trickle of saltwater coming down the creek, when that very large water hole was deep with water, quite amazing to see.

Colin was the Joker, and just as we all started to relax and come to a joint conclusion that the croc was a crock, something large and heavy splashed under an overhanging branch. With that, we all went silent with fear for what seemed to be minutes, only to be snapped out of our fear with the sound of Colin laughing his head off as he came out from behind the bush. Shirl gave Colin a piece of her mind. Great Day was held by all.

Leaving Broome was difficult, as we were having such a great holiday, but it was time to travel back to Perth so Lorna,

Colin and Shirl could meet up with their families. Brian had kindly put a two-way system in both cars so we could talk as we travelled. This was great, as we told jokes, sang out of tune and alerted each other if a pit stop was required. Our first stop on our way home was about 200 kilometres out of Broome when we came across a handwritten sign on the side of the road saying 'Homemade pancakes'. Without hesitation, we turned down the dusty track, only to come across a metropolis of cars, caravans and a bus and dozens of hungry people waiting in line for pancakes. The 'bakery' consisted of a corrugated iron canopy with two or three pit fires covered with hot plates, with a couple of people pouring large blobs of pancake mixture onto the hot plates as fast as they could go. As I had worked as a short-order cook, I realised that these people were facing a bigger task than possible, catering for the hungry travellers, so I offered to help by making our own. All good. When we had had enough and willingly paid for our yummy pancakes, I handed the mixture to the next customer, who was also only too pleased to help by making their own.

Soon, we were on our way again. We passed an amazing man. Sadly, I've forgotten his name, but he was walking, pushing a wheelbarrow around Australia to raise money for charity. All he wanted from anyone who stopped to talk to him and his dog was a small amount of water, as he couldn't carry too much because of the weight. His dog looked more tired than he did, as we gave some water and wished him a safe journey. We wanted our visitors to see some of the wonderful wild flowers and also experience the beauty of WA gorges. We arrived at Weano Gorge late in the afternoon after a slow drive, so as to appreciate the beautiful wild flowers adorning the roadside and adjoining landscapes. We quickly set up camp, and all sat around a campfire, singing, eating and endeavouring to lighten the towing load by emptying the eskies.

The next day, everyone was excited to trek down into the bottom of the gorge. Yah, everyone except Brian, Gail and me, as we could see just how steep and narrow the rock-covered track was down, but with one each on our arms and a prayer under our breath, we slowly commenced the slow descent. I was hanging on to Shirl like there was no tomorrow. Brian was helping Colin with his walking stick, and Gail was assisting Lorna with her asthma puffer when needed. Shirl was chatting, happily commenting about the overwhelming splendour of the sheer cliffs and walking like she was on a flat road in a country town. I, on the other hand, was white with fear as I could see the sheer drop with no railing. We reached the first small landing, and all stopped for a rest. It was at this point that my brother, very quietly, said to me, "Lyn, I think we may lose one or two here." I had to see the funny side of his comment and burst out laughing. Fortunately, and with the help of God, we made it down, and although coming back up was very slow and exhausting, the slow pace allowed us to stay a little safer. Needless to say, we all slept well that night.

It is an extremely long drive from Broome to Perth, but we didn't notice the time as we told stories on the two-way, sang songs, played games and enjoyed the special time together.

Thank you, my darling brother and sister-in-law, for a holiday of a lifetime, XX.

Although they never complained about sleeping in a tent whilst away, they all did appreciate getting to our home and sleeping in a comfortable bed.

The next week was full of family get-togethers and catching up with Max's boys and their families, my girls and their families, and meeting our wonderful Brady Bunch in its entirety, barbecues, love and laughter.

We had many happy holidays in our camper. One that comes to mind is the time we were travelling to Denmark to spend some time with Les and Lorraine. Max drove until Williams, and then, as he was tired, I continued driving from there. I was always happy and loved listening to music. Whilst driving not far from Williams, I saw a police car with sirens blazing, going in the other direction. *Oh, my goodness,* I thought, *I hope there hasn't been an accident up ahead.* The next minute, I heard the siren behind me, so I moved as far left as I could so they could get to where they were going in a hurry. But as they passed, one of the police officers indicated to me to pull over. I felt sick. I thought the accident must be bad. *Hope no one is hurt.* I pulled over, and Max woke up as the police officer came to the window.

I immediately asked if there had been an accident. I was reassured that there hadn't been. "But," the officer said, "if you keep driving at the speed you're driving at, there very well could be." The officer said, "Do you realise that you were travelling at 130 kilometres per hour with a trailer in tow. It is not legal to drive more than 100 kilometres whilst towing."

My reaction was, "I never drive fast. Are you sure? I hope I wasn't going that fast. I've never driven that fast. I'm so sorry. I'm really sorry." I have no idea why, but the officer said, "How you going, mate?" to Max, told me to slow down in future, and got back in his car and drove off.

Well, we certainly had a bit of a talk about when we met up with our friends at the caravan park, and yes, it was all about my bad driving.

Another holiday we spent with Les and Lorraine was a trip to Broome. Fortunately, Les never drove his ute over 90 kilometres per hour, and as we wanted to stay together, I was always driving within the law.

I love the outback and had my eyes wide open, no matter how many hours of driving we did in a day. Brian had organised a two-way speaker between cars so we could communicate as we drove. Lorraine, on the other hand, thought the drive was boring, and so she either read her book or had a sleep. Not on my watch! No chance of her resting, as every time I saw a lizard on the road or an eagle gliding, I would get on the two-way to make sure she didn't miss one thing of our wonderful adventure in the outback.

Eighty Mile Beach was just beautiful. It had been a long drive, and noticeably longer with the extra-long, bumpy drive from the highway to the beach. It was an unsealed road, and we were all very hot and exhausted by the time we parked at Eighty Mile Beach Caravan Park.

The water looked enchanting. Within minutes of us arriving, Rainy Days and I raced into the water, clothes and all and just sat and chatted and allowed the cold water to wash away the heat of the day. The need to quench our thirst was the prompt to return to our campsite and enjoy the warm evening with our husbands. Heaven on earth.

The next night, we were invited to join some of the other campers at a barbecue. Within a few minutes, a man came up to us and said, "Are you two the ladies who were swimming in the water yesterday?"

Why would he ask this? we wondered.

"Yes," was our reply.

He went on to say, "Thought you should know that it is not safe to swim here as there are a lot of very venomous sea snakes in this water."

Yikes. We didn't swim much after that.

After a few days fishing, lazing about, but not wallowing in the water, we travelled through to Broome, and although I had seen it before, I will always remember the breathtaking sight of our bright red cliffs rolling lazily down into the crisp aqua blue water of the bay. We live in a beautiful country.

At this stage, I will retread a few of my little threads in my Web of Life.

I mentioned earlier in my story that Max had affectionately nicknamed my friend Rainy Days (Lorraine), and it was actually here in my story where this occurred.

We arrived at Roebuck Bay Caravan Park feeling very hot and bothered from the long drive we had just done. And of course, Mother Nature called immediately. Lorraine said, "Back in a minute, gotta go." And off she went.

We all continued setting up the van, and had put the kettle on, and were sitting with a cuppa and biscuit in hand when Lorraine returned. Oh, my goodness, before Rainy Days (Lorraine) had time to take a sip of her tea, we all knew everything about at least two of our caravaning neighbours – where they were from, what car they were driving, where they had travelled, what their names were, how many fish they had caught, where they were caught those fish, and how those fish were going to be cooked for dinner that night.

Les, a very quietly spoken man, said, "Geez, love, is THAT all you found out?"

We all laughed uncontrollably. And from that day on, my darling friend (probably won't be a friend at all if she reads this) was affectionately known as Av-a-Chat Rainy Days. Love you, my friend.

# Why? Dear God, Why?

It is even difficult for me to find the appropriate heading for this part of my book. Other headings came to mind, such as unfair tragedy, too much pain, relentless suffering, too much for any one man, etc. But 'why, Dear God, why?' seems to say it all. As we are all aware, after someone suffers a stroke, their health can suffer in other ways as well. Thus, check-ups with the doctor become more regular. It was at one of these checkups that Max was told his heart was failing and he needed open heart surgery. Heavy black clouds were upon this wonderful man again. Max somehow regained his composure and quietly discussed all the risks he would encounter with this major surgery.

My heart is thumping in my chest as I write with the vivid memory of the fear I felt for my darling husband at that time. *Be strong. Be strong. Max needs you to show confidence and strength* was what was running through my mind.

After the operation, Max was in intensive care for five days, during which time he battled to stay with us many times. Once again, we were blessed, and with a long recovery ahead of him, he returned to a recovery ward. Max pushed himself to the limit to be able to return home. I spent every day at the hospital helping where I could, reluctantly leaving him at night. I would sneak outside food into the hospital as Max was starting to literally feel sick with the smell of hospital food. I'm sure we all know that smell.

The welcome home party was, as always, with their family, bigger than it should have been and very much louder. Max showed his strength of character, yet again, settling down on the lounge instead of going to bed just to be with his family.

This operation did take more time than Max wanted to recover from. But slowly, the black clouds turned grey and the sunshine peeked through, giving promise for positive, happy days again.

# New Opportunities

A young couple had not long reopened a deli on Old Mandurah Road and needed staff as they were expecting their first child. I was very happy, as the hours of work suited me, allowing me to be home with Max more. I loved the busyness of this deli, and I always enjoy the interaction with the wonderful customers, especially the local people. It was great talking to all the young jockeys from a Baldivis stable, who came to the deli dressed in plastic bags, trying to lose a couple of kilos ready for their next race.

We had lots of laughs, especially when I asked if they could give me a tip. They just said, "Yes, Lyn, we'll give you a tip … Don't bet!" Such great people.

I soon knew all the local customers, and within reason, knew their regular orders, which I tried to have ready for them as soon as they pulled up in front of the Deli. One lady bought every daily newspaper they produced I think, and we were in big trouble if we didn't save her papers.

Out of respect, and for the purpose of the story, I will refer to the young couple who owned the Deli as Ken and Rose.

Before very long, the business became even more busy, and when Rose asked if I knew of anyone who would be suitable to work with me, I immediately mentioned Rainy Days. Within a short time, Lorraine and I were working as a team again.

The shop opened at five o'clock in the mornings to cater for the Refinery and Market Garden workers, which was great in summer, but not so good in the winter. Nevertheless, we alternated shifts, and all was fine.

Rose was one of the hardest little workers I've ever known; she always had a big warm smile on her face, arriving every day to work with bags of stock for the shop, baby under one arm, bags of baby gear slung over the other arm, and a great big Alsatian dog running between her legs, doing its best to trip her down the back stairs. Although I didn't feel much trust being around the dog, he was a well-needed guard dog. Rose was loved by everyone and a joy to work for.

Ken was always very kind to me and, when I worked on the weekend, he would often ask me to "pick a horse, Auntie Lyn," (as they called me). He would put a bet on himself, and would always give me part of the winning, saying "bonus for working weekends." He was always thoughtful: if I was going to visit Terrie and the children, he would give me products that could no longer be sold, but would help out as treats for my grandchildren.

It wasn't very long before Rose was yet again struggling in the door of the deli with baby number two under one arm, toddler hanging off one leg and an even bigger bag over her shoulder, while still trying to get Tyson, the dog, to his designated watchdog area. We were exhausted watching her, but Rose kept giving the biggest smile to everyone she came in contact with, and her cheerful disposition never changed.

Within a short time, the storeroom in the back of the shop took on a new look. Freezers and shelving were shuffled around to make room for an enormous children's playpen, ride-on toys and all! Very well done, I thought, as before long, one little child would run into the shop with Rose close behind with another child on her hip, and baby number three snug as a bug in a rug under the other arm. Such a beautiful little mum, taking everything in her stride.

How wonderful that Rose's mum and dad, Nan and Harold were always close by to help. Probably just as well, as struggling in the door with number four baby, then number five baby and then number six baby did create a lot more trips to the car, even for this supa mum!

## Messy, Stormy Times

It was about this time in our lives when our ever-increasing family were busy building their own Webs of Life, and in such, they too were encountering life's heavy weather and storms.

Max was determined to recover fully and he and I were always there to encourage and support our family when they needed us.

Everyone's storms were different. Unfortunately, some of our children were able to avoid these storms altogether but they, as part of a bonded family, were always willing to support and encourage their peers in tough times.

Max and I worked through supporting in every way possible, with marriage breakdowns, addiction issues, abuse, pretense of a pregnancy as entrapment, suicide threats, maintenance trauma, home robbery, depression, and many moments which cannot be mentioned. However, in saying all of this, every one of our children who were themselves being blown from thread to thread by these storms, never lost sight of the love they had for Max and myself, and would run to our side day or night when needed. Unconditional family love.

# Christmas Heartbreak

Max had developed a repetitive cough, and on one of his visits to the doctor, he mentioned the annoyance of this cough. We were both a little taken aback by the urgency of the many tests immediately requested by the doctor. Although it would be an understatement to say that my darling Max was completely over tests at this stage, he did what was asked and returned to the doctor's soon after.

Only those who have experienced hearing the words, 'there is no easy way to tell you, but you have incurable cancer' could possibly understand the incomprehensible, heart-stopping, unimaginable pain Max had to endure on that day. I can't help but relive that moment when all I could do was hold on to and cry with my brave, devastated husband. Words are not enough.

I'm not sure how I drove home. My mind was trying to find some way of showing strength as I had to do everything in my power to overcome what I was feeling, to give every inch of strength to this beautiful man of mine as he battled his ultimate battle.

It was only two weeks until Christmas, and our usual big family Christmas Day had already been organised with presents piled up under the Christmas tree and recycled decorations adorning the entire living area. This memory takes me back to one of our previous Christmas days when Ceri's darling dad, Jim, dressed as Father Christmas to the delight of most of the grandchildren. Of course, there were always one or two who were scared out of their wits by the look of the big, red, hairy man! Respectful and precious memories of Jim and Joyce.

Max, for the first time, and understandably so, needed to be left alone with his thoughts. Our home was sad. I was sitting quietly with my arms wrapped tightly around him when, with tears in his eyes, he said, "I am not going to tell anyone until after Christmas." As I went to question his painful decision, he quietly but firmly said, "No, no one is to know until I tell them after Christmas."

How strong can one man be? On Christmas day, he entertained, watched all of the children's excitement, washed dishes, played games, put on a brave face, and made sure no one in the family knew that it would be his last Christmas. Sadly, even the strongest of men have a breaking point. Max could not bear the pain of telling his children how very ill he was, which resulted in him suffering another stroke, leaving him unable to speak once again. I can only imagine the pain his wonderful sons felt at that time. I was somehow able to understand his every request and did everything in my power to honour his wishes as he did not want to go into hospital, so our bedroom was made as comfortable as earthly possible to help in some little way with the pain he was suffering.

Nicole and Terrie stayed with me, assisting in every way possible, but unfortunately, there came a time when seeing him unable to get his breath after a coughing fit, I had to ask for his forgiveness and call an ambulance to take him to hospital. I never left his side, sleeping on my chair next to his bed until he was transferred to a special room. My heart is aching so badly as I write.

The room might have been a small room, and the rules around visitors, etc. many, but that room was full of all our children, and nothing or no one could come between them as a united family and their adored dad to say their goodbyes. Love forever. A never forgotten shhhh moment.

# The Strength to Rebuild my Web of Life

More than fibres were torn to shreds when my darling husband Max kissed me goodnight for the last time. The pain was so horrible that I did not even notice the heavy raindrops, and I was oblivious to the fact that I was slipping from my Web of Life without the strength or willpower to hang on. I had experienced losing loved ones before, and knew the depth of pain, but each time, the pain is greater, with no relief from that heavy, heart-wrenching ache saturating every emotion in your body and soul.

I just wanted the man I loved to once again be holding me in his ever-loving arms. The love we shared can be best described as next-level love. So very many shhhh thoughts, private and sincere. XX

RIP, my darling Max.

One of the most important things I have learnt in life is that when we are suffering, we are not to be selfish, as many are suffering just as much, if not more. So we must be strong enough to hold our pain-drenched emotions within and extend our arms and heart to those also carry this indescribable pain of losing a loved one. His sons, foremost, and my daughters, our children, showed such strength that words will never be enough to describe the admiration I have for them all.

Max had touched many lives, and his funeral certainly reiterated just how much he meant to so many. I'm sure that Stammers Supermarket and some of Coles Supermarkets were very understaffed that day, as so many of Max's wonderful colleagues showed respect by wearing their uniforms to say their goodbyes to a respected friend.

I remember mentioning how at every funeral I've attended, there is always one person who, for different reason, tugs at my heartstrings. This time, it was not just a fleeting thought. It was something so heavy and dark that I will and, sadly, can never forget. As we were leaving the grave site with Terrie and Nicole supporting me on each side, Nicole stopped and pointed to the ground in front of Max's grave, and quietly and very slowly, said, "See that plot, Mum. That is where I'll be next year." These words entered my already devastated heart like a spear. My heart almost stopped and my head began buzzing when, uncontrollably, I just said, "Don't be so stupid, Nick. Don't talk like that!" This embedded thought could never leave either Terrie or me.

For some time after, the support and comfort I received from family and friends was overwhelming, and I've always felt I've never thanked everyone enough. Thank you to everyone.

Eventually, the rain subsided, just enough for me to pull myself to a fragile but not yet broken fibre, where with a heavy heart I began to rebuild my Web of Life, tiny thread by tiny thread.

# Back to Work

Support from family and friends is one of the most valuable tools to aid with the mourning process. There is no way possible for anyone to help you 'get over' your loss as there is no such thing as getting over a loss. We all find different ways to manage our loss. None are right or wrong. It's just a way that each of us can adjust, thus allowing our lives to move forward without anyone else noticing our grief.

I saw everyone around me trying to do all in their power to protect and help me, and for a better word, to feel better. I could not accept them giving up their lives any more to assist me. One of my ways to help myself was to talk to people. It didn't much matter what we talked about, just like general stuff associated with life's goings on, helped me adjust my thoughts and being with people who didn't know my grief was another way I could feel some normality again. My wonderful friends from golf were instrumental in my grieving process. Golf is more than a sport; it is also a fellowship. And I want to thank all of my beautiful friends. Thank you.

I started work back at the deli, which for me, was the best medicine. At first, I couldn't get my head in the right place, but I'm not one to give up easily. Early starts, lots of work, noisy customers, grumpy customers, happy customers and aching legs after standing on them all day. Wonderful. I could breathe again for a short time, whilst I had to concentrate on getting orders right, add up the purchases in my head correctly and still take the time to interact with our valuable customers nicely, I was able to push through the painful thoughts for a short time and join in with life again, be it for a short time.

Each day at work gave me a way of being able to slowly store my grief and overwhelming pain in a special part of my heart where I, and I alone, could visit in a heartbeat. Shhhh moment.

# Nine Little Words

In a previous part of my story, when I was talking about my days at high school, I mentioned that nine little words uttered by one boy to his classmates, just loud enough for me to hear, affected my life so much that I would have a reason to revisit those threads later in my book. We all inherit something that we're not so chuffed about from our parents and our family genes. Poor Nicole was the one who inherited my nose. As I've mentioned before, hate is not a word I like using. But Nicole also disliked her nose and felt uncomfortable with photos of herself, and suffered the same inferiority complex as I had, and I would go so far as to say my mum had suffered also. Nicole, however, also had spunk and lots of it. She worked hard, and as soon as she had saved enough money, she booked herself into hospital to have Rhinoplasty surgery.

The result was transforming, not only for her outward appearance, but certainly for her soul. Nicole's whole demeanour lifted, and she had sparkle back in her eyes; possibly no one else even noticed, but for Nicole herself, the operation was very worthwhile.

With this in mind, I was going through a low, sad time in my life, and my beautiful daughters were never far away and always engulfed me with love and support and encouragement, always united, helping each other in times of need.

One day, Nicole came to me and said, "Mum, I can get you in with my doctor to have a Rhinoplasty. You've always disliked your nose. You should do something for yourself for once. Please say yes, as I need to know by tonight if you want it done."

This was not a decision one would make in minutes, but with the many underlying issues that have been engulfing our lives for some time, and the fact that those nine little words had haunted me all my life, I said, "Thank you, yes, book me in!" Sadly, I gave no thought as to how this may affect my mum and others in my family, which it did. Another one of the hundreds of mistakes I made throughout my life.

The mistake here was not that of going ahead with the operation, as I was extremely happy with the result, but the mistake was not allowing others close to me to talk over such a change. To this day, Mum often says, 'It was such a shame you changed your nose. I often wonder how you would look now, if you hadn't." With that said, I am pleased I did have the operation, as it has somewhat alleviated insecurities, and I no longer have to revisit those haunting nine little words whilst visiting threads of the past in my Web of Life.

# Life Changes Ahead

Paul was one of my regular customers, and I took pride in making sure his order was ready and waiting as he walked into the deli. He was a very hard-working market gardener, and always called into the deli on his way to the markets to get his standing order of three wee William cigars, 600 ml of Master's iced coffee – not Brown's coffee – no, Browns was rubbish – and a pepper steak pie. Every now and again, just to keep me on my toes and with just a hint of a smile on his face, he would quietly say, "I might have a beef and salad roll today, please." I had to win this game, so after that, I always had both his lunch choices ready.

It was very easy to know at what time he would arrive, as the driveway from the market garden was only a short distance from the deli, and I could always see the big truck slowly descending the long, sloping driveway to turn onto Old Mandurah Road. One Saturday, I worked a different shift, and Paul walked into the deli for the first time not in his work clothes. What surprised me more was that he was wearing an RGC golf jumper. The Sainsbury's gift of the gab jumped into gear and I asked, "Are you a member of Rockingham?"

"Yes," was the simple reply.

I went on to say, "I've been a member for many years. I'm not a low handicapper, but I love the game."

Paul picked up his three wee Williams cigars and quietly said, "We might have to have a game one day," and left.

Like most regulars, Paul had casually chatted to all of the staff on and off over the years. Thus, he was aware that I had not long lost my husband, and he was very sympathetic, polite and respectful to me in every way. Weeks later, he asked if I would like to play a game of golf, which I was delighted about, but also nervous about, as I had been told that Paul was a very good golfer. The game was very enjoyable, after which we went into the clubhouse for a drink. We chatted for quite some time, and although I, of course, did most of the talking, it was amazing to hear more of Paul's working history, golfing history. But more importantly, I couldn't help but notice Paul's charming, quiet demeanour, allowing me to feel free of expectations, secure and relaxed, able to be just the person, a glimpse of feeling myself again.

The next time Paul came into the deli for his lunch order, I noticed his slight grin almost reached a smile when he said, "Good morning."

I was very happy working at the deli, but through necessity and common sense, I had been giving a lot of thought to planning my future financially. I was still young, and after losing my superannuation and life's earnings with the loss of Trendy Tots, and, although I owned my home, my savings were limited. Therefore, I realised that I may have to consider obtaining full-time employment with long-term security prospects to enable me to retire comfortably when the time came. I was confident with my resume, and knew that I was not afraid of hard work, and even studying if required, but I also knew I needed to give myself a little time before taking this step, as many more of life's storms were hovering overhead.

The friendship between Paul and me had deepened. Our conversations extended beyond the time of day, and in such, I was able to find out that his market garden was, in fact, a hydroponic gourmet lettuce farm owned and run by Paul and his partner Rob. There was also a silent partner, Brian. I felt very comfortable that Paul was someone I could confide in. Therefore, I'm sure he discovered more about me in a short time than I knew about him.

For many years, I had always felt that Paul was a good man. Don't ask me why the word 'good' comes into mind, but well before I knew anything about him, other than his liking for wee William cigars, my mind knew he was to be trusted. He was a good person – come to think of it, maybe my love of the scent of perfume cigars had something to do with it.

My life was busy with work, kids, and many visits to see Mum, and I tried my hardest to keep her spirits up as her loneliness since losing Dad was something she had no control over, and we, as her family, could only give suggestions and support to try and help her in some way. This was not the easiest time for me, as I myself missed my adored dad so very much, and privately cried buckets of tears as part of my grieving process, along with the added heartache of losing Max, I found it very difficult at times. Thank goodness for family, beautiful babies, sunshine and my very intuitive, cuddly cat.

Paul had called in for a coffee, and as we sat in the courtyard, he told me that his partner, Rob, had decided to sell his half of Balhill Water Gardens, which was the name of the business, and asked me if I would be interested in joining together with him in buying Rob's share of the business, which would give us both a very good income and secure our future together.

Most people would think this ludicrous, but as I possibly think a little outside of the square, my first thought was 'a hell of a risk'. Then why not find out more? Paul said he would provide all of the books and the accountant's details so that there was no doubt as to how the business was travelling and expectations for the future. My second thought was "Ring Brian," my confidante and wonderful brother for advice, as this would mean me selling my home and Paul selling his unit to be able to finance such an undertaking. Much homework had to be done.

Brian was his usual, thorough in investigation, constructive in advice and supportive as a loving brother, as I expected. Love you, my brother. He said, "Lyn, if you think you and Paul can make it work, and I see no reason why you shouldn't give it a go, if that's what you want."

The enormity of selling our family home, giving up any small amount of security I had at the time was second to none as far as anxiety goes. 'But something good always comes from something bad' was another one of those silly sayings that I was drowned in as a child, so I knew something good was around the corner. Surely, the power of positive thinking.

It took quite a while to sell both properties and have all our ducks in a row, but in the meantime, I, once again, was almost blown away with having to rewalk one of my threads of my Web of Life during the takeover of Balhill Water Gardens. There were papers to be signed and many details to be discussed. So Paul had arranged for me to meet his partner, Rob, and his wife at the home where Paul lived on the Balhill property. Rob's surname had never come up, until we were driving to meet him and his wife. I asked, "What is his wife's name? … just to be polite and prepared," to which Paul replied, "Nola. Rob and Nola Stammers."

I was in disbelief. I think I just went quiet for a minute, then said, "I know Rob and Nola very well. Max worked for them at the supermarket. I had heard that Rob left the supermarket business and was doing something else, but never in my wildest dreams did I think that the Rob you are partners with is *that* Rob."

Naturally, this made doing business with them very positive and friendly, with a confident outset for both parties.

# Could a Wish Come True

I loved Paul's quiet, level, calming way. I soaked up the non-expectational, uncluttered, considerate, trustworthy, honest Paul. It was exactly what I needed at that time in my life. Although Paul always erred on the side of privacy, he did tell me early in the piece that he and his five sisters and one brother were born in Kenya, Africa. Paul told me his father was a Baptist missionary, and how very difficult it was for his mum, raising seven children, surviving mainly on what they grew themselves. They had to be self-sufficient, relying on a few chickens, sheep and a milking cow, along with corn and the vegetables they managed to grow to feed the family of seven. My mind immediately revisited an early part of my Web of Life, in fact, primary school where I was sitting on a wooden bench in a little dirt floored shed with a lovely lady who was taking our Scripture lessons, telling us about the missionaries in Africa, followed by us singing, 'What a Friend We Have in Jesus'.

This was one thread of my school days that has never left my mind, and now to be hearing from Paul, a man I was going to go into a relationship with, that his dad was one of those missionaries seemed, in some convoluted way, a sign of connection to cuddle my mind. Even more, Paul then told me that his five sisters still lived in England, and went on to say, "Hopefully, you'll be able to come with me when I next visit them."

Oh, my goodness, my two childhood wishes, one to be a missionary in Africa and the other to one day go to England to see where my dad was born could possibly come true. Certainly, I was never going to be a missionary, that was for sure, but to think that my other childhood wish to one day travel to England could actually come true was beyond my wildest dreams. My heart skipped a beat.

# Gentle Arms of Future Happiness

The day Paul asked me to marry him had started out like any other day for us. We were busy sorting things out, packing and discussing the move to Balhill when we took a break to have a cup of tea. Paul, in his quiet manner, took a sip of his tea, put the cup down, looked at me and said, "I would like you to marry me."

There was no doubt that our special love had grown into something beautiful. But with everything else that was going on in our lives, getting married was something I had not considered, and hearing the word certainly took me by surprise. I remember asking if I had heard correctly, to which Paul replied, "Yes, I am asking you to marry me."

This time, it sounded very real, and I at once felt flustered and said, "But, Paul, what about all the issues we've got to sort out? Are you really sure you want to marry me?"

He replied, "Yes. I wouldn't have asked if I didn't want to marry you."

I had to take a breath with a million thoughts going through my head, Paul, up to that point in his life, had very few problems, with only one beautiful, self-sufficient daughter to consider, compared to the increased issues of my very beautiful, very large family, who were always first and foremost in my mind, and this closeness would never be able to change that. This gave me much to think about, considering all of these thoughts and more.

I simply said, "Paul, you know if you marry me you are marrying a job lot – two daughters, their husbands and children, three stepsons, their wives and children, two dogs, five fish, a cat and a budgie as well."

He gave me a gentle kiss on the forehead and said, "Yes, I know."

With that, I wrapped my arms around him and said, "I would love to marry you."

## Magnetic Attraction

It didn't take long at all before Paul and I realised that in many ways, we were polar opposites. Strangely enough, we actually both embraced this fact, both seeing a new and positive side in each other that we could benefit from in our own lives. The first time Paul asked me to dinner at his home was a good example of just how far apart our way of life really was. I was excited about seeing Paul and wanted to look tickety boo. We had spoken over the phone, and I asked if sixish to arrive would be okay. All good. I had plenty of time to get ready.

About five changes of clothes later, and lots of umming and aahing as to which shoes looked best, what perfume would be best to suit the occasion, and of course, getting my hair how I wanted it. I glanced at the clock and saw that it was getting close to six. No worries. I thought it only takes fifteen minutes to get there, so I'll be just right about six.

When I drove up towards the house, Paul was waiting on the driveway, looking very serious, which worried me, as I thought something bad had happened. I quickly got out of the car and asked, "Are you all right? Has something gone wrong?"

With that, he said, "You are late. I was worried that something had happened."

I quickly checked the time and said, "I'm not late, am I? We said sixish, I'm sure."

Paul's reply to that was "Yes, but it's nearly twenty past."

Oh, my goodness, my first insight into how different our lives *had* been. Before this, I had never had the privilege of expecting a 'time set' to be in stone. When any of my family said they would be arriving to my home about 6.30 that was simply a thereabouts time, due to the fact that they quite often had to travel hundreds of kilometres, and could encounter many variances in their travel before actually arriving at my home "about 6.30". Besides, as long as they were coming to visit, I didn't care what time they got there. I had certainly become very blasé and possibly too relaxed about many things.

Paul, I found out, was extremely astute and would always be ready early and arrive and at an appointment two minutes early, never late, even by one minute. Paul had lived on his own for most of the time since he and his wife had split some ten years previously. I believe he did have one or two relationships, but he kept his personal life to himself.

Introvert would possibly describe Paul best, although I feel that word is not quite right because he was just a beautiful, kind man who wanted to do things in life properly. Having had a Christian upbringing, gave Paul and his brothers and sisters a strong mindset of doing what is right, honest and good. From the time that they were born, they followed the teachings of their father and mother, who were Baptist missionaries in Kenya. It goes without saying that I, on the other hand, would certainly be described as an extrovert. If you've suffered reading my Web of Life, you'll know for sure that never a true a word spoken. I talk too much, saying things I shouldn't. I knew, however, that we could and would give and take and we would have a happy life together.

Showing love and affection was very straightforward for me, but Paul's reserved, quite private ways, made it difficult for him to relax and give in to his feelings. These feelings were there, just hidden under years of holding back, so that no one saw him doing anything improper in any way.

I decided, possibly out of need, that I could somehow break down these barriers and allow Paul to find more of the soft things in life, laughter and happiness. He had already shown an abundance of love, a giving love, not a selfish love, and adored his beautiful daughter, Marika. He was a caring, loving brother to his siblings, and always gave a helping hand privately, preferring little or no recognition of his kindness.

Paul was such a kind person that even a red back spider could cross paths with him without a fear in the world of being squished, come to think of it, any animal, insect or reptile, would not have a care in the world if they crossed paths with Paul. He would simply walk around them carefully, gather them up carefully, or open an escape route for them to ensure their freedom and safety.

I remember one summer night, just as we were about to turn out the bedroom light, I saw a great big wolf spider on the wall above the bedroom door. I quickly said, "Paul, don't turn the light out. There's a spider in our bedroom."

The very tired response was, "Don't worry about it. He won't annoy us."

He proceeded to turn the light off and flop into bed after a very long, hot day at work. I was brought up on a farm with plenty of critters, but I was hoping that Paul would have done his usual and take this extra-large furry intruder outside. Like a kid scared of the dark, I strained my eyes for hours waiting to see if that big daddy of a spider would decide to share our bed. Exhaustion from the day's work obviously took over my mission of spider-watching when suddenly I was woken by what felt like a monster falling from a height and landing on my thigh. I didn't realise I could jump so high after giving that big boy the backhander of his life and screaming for Paul to turn on the light.

Of course, Paul's expression never altered. As he put on his dressing gown, found a cardboard box and gently scooped up the slightly worse for wear night intruder, took it outside, got back into bed and simply said, "Alright, now, dear." Gotta love that man. XX.

I had always been a touchy, touchy, lots of cuddles and kisses and hugs type of person, and needed this affection in my life. Paul's love and affection was on a deeper, very reserved, private level. *A few gentle, persuasive changes required.*

I always felt like a cuddle and would quite often walk up to Paul with the idea that he would put his arms around me and we could share a 'moment'. Sadly, most times, the response was not forthcoming. So after a short, very short time, I decided that I would need to be proactive. I wanted more affection.

My new approach to this hiccup was I would walk up to him, tell him I loved him, ask for a cuddle, and then, literally, I would lift and place his arms around me repeatedly, all the while saying, "You love me, don't you", until he couldn't help but laugh, knowing full well that my persistence would not go away. Yes, he loved me.

Breaking down these well-embedded barriers was special to me, and you know what … I think they were special to Paul also.

I am no different from most of us, I'm sure, and love being told "you look nice." I thrive on a compliment, even if it's just a formality. I'm easily pleased. Vanity is not a good attribute, as we know, but it is nice receiving some sort of acknowledgement for one's efforts to please.

When we were going out, Paul would be dressed and ready hours before the event, sitting in his chair reading or doing his Sudoku, waiting for me. After many changes of outfits, hair adjustments and shoe changes being the norm, I would walk out, stand in front of Paul and ask, "Do I look nice?

Paul would lift his head and quietly say, "Good, dear."

'Good, dear' was not what I wanted him to say, No!

This, too, became another one of those times when poor Paul met his match with determination. When these 'good, dear' words occurred, I would simply say, "No, not good enough. We'll try that again." And I would walk back into the bedroom, take two minutes to contain myself from laughing, and walk out again and say, "Do I look nice?"

If this failed to get the answer I was looking for, the next time I would run out and straddle him in his chair, shake his shoulders until he was almost crying with laughter, eventually saying, "Yes, you look very nice."

Job done!

## Catastrophic Pain and Suffering

There has never been a right moment when I have been able to control my emotions enough to write about the most devastating, soul-destroying, heart-crushing time to have ever happened, not only to me as a mother, but to a young son, sister and an entire family who all had to endure the ultimate pain and longtime suffering. My beautiful daughter Nicole had been unwell and suffering for a long time, and help and love had come in many different ways, and perhaps it's acceptable to say, left-of-centre forms. To many judgmental people, her boyfriend may have not appeared to be suitable, however, to us, he was a blessing for some very important reasons. Nicole, for the first time in ages, was happy. Her boyfriend loved and spoiled her, and he understood her, giving her the support she needed. Nicky would bounce in the door with an arm full of clothes and Nicky-type ornaments, shoes and all sorts of things that her boyfriend bought her.

It was wonderful to see her happy.

Nicky hadn't been in touch by phone for some time, but late one afternoon, I received an unusual phone call from her.

"Hi, Mum. Just thought I'd ring to say hi."

I was delighted to hear her voice, but there was something hidden in the way she was talking, which I couldn't help but make a mental note of as I often did. She went on to say, "Mum, Simmy's a great dad to Luke, isn't he? I love Simmy."

I answered "Yes, he is."

"Bernie's a great person. I love Bernie. Terrie's a beautiful sister and a great mother. I love Terrie. B's a great neighbour. This person is a good person. That person is a great person ..." and she kept telling me that she loved all of these people. She then went on to say, "Mum, do you know how much I love Luke. My Luke is very clever. He's going to be someone very special."

I said, "We all know how much you love Luke, and you're right. He is very clever."

Nicky said, "Bye. Love you, Mum."

That was the last time I heard my daughter's voice.

When we talk about drugs and their effect on everyone – the 'everyone' quite often doesn't include the one suffering the most. We become caught up in the way someone suffering from drug addiction affects our lives, and how it disrupts what we want or would like in *our* precious lives. But we quite often don't consider the one suffering the most. Nicole was suffering, but getting better isn't as simple as 'having a heart transplant', then you'll be better. Once again, (and I myself can only imagine) but without a doubt, only those who have walked this walk and experienced such depths of destruction could possibly know this pain.

People can be and are often very judgmental, especially about the parents of someone suffering. I've heard people say things like, 'I wouldn't put up with that', or 'it's the parents' fault; they were too soft', or 'I'd just kicked him/her out', and many more comments that are of no value to anyone. However, (and sadly for those it happens to), I have noticed throughout my life that those who judge, many times in the future, learn to live with the same situation.

All families do their very best and try everything within their power to help solve this horrific, life-destroying scourge of our times, including preventing, by every means possible. But as we know, and as much as we think (and certainly hope) it won't happen to us, it very sadly sometimes does.

Like any habit in the world, people unite, encouraging others when experimenting any habit, be it smoking, drinking, drugs, sex or rock and roll, we all need the feeling of safety in numbers, which, for some reason, gives us a false idea that it can't be bad if everyone else is doing it. Encouragement from others, just at the wrong crucial moment in someone's vulnerable life, (not always), but very often is when we go down the wrong path in life.

To all who are suffering, either the ones suffering themselves or their families, my heartfelt and sincere thoughts are with you all.

I will always be proud that I was one of those parents who saw past the ugliness by seeing the beauty of my daughter, who was a precious daughter, mother, sister, granddaughter, and auntie, who was loved by all who knew her. Nicole was kind, thoughtful, and loved her son unconditionally.

I am in no way covering up or disregarding the horrible times that occurred during this time in our lives, but my heart only reflects on the fact that if I or anyone else was suffering, my adored daughter would have been suffering much, much more.

I remember going to visit Nicole one day, and as I walked into the kitchen, Nicole said, "Be careful, Mum. Don't break Luke's train track."

The train track went around the kitchen floor, under the chairs and over the table and down the other side. She would spend hours drawing games, like Snakes and Ladders, and making up stories, and they would write a book together, and Luke would illustrate the book. If Luke was playing on the floor with his Thomas the Tank Engine, no one was allowed to move or upset his play. With all that was troubling her, Nicky did everything in her power to do the best for her adored son. When things became very dark, she and Simon shared Luke to ensure he suffered as little as possible. Simon adored his son and also did all in his power to ensure Luke had the best start in life.

I was very fortunate to have been given the privilege by my daughters and their husbands of sharing in all of my grandchildren's lives from the time they were babies. Thus, a strong bond was formed and will remain eternally.

Paul and I were planning our life together, and I was slowly moving in with Paul at Balhill Water Gardens. The home was only small, but I thought it was adorable, and the views from the top of the hill were just delightful. The sun sets over the lake took your breath away.

We were busy putting a large wardrobe together in the bedroom, as Paul was a minimalist, and the robe he used would not hold my 'more than anyone would ever need' volume of clothing, shoes and handbags. It was time for a cuppa, and as I walked out into the lounge room, I noticed a news flash on the TV.

"A man and his pillion rider had been killed when a utility being driven on the wrong side of the road collided head-on with their motorcycle on Albany Highway, Gleneagle."

I took a quick look, as I had never heard the name Gleneagle before, and just wondered where it was. As I looked at the screen, they were showing the photo of the bike with things strewn around the site. For a split second, I thought, 'That looks like Nicky's jacket on the road.' But because I had a habit of thinking the worst, I thought, 'Don't be silly. There must be hundreds of jackets that look like that.'

With that, I proceeded to make a cup of tea.

The phone rang.

It was Terrie, who was living in Cunderdin at the time. I was always happy to hear from Terrie, but this was different. Terrie's voice seemed different when she asked, "Is Paul with you, Mum?"

I replied, "Yes, darling. Why?"

"Mum, I've got something to tell you." Terrie paused, which prompted me to say, "What? Is everything okay?"

Terrie's reply was "No, Mum. Nicky's boyfriend has been killed on his bike."

I felt sick and said, "How dreadful! Nicky will be devastated. She loves him so much. Does she know?"

With that, Terrie started to cry and said, "Mum, I've heard they think the pillion rider was Nicky."

This message was a long time ago now, but some things time just cannot heal. This is not something that anyone would find easy to write about, but I will be as honest as I can as I relive this most devastating moment in my life. My heart is pounding, and I feel very distraught and quite numb with what I'm about to share with you.

I remember going completely numb. My ears were buzzing. I couldn't breathe, and I couldn't get far enough down. I was crawling on the floor wanting to be under the carpet, with flashes of Nicky's leather Jacket moving in and out of my mind. Terrie was crying, saying, "Mum, I love you. I'm coming down. I'm so sorry, Mum, I'll be there soon."

Paul ran to comfort me. Millions of distorted thoughts were running in and out of my head as I tried to talk, but just couldn't get words out. "What about Luke? How can this darling boy find out that his mother has died? This is too much. It's not true. She hasn't died. What about Mum? I can't tell her. The pain is too much. My darling, I want to cuddle you. Nicky, don't go. No, no, it's not true. What about her nephews and nieces? It can't be true. What if it isn't her? No, it's not her. Hurry, Terrie, I need you."

Paul helped me off the floor. I was a blob of nothing. I couldn't see or hear anything. I just wanted to go back to my home to phone someone (I didn't know who) to find out that it was all just a big lie and Nicky would come home.

I didn't know who to ring. I tried the hospital. I tried the police. No one cared. I was crying, not able to talk or think. No one could tell me anything. For what seemed like a lifetime, I rang and hung up and rang again. My darling Terrie arrived, and we held each other, cried and cried some more before, somehow, I was put through to Major Crash.

This is not an experience I would wish on my worst enemy. I explained that I was trying to find out if it could have been my daughter who was killed along with the rider in the motorbike accident which had occurred on Albany highway, Gleneagle. The officer I was talking with seemed very blasé, and said "Just a moment." At this stage, I think he thought he had put my call on silent. But unfortunately for me, he hadn't. He yelled out to someone, with me being able to hear, "Ah, what was the name of that girl who was killed at Gleneagle, who was unidentified?" Someone answered, "Yeah, they think her name was Williams. Yeah, that's it. I think they said Nicole Williams."

The officer then picked up the phone to me and said, "Her name is Williams."

Before he could speak again, I said in a controlled and articulated but quiet voice, "That is my daughter. You were speaking about my daughter. She is not just 'that girl who was killed', she's my beautiful daughter. Please have some respect!"

At this point, I became numb and cold and couldn't breathe. Terrie hugged me.

There was no hope of gaining any grip on my Web of Life. This storm was too strong, and I slipped down and down with no strength in my heart to hang on. I am very aware that many thousands of mums have experienced this indescribable pain of losing a child. In fact, three of my cousins have also felt this endless heartache and pain. Many of my closest friends have also had to endure the unthinkable pain of losing a child, and as with any part of life, only those who have felt this heartache can understand fully. Heartfelt love and thoughts.

Of course, finding out about the death of your child is only the beginning of the pain. The enormity of being part of everyone else's pain is inevitable, and many times, in the case of Nicky's son and all who adored her, this then becomes the greatest of pain. I was witness to my family crumbling in despair and suffering. I could not be selfish, as I was not the only one who was filled with this relentless heartache. I had to be strong. Yes, my darling dad had taught me to think of others and be strong. *Others still need you to be the strength of the family.* Dad was the strength for us always. And now I must be the strength in my own family.

*Nicole and her adored son Luke. Every picture does tell a story. Shhhh moments for a lifetime.*

# A Loss Like No Other

Recovering from the pain of losing a child is impossible. No one actually recovers. They just push their pain to a private place within. This pain stays forever. The effect something like this has on a family is too much to put into words. All that followed after losing our beautiful Nicole, including the heart-destroying funeral, fighting for justice, appearing in court, actually seeing the person who was responsible for your daughter's death, watching your darling, eight-year-old grandson slowly burying his devastating pain and suffering within, trying to protect his dad and family the only way he knew how, watching your eldest daughter write an Impact Statement so graphic and disturbing that it debilitated her life as she knew it. These, and many more, were just some of the heartaches to follow, impacting all of our family.

My, perhaps obscure, faith was something I reached out for like no other time in my life. Yes, we have a friend in Jesus.

Times like these are also when we understand the true and deep meaning of the love of family, as this love cradles us, allowing us to grieve in our own way and time.

# Balhill Water Gardens

Working on the lettuce farm was so good for my soul. I was out in the fresh air, able to smell the perfume from the gum trees as it drifted on a gentle breeze through the garden, allowing me to close off from reality momentarily, thus taking my innermost thoughts to a spiritual place of reflection. Hydroponic lettuce farming was hard but wonderful work. We had seven staff working on a picking day as we rotated 1,700 lettuce in a week. In summer, we began work at 5 am to avoid the heat; the first truck would be stacked with crates of lettuce before 9 am, ready to set off to the Canning Vale markets. By the time the truck returned, we had almost finished picking another truck load. There were 240 free-standing beds, and as the beds were picked out, they were washed and young seedlings were replanted in each one. The empty seedling beds were then also replenished with new seedlings. And so it went.

Dave was our manager, and our garden was in good hands. Dave was a reliable, dedicated, hard worker, and kept an eye on everything at all times. Leanne and Reggie were part of our great team. A reverse osmosis machine kept the water purified so the lettuce had 99% pure water fed through small tubes into each bed. Specially mixed fertilizer was mixed and fed throughout the water tanks twice daily. It was a 24/7 business, and I love being part of it. Summer was difficult, as if the tubes to a bed became blocked with silt, the lettuce would drop in within minutes. So everyone was trained to rove the gardens looking for wilting leaves. When this happened, the tubes were disconnected and blown clean so the water could run again. The pumps went all day and night, and quite often Paul would do a walk around during the night in summer, and quite often we were unclogging tubes in the moonlight. So romantic!

Paul decided to hire a truck driver so he could remain working in the garden after a pick day to allow everyone to leave work a bit earlier.

Once again, I revisited some of my previous threads in my Web of Life and explained to Paul that Keith, Dad's cousin who had come to live with Nana Hattie when I was a very young child, was now living in Perth and might be looking for a casual job. Presto, a happy reunion. It was so good seeing Keith on a regular basis again, and the job suited him at the time.

Working in the garden certainly helped keep me fit. Lugging crates of lettuce up the incline of the garden and struggling with the extra big and very long garden hose when cleaning the beds put muscles on your muscles, that's for sure.

Of course, as Paul was a member of RGC, he took Thursdays and Saturdays off for golf, and I had Wednesdays off for my golf day.

Once a month, Rob (Paul's ex-partner) would give Paul a two-day break. Paul would often go to Albany to see his brother, Bill and his sister-in-law, Elizabeth. The first time I went with Paul, I couldn't believe how alike he and his brother were. Elizabeth and Bill had the most beautiful property on the outskirts of Albany, and the garden was out of this world. I was welcomed with such warmth, and once again, I benefited so much by getting up and close to nature. It was very uplifting.

Another time we visited Bill and Elizabeth, the Albany amateur wine makers group were holding their annual wine Awards, which included lots and lots of wine tasting. Elizabeth had been using the abundance of fruit from their orchard to make many flasks of fruit wine, and the wine awards were a good chance to compare and get ideas, plus have one or two sips of delicious wine. What fun!

Bill and Elizabeth, like Paul, appeared on face value to be very controlled and proper (for a better word). And I'm telling you, they certainly let their hair down at the wine tasting, and boy, did we have some great belly laughs. They both made me feel like I had been part of the family for years.

I met Paul's beautiful daughter, Marika, when she was visiting her dad at Balhill, and once again, I was met with a sincere, genuine warmth. Marika, like her darling dad, was quiet, thoughtful, kind and sincere, and like her dad, I'm sure she didn't know what hit her with my nonstop chatter and openness of conversation, and this was before she met the job lot. Oh, my goodness, more gentle blending needed.

# More Fun than Golf

The end-of-year Golf Presentation night is another night of frivolity. This photo was taken when we did a skit called (hard to guess, I know) 'Ladies of the Night'.

*Left to Right: Paulette, me, Lyn Van., Lyn Mac., Di, Denise*

*Three clubs and a putter day. Yes, we played golf in our silly outfits*

*Winners are grinners. Colleen and I on presentation night*

I always say "I love golf," but I think what I really mean these days is I love all my friends at golf! These are photos of my wonderful friends at Dunsborough.

PS. We did play golf as well, I think!

"Rocking Rainbows" was the theme we had to dress as for the presentation night of Regional Senior, which was held at Dunsborough 2024. We had so much fun, even the golf was fun. Our group was last to hit off on the Saturday. Therefore, it was late and dark when we were playing the last few holes of the competition, so much so that many of the locals lined the sides of the last fairway with torches to help find our golf balls!

We did have a few ladies in our group that played well and won a trophy, but (sorry, my friends) the highlight for me was that Rockingham ladies (oops, possibly didn't act like ladies that night) won the Best Dressed! Yay!

*Left to Right: Karen, me, Sue, Beth, Carmel, Wendy, Barbara, Denise, Mary and Julie*

# Gentle Changes

Both Paul and I found out early in the piece that we both needed to consider each other's ways of doing things, and the fact that at our age, old habits die hard. At first, we struggled with all sorts of things, most being small trivialities, which, in the scheme of things, didn't matter much anyway.

Having grandchildren running around Balhill was a big adjustment for Paul, along with the huge increases in visitors coming and going at all times, and the added noise, more noise, I'm sure, than Paul had heard in years. But gradually, family coming and going, meals at odd times, kids hitting golf balls out of sight and lighting cracker stoked fires in hollowed out black boy stumps and Beau, the cat, settling into his new home, 'somehow' became slightly less stressful for Paul, and sometimes I think he actually enjoyed a tiny bit of this craziness.

My adjustment was coping with the quiet, especially the no-conversation times as Paul worked in his office for hours, and when he wasn't working, he would sit and read for more hours. This I certainly found difficult to adjust to. Fortunately, I had plenty to keep me busy with work, housework and a very large property and house garden to care for. I always kept myself busy, but the no interaction with someone reading took me years to come to grips with.

Paul was never possessive of my time, and therefore, I knew I could not be possessive of his time. We adopted easy solutions to little hiccups. For example, when we travelled in his car, the radio was always on classical music, and when we travelled in my car, the radio was 96.5 and loud! Who said adjusting was difficult?

One day, Paul had been to Rockingham City to do the banking. When he arrived back, he said, "Have you renewed your passport?"

"Yes," I replied. "Why?"

He explained that his sister in England was not well and he wanted us to travel to see her in the near future. I was so excited and happy.

"Are you really going to take me to England?" I asked. Paul's reply was "Yes, but we will have to get married first."

We had not long been engaged, and it was far too close to my beautiful Nicole's passing for me to contemplate a wedding. A compromise was agreed to, and our wedding was planned for later in the year. I did, however, ask Paul why the need to have our wedding before our holiday. Paul's faith, although slightly hidden, was very strong, and he explained that out of respect, he wanted us to be married if we were staying with his sisters. I love Paul's consideration and care for others, and many of his genuine, thoughtful, kind ways reassured me that I also would always be respected, cared for and loved.

This was a busy time in the lives of our children.

Terrie's ever-present walkabout urges, accompanied sadly by unforeseen circumstances, had once again prompted more house moves from Cunderdin to Southern Cross, from Southern Cross to Darken and from Darken to Williams!

My old trailer had its time cut out, but the fun we always had made up for the sheer hard work involved in the roller coaster quest for Terrie to find the happiness she deserved and be able to settle in her life. The move to Darken was the quickest ever, and we still laugh about it today. We arrived at the little house late in the morning, four kids in tow, as it was school holidays, and Luke was staying with his cousins. As per normal, Terrie's expectations were to have the house completely set up before bedtime that night. Boxes were flying everywhere. The dog was running excitedly in between everyone's legs, and the newly bought remote-controlled Hot Rod toy screeched up and down the dusty driveway to the delight of the kids, big kid included. Hours later, food or the lack of it was on everyone's mind. No problems. We'd just duck down the street and get something. A couple of loaves of bread later, plenty of polony slices and a bottle of good old tomato sauce, and the job was done. Before very long, the shower was running red hot with sweaty kids in and out. The washing machine was thumping away with sweaty clothes from those same kids, and it was sit-down, relax time. Terrie then asked if the kids would like some ice cream, which she had tried to keep cold on ice. Luke has never forgotten his holiday at Auntie's house in Darken, and to this day, we still have a laugh. "Yes, please," was the quick reply. With that, Terrie, who was understandably exhausted, tipped a two-litre tub of Peter's ice cream upside down on a dinner plate, cut in four, flopped each quarter onto plates and yelled "Sweets are ready!" The kids' eyes almost popped out of their heads as they hurried off, all looking like the cat that had swallowed the canary with more ice cream on their plates than they had ever eaten in one serve before.

The next day was much the same, with touch-ups needed everywhere, shopping to be done, and the never-ending fights over whose turn it was to have the remote control. Naughty Nanna, I know, but I was very grateful when that dune buggy shat itself, I must say: No more fights. Yay!

Eventually, it was decided that we would go for a walk to look around town. The main attraction wasn't the school, which was Terrie's main concern; it was, of course, the swimming pool. Sadly, it was too late that day, and reluctantly, with four kids scuffing their shoes along the dirt in disappointment, we moseyed on back to the house.

I had only returned home to Balhill a day when Terrie rang and said, "Mum, guess what?" Her husband had been offered a job in Williams, with a house included in the package, so they would be moving the next weekend. A removalist truck was arranged.

Paul and Ceri were at a time in their lives when their children were growing up, playing hockey, socialising with friends and getting into the party scene. And party they did. We were always invited to be part of each special event, and I just loved joining in with the fun, especially as most were the dreaded dress-up parties. We spent happy family time celebrating all sorts of occasions at Paul and Ceri's home; Mike had finally found the love of his life, Jiang, and he celebrated his happiness with a traditional wedding in China. Jiang is a treasured part of our family. Seeing Mike happy gave me much joy.

Greg waited a long time to be with the love of his life. He had met Susie earlier, but family tradition saw Susie go back to Slovenia, which was heartbreaking for Greg, but fortunately, God works in mysterious ways, as Paul's sister would say, and one day, sometime later, Greg and Susie were happily reunited, and not long after, became husband and wife. Their wedding was very special, and I remember so clearly the wedding party held at Susie's parents' home. The music was loud. The party was in full swing when Susie's mum started making loud la, la, la, la, la sounds as she was smashing plates on the brick pavers. Susie quickly put a stop to this, explaining to her mum that although it was tradition, kids dancing in bare feet and broken glass could end badly.

Greg and Susie blessed us with a beautiful granddaughter, Lisa, followed by Amy, and to our surprise, a third grandchild, Max, arrived, completing their happy family. We were invited to join in with so many happy get-togethers at Greg and Susie's home.

On one such occasion, I remember asking where John (Susie's dad) was, and Susie replied affectionately, "Dad's in the shed with all the wogs, cooking goulash."

When I went into the shed, John and his family were all sitting around a gas burner strategically placed on a piece of tin with a large pot of food hanging from a tripod. I just love tradition.

# Our Wedding

Balhill was the perfect setting for our wedding, as our home was on the top of a hill with views overlooking Lake Walyungup, also giving glimpses of the ocean. The sun sets never let us down, and I always felt like the luckiest person on earth to have a view like this as part of my everyday life.

Once Paul and I decided where we were going to have our special day, Paul put full trust in me, as he always did, to organise our wedding day as it suited me. When I was asked if he would like lights or flowers or, in fact, anything, where I thought he might like to have input, he would simply say, "If you would like that I'm happy."

Within days, the big white marquee was erected in the middle of our extremely large front lawn and was set up with a dance floor, an area for a DJ, and white chairs for our small number. Oops, that's a fib, perhaps not so small number of guests. It wasn't my fault that the numbers blew out just a tad, remembering family alone accounted for about fifty people. Oh, well, phone the caterers again.

Our day was just perfect. The sun was shining with the perfect, gentle breeze whispering through the trees, and although a storm was forecast for later in the evening, nothing could dampen our wedding day.

As I mentioned, Paul didn't talk about his past life much at all, but as I also mentioned, I was usually ever so gently, able to persuade and extract information from Paul when required. Of course, being an open book and never being able to understand why others aren't the same. I often wanted to hear what, in fact, amazing, important things occurred in Paul's life that I felt were extremely memorable, and should be remembered with pride. One thing that fascinated me greatly was that, because he was born and grew up in Kenya, he and his family were able to speak Swahili. How wonderful. I had been fascinated about Africa from an early age, and I was now about to marry a man who could actually speak one of the African languages. A wish comes true.

This made me want to be able to tell Paul in Swahili that I loved him. Who better to help with this other than Bill, his brother. Many, many phone calls and many more belly laughs later, the most important words I ever managed to learn, perhaps the only words were on paper so I could practice the accent to some level of accuracy. The difficult part of this was that not all cultures expressed their love for each other in words, and Bill and Elizabeth, because of their reserved natures, couldn't explain to me that what I was asking from them would not be appropriate to say in front of a minister of the Lord. I'll let you imagine for yourself about this. Certainly a shhhh moment.

Our adored daughters gave us away. A Salvation Army Minister performed the service with a touch of humour and advice. Towards the end of our vows to each other, I nervously looked into Paul's eye and said, "Nakupenda sana," and by the big smile on Paul's face, I'm sure he didn't have a clue as to what I was attempting to say. But who cares? I did get a smile and a hug. What else matters?

We danced and enjoyed the wonderful finger food, which was in abundance, and soaked up the well wishes and love that surrounded us as the evening went on. We were blessed with our own, what seemed like, fireworks display as lightning danced over the lake in the spectacular show, with every strike being followed by many oohs and aahs from our visitors.

*Our Wedding Day*

*Paul Bayless Maxwell and Lyn Margaret Maxwell*

*Marika, Paul, me, Terrie and the Salvation Minister*

*Every picture does tell a story. I am sure Paul is thinking 'What have I done.'*

*Family photo*
*Left to right: Marika, Bill, Paul, Anthony, Damien, me, Elizabeth, Tara, Molly, Robin.*

*Mum, me, Paul and Auntie Shirl*

*How I will always remember my cousin Stephie*

## Holiday of a Lifetime

The sheer excitement of actually going to England was so overwhelming that I was in disbelief and it wasn't until we walked through the entrance of the boarding tunnel to board our plane that I accepted fully that it was true. Impulsively and to the embarrassment of my husband I'm sure, I turned around and yelled back to Brian, "I'm going to England!"

Window seat please.

After some hours into the flight, I noticed that I could actually see interesting forms below, which looked like blocks of brown earth and all sorts of interesting shapes. Later in the flight, to my amazement, I was able to see snow-capped peaks, and I couldn't believe how interesting looking out of the window could be. It was only when heavy turbulence occurred that I pulled my squashed-up face away from the window, instantly needing reassurance. Paul had the most calming way about him, and he simply tapped me on the hand and said, "Just normal. Nothing to worry about," and continued reading his book with a repeat of the ever so gentle tap to my hand every now and then, just to keep me from disrupting his reading, I'm sure.

After circling Heathrow Airport for some time, we finally landed safely.

The overwhelming, warm and kind, sincere welcome we I received is something I will never forget. All of Paul's beautiful sisters made the huge effort to be at the airport to greet us. This was no mean feat, as they all lived in different areas of England, and as our flight didn't arrive on time, it meant that they had been waiting for hours. Within minutes of meeting them all, I was handed a cup of thermos tea and offered a piece of homemade cake. This was very much appreciated, as we were both feeling very dry, and I just loved the thermos tea. However, it was the bubble of warmth and kindness that I could feel encircling me that left a special lasting memory.

The planning that had been done to ensure that my experiences whilst in England were the very best possible was so clear in every kind thoughtful gesture by all of Paul's family.

We stayed with Paul's sister, Constance, and her husband, Ernie, in a beautiful, green, manicured garden area where I was blown away by all of the two-storey homes. I had once thought that everyone in England must be very rich to be able to all live in two- or three-storey homes.

Constance was an avid golfer, and, like Paul, took her golf very seriously, and did I mention, they were both also very competitive. We played golf on some breathtakingly beautiful courses, and the weather was perfect. When not playing golf, Constance and Ernie filled their days with visiting as many amazing landmarks as possible in and around London. The spectacular cathedrals, century-old Manors, art galleries, parks, castles, antique shops, Buckingham Palace, the Eye in the Sky are all memories I have forever.

I don't think I would ever be able to show the appreciation I feel in words for these experiences. But thank you, with love.

Paul's sister, Mary, and husband, John, lived in Eastbourne. Constance very kindly drove us down to spend time with Mary and John. Elizabeth, another of Paul's sisters, lived close by, so we would be able to spend time with them all.

Once again, an undeniable warmth and kindness greeted us as we were shown to our room. Mary had not been well for some time. Apparently, she had been unwell earlier in her life, but she had cleverly hidden any signs of discomfort while we were with them, so we would not worry. Mary and John were excited to be able to take us to the foreshore to see the famous Red Arrow show their precision flying skills. This was certainly a once-in-a-lifetime experience. How very fortunate we were to be visiting Eastbourne just at the right time. We walked out to the very old pier, watched a glassblower show off his skills, visited the souvenir shop, saw the children's old amusement park, and had a cup of tea in the sunshine. Yes, everywhere we went, the sun was shining. Another day, we visited the amazing Eastbourne Flower Show, which was out of this world.

We spent time with Elizabeth and met her beautiful grandson, Sebastian.

Paul and I visited England three times together, and each time my emotion/love grew deeper for my beautiful sister-in-laws and their families.

Perhaps one of the most memorable times in my life was on one of these visits. I had enjoyed a wonderful visit with Constance and Ernie. Phillip and Lillian had arranged to take us out the next day. Phil asked me if there was anything I might like to do whilst visiting England. I replied that one day, when the time is right, I would like to find where my dad was born. I understand that this was something that would take much more time than was possible during our time-restricted visit with them at the time, but I mentioned that I would be very grateful to see some of the beautiful countryside if that was at all possible. Phil asked if I had any ideas when my dad was born, and thanks to my dear Aunt Doris, many, many years before telling me a few hidden secrets about Nanna Hattie, one of which was where Dad had been born, I was therefore able to tell Phil the name of the farm at least. Lil and Phil reassured that a drive up the country would be perfect, and they would pick us up in the morning.

Our family 'tourist guides' arrived early the next morning.

Before we had reached the bottom steps of Tudor lodge to greet them, Phil, holding a rather large book in his hand, said, "Well, Lyn, I found two Frost Hill Farms, but I think the one on the outskirts of Overton may be where your dad was born. So we packed some sandwiches and a thermos of tea for our journey, as it will take a little time to get there." I could not believe my ears. These beautiful people had gone to all that trouble for me. Tears welled in my eyes with the overwhelming thought that my lifetime wish could, just maybe, be granted.

The drive was something else, as we began from Tudor Lodge in the busy part of North London, with cars, buses, bikes and pedestrians going everywhere, and roads so busy it was hard to believe that anyone managed to get to where they were going safely. As for the numerous roundabouts, how anyone was able to exit when needed beggars' belief.

Phil was confident and relaxed, and before very long, we were driving along some narrow country roads with nothing but green paddocks – oops, sorry, 'fields' – for as far as the eye could see. How truly breathtaking. We drove through the most beautiful villages, little villages so old and quaint that it was enough to take my breath away.

We stopped at the town of Overton, which was a name that I had heard discussed many times around the kitchen table when I was a young child, staying at Nanna Hattie's. Lil and Phil were so patient and kind, taking us to the library, chatting with the librarian about the history of the area and the local families who had lived in the area. In no time at all, the Sainsbury name was on the table in front of us in books, newsletters, band announcements, with old photos of the Sainsbury brothers (Dad's uncles).

My excitement went through the roof. How could this be true? I had heard of people taking years and years to find out this information. Phil and Lil suggested we have our lunch before driving to where Phil hoped we might be able to find Frost Hill Farm.

Paul could sense my excitement, and at the same time, he was composed enough to realise that we might not be able to actually find the house. He squeezed my hand and said, concernedly, "Settle down." There was no way on earth that I could remotely settle down. But out of respect for Paul, I replied, "I am." What a non-truth. Sorry.

A very short time later, we were once again surrounded by picturesque fields of green and gold. Halfway up the next incline, lo and behold, right before my eyes, I saw the house where my darling dad was born. There it was, standing in all its glory, bathed in history and hidden stories. The amazing thing about the very old buildings in England is that they look exactly the same as they did hundreds of years ago.

My emotions became very real, and I couldn't thank Phil and Lil enough for making my wish come true. I was floating, thoughts in all directions, when Phil suggested I knock on the door and see if the new owners could recall the Sainburys living there.

I didn't need much encouragement and went to the back of the house and knocked. A very kind lady explained that she thought she had heard that name, but to be sure, she explained that I should go back down the hill a mile, where the old caretaker of the house lived, and he should know. And she added, "He knows everything." I couldn't thank her enough. I was worried that I was imposing on the kindness of Phil and Lil a little too much, but they insisted that they would be very happy to see if we could find out more.

Sure enough, the caretaker did know the Sainsburys, and yes, that was their home, and that the most valuable words to me were, "Yes, I know Willie. He and his cousins would run around everywhere." He went on to say that he had worked for them for years. Then, to our astonishment, when asked about Nanna and all of her brothers, he said, "Yes, I knew them all. Lazy lot they were – spent all day working out what to do, and then did nothing!" Interesting, for sure, but not quite what I needed to hear. Phil, Lil, Paul and I had a laugh about it and thanked him for all his information. Just as we were leaving, he said, "By the way, I believe one of the old cousins, Ben, is still alive and living just up the road in the village of Hannington." He went on to tell us the exact address, and the cottage he lived in was called Rose Cottage.

Could there be any more surprises? Yes, Phil insisted we drive to Hannington. Paul and I were, by this time, completely overwhelmed by the generosity and time, and tried to convince them both that they had done more than enough. Within a short time, we were all standing in front of the most adorable, thatched-roof cottage opposite the village green.

In breathtaking anticipation, I knocked on the very small front door. Within a short time, a white-haired man opened the door and asked in a West English accent, "Can I help you?" There was no doubt in my mind that this man was Dad's cousin, Ben. He even had the same hands as my darling dad, looked like all of my great uncles, spoke like them, and yes, he was my second cousin Ben. After introducing ourselves, he invited us all in for a 'coopa tea'.

I couldn't believe my eyes as I sat down. I looked into a basket of photos next to the lounge only to see it filled with photos of Nanna Hattie, Uncle Monty and his brothers and dad!

Ben was certainly a Sainsbury, and it was difficult to leave, but contact promises were made and warm hugs exchanged, sealing a dream of a lifetime come true.

I will never in my life be able to thank Phillip and Lillian enough for the extreme effort of love they extended to me to

give me complete fulfilment of a lifelong wish. Thank you. XX
England felt like home.

During our wonderful visits, I was able to spend time with all of my sisters-in-law and their families. We had a very special visit in Eastbourne, staying with Jeanie. I will never forget the happy times, walking on the downs, looking out over the channel, admiring the white cliffs and Lighthouse which had been moved backwards to avoid falling into the Channel, and thanks to Jeanie, learning lots more about Paul. Jeanie was always happy, and we got on so well, chatting the whole time. We enjoyed a delightful stay with Jonathan and Julianna, Sebastian's dad and mum.

I couldn't get over the fact that Julianna's piano was a grand piano. Jonathan was full of surprises for us also. He had two Lamborghinis in his carport. Is that possible? I remember thinking to myself, to our delight, Jonathan reassured us that it was possible, and he took us for a fast drive in one of these amazing sports cars. Oh, what a feeling!

Another time, Constance and Ernie took us to Constable country, as the family knew I loved painting. The area was so picturesque, and my camera was working overtime. This was another very special day in my life. I was truly blessed to meet Elizabeth's family, Lil's and Phil's families, and although I didn't meet everyone, I have since been able to meet Ruth and her husband through modern technology.

*This is one of those "who knows who" photos. This is a photo of one of our second cousin, Charles Sainsbury-Plaice, with Prince Charles.*

Our cousin Charles is now King Charles' photographer.

This photo was taken during my first holiday to England, where I was able to meet Ben Sainsbury, one of my dad's only living cousins at the time. Paul's brother-in-law, Phillip, and Paul's sister, Lillian, somehow not only found Frost Hill Farm, where my dad was born, near Overton, but also found Rose Cottage, where Dad's cousin Ben lived.

Truly a wish come true.

Ben was 91 years of age, and so much like all of the Sainsbury brothers that I had known when I was growing up. Please note the photos in the basket next to the photo of Ben and me. When I first went into the house, I noticed so many photos of Nanna Hattie and Dad in the basket. Ben and me, such a wonderful memory.

*Ben showing off his old tractor. The Shed was a typical Sainsbury shed. So uncanny.*

*Frost Hill Farm. Frost Hill farmhouse, where Dad, William Whistler Sainsbury, was born in 1918*

*Rose Cottage, where Ben Sainsbury lived until his passing in 2005*

*Paul sitting in one of Jonathon's toys*

*Paul's beautiful sisters: Elizabeth, Constance, Mary, Lillian, Jeanie*

## Balhill Water Gardens continues

It is very hard getting back to normality after such a wonderful holiday break, but within a few hours of getting off our flight, we were hard at it once again. Fortunately, lingering thoughts of an unbelievable holiday helped with the transition.

Summer was particularly heavy going, not only with the heat and risk of so quickly losing a bed of lettuce, but also with the threat of fire. Our acreage was set amongst trees and, with only one road out of the property, fire prevention and procedures were first and foremost on our mind.

One day, during the busiest part of the day, I knew I could smell smoke. As I mentioned before, I have a heightened sense of a smell, so much so that everyone around me said, "No, I can't smell anything."

This was not good enough for me, and I stopped picking and ran up the hill to investigate. Sure enough, the man next door had ignored the total fire ban for that day and had been grinding metal in his shed. The fire was already through our fence. Within minutes, the sprinklers were on. The fire brigade had been called, machinery moved to the safest area possible, hoses at the ready, and with that done, we could do nothing but wait to fight the fire with wet bags if necessary. The local fire brigade arrived very quickly, and thank goodness for that. As the fire roared down the hill towards the garden at a great speed, mopping up went well into the night, and even the next day, some of the tree stumps were still smouldering.

Another time, I was on my own on a Saturday when our neighbour came over to warn me of a fire a few doors down. And as everyone's properties were crisp-dry, a small fire could turn into a massive threat. Within a very short time, I rang the golf club to alert Paul, and then commenced to move the truck forklift and turned on the sprinklers. This time, we were fortunate as the fire didn't reach our property.

Winter had its own disadvantages. Many mornings, the garden was so cold that ice formed, not only on our poor little fingers, but also on the lettuce leaves. When this happened, we were unable to pick as the lettuce would bruise and be unsaleable. The garden was completely covered with hail cloth, which did also help with the many frosts.

Speaking of hail cloth, oh, dear. One particular day, I was moving the forklift to get a new empty pellet without a care in the world, until I noticed everyone in the garden running towards me, yelling, Stop! My heart and the forklift stopped at the same time as I thought I had run over someone or something. Dave was standing in front of me, shaking his head and pointing upwards. Oh, no, I could see sky. I had raised the fork too high, and the extender had, unbeknownst to me, hooked into the hail cloth, ripping metres and metres of it wide open. Not good.

Paul simply said, "We'll have to fix that after the pick."

Dave will never know how much I appreciated his kindness and help. He stayed back and worked with Paul, sewing the hail cloth together with twine. This was extremely difficult, standing on crates with their arms outstretched above their heads, pulling the heavy hail cloth together and trying to finish before dark. I was very careful every time I used the forklift after that, or should I say, when I was permitted to use the forklift, Dave seemed to always be first at the forklift after that.

Paul never let me know if he felt unwell. He would visit the doctor, always on his own, but I was aware that he was getting more and more exhausted after a day's work.

He worked long days and worked hard, but the telling point was the walk up the hill to our home, which was really the indicator to me that Paul was not well. Sometimes he could hardly put one foot after the other, and he looked pale and unwell. I knew, however, Paul's independence and unselfish need for privacy would not allow me to put pressure on him about his health. Therefore, I took every precaution to tackle a subject gently and lovingly. It took me days to think of a way to find out what was wrong without actually seeming to be trying to find out what was wrong, if you know what I mean. Eventually, Paul explained that "everything is okay, but I should take it a bit easy. Nothing to worry about."

At least, this was a start, and gave me an idea of how I should approach or react in the future.

We had many more wonderful visits to Albany, and we were also able to catch up with Marika in Bridgetown as much as possible. The sincere, kind, thoughtful qualities I love so much in Paul almost repeated themselves in his beautiful daughter. Marika worked for the Department of Conservation and Land Management. She is dedicated to the protection of endangered Australian mammals, and just like her darling dad, wouldn't kill a flea.

I'm very sure, Marika wondered what on earth her dad was thinking when she first met me. But after a short time together, Marika and I developed a warm, sincere bond, which has grown every day since. Love you so much, Marika. XX.

We enjoyed many wonderful meals at the cidery, going to the market by the river, walking in and out of quaint, interesting shops, and enjoying beautiful meals at the local restaurant. Most of all, I loved the happy time sitting on the verandah with the sweet perfume of nature flowing gently as we sipped a locally made wine or two.

*Balhill Water Gardens, showing lettuce growing hydroponically*

*Lunchroom Fun*

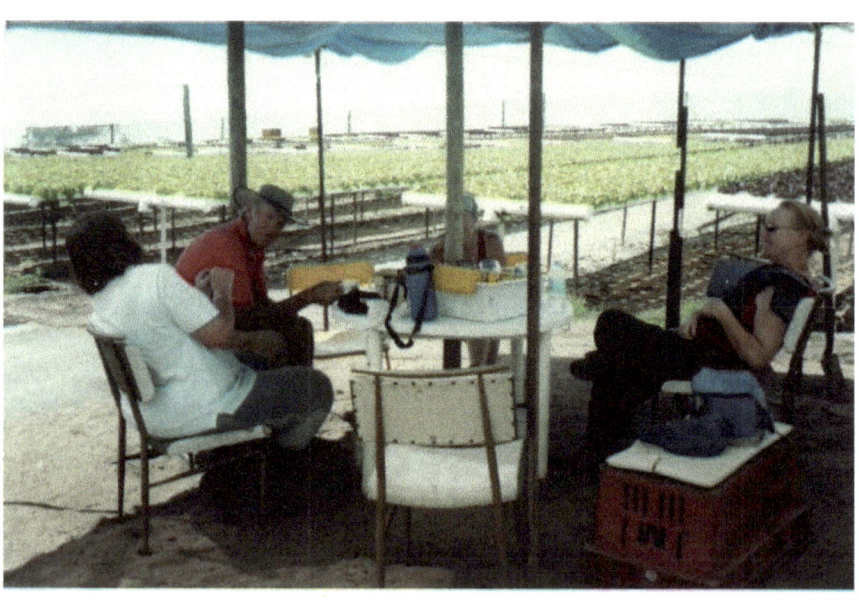

364

*Keith Sainsbury in the truck.*

*Marika, Paul and me*

*Left to Right: Elizabeth, Lyn, Elaine, Marika.
In front: Audrey.*

*Marika and Andrew*

*Elaine, David, Andrew and Marika*

# Goodbye to Balhill

Over the next year or so, sadly, Paul's health concerns became worse, and his doctors told him that he should think about giving up the physical work he was doing and perhaps accept something that would put less strain on his heart. Although Paul always seemed to have total control of his emotions, I knew that, and understandably so, even thinking about selling Balhill Water Gardens was heart-wrenching for him. Paul had built the business from the ground up, literally, and had studied hydroponics gardening in New Zealand to ensure that the business would be the best possible which, according to all accounts, Balhill Water Gardens was known throughout as one of the best examples of hydroponics gourmet letters production in WA selling was very sad for me in a much less impactive way, I know, but nevertheless, I felt Balhill was somehow close to farm life again, and I had worked hard to build our home into a welcoming family home. Our wedding was held there. The grandchildren had been able to have room to play and be kids. Many special reunions with their families were held there. But most of all, it was where our love for each other grew stronger and stronger. Our love had been built on trust and faith and had grown into a deep, sincere, emotional love where we both felt safe and unconditionally loved.

We asked my cousin Diane to help with organising the sale of our property, which she accepted willingly in her adorable, happy way. We were delighted when a family from Zimbabwe put in an offer to buy the business. The sale was slightly involved, as these beautiful people needed all the permits in the world to be able to buy a business in Australia. Paul, knowing full well the situation in Zimbabwe and his compassion for others, helped where at all possible to secure a new life with this family. Their children melted my heart. They were the most well-mannered, polite, mature children I had ever had pleasure to meet. They had, sadly all been traumatized with the brutality they had seen before leaving Zimbabwe. They say children are resilient, and these children were proof of that. I remember so clearly when we were working in the garden, when we met the family, we were introduced to the parents, who in turn introduced us to the three children. This adorable, tiny, little, frail boy extended his hand to me and said in a totally unexpected, strong, manly voice, "Pleased to meet you, Mrs Maxwell." Tears welled in my eyes instantly, and it took me all my strength to contain myself from just picking him up and hugging him. Both Paul and I were engulfed with the strong need to help these hard-working, worthy people with all the red tape, needed to be able to start their life in Australia, along with the utter confidence that we were offering them a truly profitable business. Grant and Barry were very familiar with this sort of business, as they had successfully owned and operated a commercial long-stemmed rose business in Zimbabwe, until being forced out by the unrest and danger to remain in their home. Our wish was granted, and sadly but also pleasing, Balhill was sold to some very worthy new owners. Paul stayed and collaborated with them to ensure a successful changeover which was expected as part of the sale. To my surprise, one night, as we were going through our immediate plans, Paul said, "First, you better go and buy us a home to live in." I couldn't believe it. Paul actually had so much faith in me that he entrusted me to purchase our home. Fortunately, I had been involved with selling and buying homes in the past, and certainly with the ability and help from my cousin. I couldn't wait to get started. After studying the areas carefully and looking at every house available within our price range, I noticed one of those too good to be true advertisements. I rang at once and simply asked, "What is wrong with that house? Is it near a deli or train or bus stop?"

"No," was the agent's reply. "It is a nice house," and he continued to ask me, "Do you like dado?

Oh, what a strange question, I thought. I love dado – it reminded me of Sunnyside.

Dad had used dado boards on most walls whilst building our home on Sunnyside. I just had to see this house. I insisted Paul come with me the next day, as I had a good feeling about this house; besides, curiosity was almost killing the cat. As we approached the house, I couldn't believe my eyes. It had great street appeal, and I couldn't wait to see inside. This was no disappointment. Sure, the entry was painted bright orange and the family room dark blue and vivid yellow, with red and white striped wallpaper in the lounge room to add to the mix, but my eyes only saw a magnificently designed home that would be a dream come true if it were to be our future home.

Paul simply said, "Isn't it a little big?" to which I said, "No, darling, it's just perfect."

Yes, it did have dado boards, which only added to the appeal for me, a wonderful, bright home, to say the least, for our future. Paul had worked all his life, never being afraid of changing direction and learning invaluable skills as he went. I loved this ability. I loved his ability to calmly take on new challenges with confidence. Such an inspirational trait.

In saying this, I didn't expect his keenness to change direction so quickly. We were busy organising our move and finishing up at Balhill when Paul mentioned to me that he had noticed a great business for sale. My *first* reaction, without thinking, was "No, no way. I don't want to take another risk. I'll just find a job and let someone else wear the pressure."

Paul just smiled and went on to explain that it was a bedroom furniture shop, and said, "You would love it, as you're a great salesperson."

The next morning, Paul wrote down the address and said, casually as he handed me the piece of paper, "If you've got time, pop down to Mandurah and have a look."

Paul was not only the man I loved, but he was also the man who knew me, perhaps better than I knew myself. Sure enough, I drove along Pinjarra Road in Mandurah and turned into a large car park in front of Better Beds. As I parked the car, I remember thinking 'what a great location'. I entered through welcoming self-opening doors to the most well-presented, tastefully decorated shop of its kind I think I'd ever seen. As if that wasn't enough, I was then greeted by a professionally-dressed young man with the biggest smile ever, inquiring if he could help me in any way. Sold! I was bursting with excitement, and the second Paul walked through the door, I gave him a kiss and said, "Yes, I would love that business, as long as Rino the salesman comes with it."

Better Beds was an extremely rewarding business in more ways than one. It was less physical work for Paul, if he allowed it to be. That's another story, but it was such a happy and uplifting workplace for me. I absolutely love selling and having people around in our own business, allowing me to chat and use the time how I thought best was just perfect. It was a very good and profitable business, and we kept things as they were in the main, improving where we could. Paul, as I said, was never one to overdo emotional praise, but he often told me I was the best salesperson ever, and often expressed this to others. I felt very humbled by this praise, which gave me confidence and, of course, a happy feeling within.

We owned a delivery truck, which came with the business. When Paul was at golf, I drove the truck to and from work. It was easy to drive, and I loved being seated high as I could see and read all the traffic ahead. But I also, on the odd occasion, exceeded the speed limit, and noticed a few flashes as I drove down Ennis Avenue. Say nothing.

Paul had an agreement with our truck drivers that if they received a speeding ticket, they would pay the fine. It became a bit of a game, and sadly, the game became all about me. All of the staff would hover over Paul as he opened one of the received-too-often blueys that had arrived in the mail, with high expectations and hope that the offence had occurred on a Sunday, which would mean I was responsible.

"Yes! Yes!" would ring out if the driver was me, and the truck drivers would let out a sigh of relief as Paul showed a slight grin and handed me the fine to pay. We had wonderful staff and lots of fun. Thank you to all our wonderful friends.

We kept most of the suppliers as the furniture was, at the time, mostly Australian-made. How wonderful that we were able to help our family out with special terms and conditions when they purchased mattresses or furniture, which gave us much pleasure.

Our mattress was very old, and after lying on all of the amazing mattresses in the shop, I mentioned to Paul that it would not be good for our customers to realise that the mattress we slept on was very old. Paul's answer to that was, "But I like our mattress."

Slow, gentle, loving persuasion needed again. I know Paul was very wise to the fact, but he humoured me anyway.

Just for fun, I must have tried every mattress in the shop 50 times until I found our new mattress. Yay. Clive and Nathan delivered our mattress, and I couldn't wait for our first night's sleep in luxury.

Paul closed his eyes and slept as he always had done. I, on the other hand, should I say it, couldn't get comfortable. I didn't dare mention a word to Paul, as I thought it was just the first night, and I would soon get used to the new feel after a week.

I thought I'd ask Paul if he was enjoying our new mattress. He replied, "It's fine, dear."

Now what was I going to do? After a few weeks of sneaking one of the kids foam mattresses to the floor beside our bed and sleeping soundly on that, I explained with egg on my face that perhaps the most expensive mattress was not necessarily the most comfortable for me. How embarrassing.

Clive and Nathan politely exchanged the mattress for me, and although I knew it was the butt of their jokes for some time, I didn't mind, as I finally had a great night's sleep.

We were very fortunate to have won People's Choice at the town of Mandurah's Small Business Awards. This was so exciting, and all our staff were there on the night to receive our award. Remember the wonderful times with wonderful people at Better Beds.

# Fun Parties and Dress-Ups

For some unexplained reason, in the 2000s, it was the thing to always have a theme to a party or festive event; everyone had to dress up in theme when going to these parties, and with our large family, parties, especially birthday parties, occurred very frequently. We all loved the fun and excitement of dressing up and going that extra mile to make each party the best it could be. Well, that's a little fib, as Paul, my quiet, reserved, proper at all times, darling husband, did need quite a substantial amount of coaxing to step outside of his comfort zone.

When it came to dressing up, it was considered, by all who thought they knew Paul well, that the idea of him joining in with these over-the-top festivities was ludicrous and would never happen. Who said? Paul had no idea that he was married to a very persuasive person, accompanied by many very persuasive party organisers, whereby anything could be and was possible.

One of the most memorable of these was at Amelia's 18th birthday party. The family just couldn't believe that Paul embraced his character so well and never even flinched when he was prompted to join in the many photo shoots.

Never too far away, another party. The theme for this party was film characters. This was an easy one for me, as I loved the movie Pirates of the Caribbean. Off I went to the costume shop with a request for the young salesperson for a costume for my 72-year-old husband, which would make him look like Johnny Depp. Politely, the salesperson did his job to perfection, and without even showing the slightest grin at my request, gathered up everything that was needed, and before long, I left with the prospect in my arms of being married to Johnny Depp for a night. Practice makes perfect, they say. And maybe they're right. Paul took on his character with gusto, only fading slightly late into the evening, with perhaps one photo too many.

Happy memories. XX.

*Who would have thought? Yes, here he is, the quiet, reserved, 'always proper', Paul Bayless Maxwell enjoying every dress-up party we gently encouraged him to attend.*

None of his children or grandchildren could believe this one. Yes, I know he could have been used as Johnny Depp stand in.

*Yes, and there's more dress-ups. Rhiannon, me, Amelia and Paul.*

*Paul, Terrie, me, Paul, Jayke and Gail in the background*

# Happy Memories Waikiki

Our home in Waikiki brought us so much happiness and joy. It was a wonderful family home where everyone was welcome. Goodbye orange entrance, goodbye blue and yellow walls, red wallpaper and hello a lick of neutral paint and love of tasteful decoration.

With thanks to our family for their hard work to help create our beautiful home. Within days of living in our new home, Paul realised why we needed a larger home. Most of our children lived in the country, and nearly every weekend, one, two or more families came to Perth for one reason or another, and of course, stayed with us. I absolutely loved their visits. I couldn't wait until they arrived. We often had all bedrooms full as well as air mattresses everywhere, prams, port-a-cots and sometimes a dog or two thrown into the mix. Meal times were like a production line with different cereals all lined up on the kitchen bench, accompanied by many different spreads for the loaves of toast needed, bacon and eggs always at the ready, and that was just for breakfast. Just as well my mother-in-law had taught me how to make a pound of mince feed a multitude, as the good old potato pie came in handy often as a quick and filling lunch. We had barbecues galore and every salad imaginable. But all of this busyness made my heart sing. I couldn't have been happier. Paul slowly adjusted to the noise and a temper tantrum or two displayed by kids who were testing boundaries.

Therefore, I'm very sure he often longed for his quiet home

on the hill with peace and tranquillity. Fortunately, Paul had his own innovative way of achieving some sort of normality for himself. We all lovingly and respectfully laugh about it often when remembering those special times. Paul watched sport on the TV, all sports – golf, tennis, bowls, rugby – but most importantly, the Eagles, AFL football. Paul had his own special armchair, and all the children knew that when Pop Paul was watching the Eagles, they played outside or sat quietly and watched the Eagles play with him. Unfortunately, the kitchen and family room were only divided by a half-brick wall. When I was cooking in the kitchen, which was very often, the girls always came in to help. We tried to talk quietly so Paul could hear his game. But of course, as us girls do, we had a laugh or two, and the dishes do cling from time to time. Plus, have you ever tried to pop a cork on a wine bottle quietly.

Without realising it, we needed to raise our voices a bit at a time, as Paul had been slowly but surely turning the volume up to drown us out. As you can imagine, within a short time, the kitchen and family room became so loud that I'm sure our neighbours must have thought they were living next door to Optus Stadium. Paul just sat in his chair, said nothing, but I'm convinced he felt a little smug when all of us girls excused ourselves and moved out to the patio, wine glass in hand.

After selling Better Beds, I went to work for Morton & Rino, earlier owners of Better Beds at their new business, Bedroom Gallery. Morton's shop was in Canning Vale, and although it was a distance from Rockingham to travel, I enjoyed working with the wonderful staff and developed a lasting friendship with them all. Sadly, it was about this time that Paul began having what he referred to as 'turns'. I was not convinced that the dizzy spells and certainly the fall in the bathroom were just turns and nothing to worry about, as Paul would say. Unfortunately, even gentle persuasion didn't prompt him to visit the doctor, and Paul began trying many natural ways of improving his health.

Paul never gave up on life, and played golf three times a week, read daily, played Sudoku every day, and joined in with the great-grandchildren, sports days at school and was often coerced into taking them to the local park to play.

Paul still missed working. Sometime after I began working at Bedroom Gallery, Morton and Rino decided to branch out and accept the opportunity of opening another bedroom shop in O'Connor. Before very long, this once again beautifully presented business was up and running. Morton did offer his staff the opportunity to move over to the new shop or stay in Canning Vale. Having two shops in different locations presented many unforeseen issues, and before very long, Morton and Rino were working more hours and feeling the pressure as they both had family commitments and didn't feel they were benefiting from the added pressure of two shops.

One morning, I arrived at work half an hour early, as I always did, and made a coffee for Morton and myself. We began chatting about the program for the day, when Morton said, "Lyn, I've got something to ask you."

I was curious, and he went on to say, "Would you and Paul be interested in buying the shop in O'Connor?"

That night, as soon as I had mentioned that Morton was offering us the opportunity of purchasing the O'Connor shop, and before I had time to express my thoughts – should I say, fears of going into business yet again – Paul said, "Could be good. Ring Morton and set up a time for a meeting."

Within two months, Paul and I owned a new bedroom shop, Bedroom Trends, O'Connor. Yes, Paul was going to just do the book work with no heavy work or physical lifting, etc. Paul didn't tell lies, but he did stretch the truth a wee bit with these promises to me. God love his cotton socks, the shop was amazing, and I just loved every minute of being with customers and, of course, making sales, and especially the friendships that grew with every passing day.

One day, whilst at work, I received a phone call from the Rockingham Police. My heart missed a beat as I thought, "Why would the police be ringing me? It has to be bad."

The officer went on to explain, "Your mum had fallen in her home and is in the ambulance on her way to hospital, but she's okay, but ask me to phone you.

I was in the car within a minute, with all sorts of things racing through my mind, knowing Mum would be very frightened and upset. My darling little mum was a mess. Her face was swollen beyond belief, and her hands and arms were bruised, and she had blood on her body and clothes. Mum was insistent that she didn't fall, but tripped over the bed clothes and fell and hid her face on the dressing table drawers, which was evident as the handle of the dressing table was broken off as a result of the accident.

Mum was eighty-five and living on her own, which had played on my mind for some time. She was a very nervous person, and I felt the need to visit more and more often. Every time there was a storm, Mum would call as she was frightened, so much so that she would hide in the en-suite because she was frightened of the lightning. This was not the only reason I felt Mum needed to find somewhere more suitable to live, although it is very difficult for me to believe that some people find the need to be very unkind to others, but sadly, they do. The man who lived across the road from Mum didn't like the trees that the Shire Council had planted on Mum's verge. Sure, they did drop leaves, and sure, the leaves did blow across onto his lawn, but certainly there was little Mum could do to change this, as they were trimmed regularly by the Shire and the wind had a mind of its own as to which way it blew. The man was not nice. He would wait until Mum was asleep and bring the leaves and sand that he had swept off his lawn across the road and pile it up on Mum's doormat. Mum became terrified that he would do worse, so I contacted the police. This did not seem to make any difference. So Terrie and her husband knocked on his door and had a little chat to this nasty man, which did help us substantially. Say no more.

Paul was very upset as to what was going on, and so he and I spent many hours working out what we could do to help Mum. Mum was a very active, capable, alert 85-year-old lady, and going into any care facility was totally inappropriate for Mum at that time. But living in a big home on her own was also not suitable, as I felt the need to spend more and more time visiting, which in turn, took me away from Paul and our life together.

I was having a cuppa with Mum one day when I said, "Mum, I know it's possibly not a good option for you, but Paul and I have measured our backyard and we have got room to build a granny flat, if that's something you would consider."

Within a few minutes, Mum said, "Actually, that's a good idea, as long as it's okay with you and Paul. Done. We discussed this with Brian and Gail, and their input was positive as well. And before long, our shed was gone and a concrete pad was poured. Mum's beautiful new home was ready to live in before her birthday.

Mum commenced living with us in her attached granny flat from the age of 86. This arrangement was fantastic, as when a storm occurred or Mum needed help, I could just walk through our laundry door into Mum's home and reassure her all was okay. Paul was, without a doubt, the most considerate son-in-law possible. Never once did he object to me spending time with Mum. In fact, he always questioned me if I hadn't been down to check on her when I arrived home from being away from home.

Bedroom Trends was a perfect business for us, and all was going well. But unfortunately, within two years of us taking over, there was talk of a recession, which made me very nervous. I suggested to Paul that we should sell as we had worked hard for what we had, and I didn't want to risk losing our retirement fund, even if it wasn't quite enough.

Paul was always very careful and competent with financial issues and never let us down. But this time, when he said he thought we'd be okay to continue, I still felt unsure, and for the first time, questioned his thoughts. Perhaps deep down, I was also concerned about the ever-occurring turns he was having, and just thought it was time. Paul and I struggled with this discussion, and I signed the paperwork to sell our shop first, with an agent having to wait some time for Paul to sign.

**Bedroom Trends**

*Bedroom Trends with Lyn and Paul*

*Paul and Terrie*

*Below: Bohdi, Terrie, Deegan, Ash, Van, Quade, Jamal, Kaelyn*

*Above: Jamal, Kaelyn, Terrie, Paul, Quade*

*Cody, Sophie and Luke*

*Luke, Jayke and Deegan*

# Walkabout Again

Terrie had moved from Darken to Williams and then, so her eldest son could start his apprenticeship in Narrogin, Terrie decided to buy a home in Narrogin, which would also give her other children a high school to attend without having to catch a bus.

With a little help from Auntie Muttwyre, as was Terrie's favourite saying, when things were tight, the deposit for her home was achieved, and you guessed, moving again. Paul and I visited as much as we could, and as always, Terrie's home was warm and welcoming. Two teenage boys, and one girl who thought she was a teenager, certainly kept Terrie on her toes, but nevertheless, she was very happy in her home, and I'm not sure, but I think Terrie stayed the longest time ever in that home.

Jayke was looking for his first car. Cody was trying to scare us all to death by being a daredevil on his push bike. He and his mates had formed a little group who built jumps in the bush, and with little or no protection, they rode full speed up a precariously held together ramp and did somersaults into a pit full of old foam and mattresses. Cody took me out to watch one day, and I know I've always considered myself a 'with it' Nan, but I almost collapsed with fear and had to leave. When I think about it, even now I feel sick. There were star pickets holding up sharp bits of jagged tin with rusty drums as stands and gravel on each side, with the landing pit just large enough, if they made no mistakes.

Terrie worked at the local supermarket, and it was there she met her husband, Paul – not to be mixed up with my husband, Paul.

Terrie and Paul were married in a very old quaint church in the town of Quindanning, with Jayke, Cody and Sophie in the bridal party. It was a beautiful, happy day, and the setting was just amazing.

The reception was held at the bowling club in Narrogin, and what a happy, different reception it was. The bride and groom sang karaoke, and everyone joined in. Fish and chips were served straight from their own fish and chip shop. The Swinging Seagull in Narrogin. The children joined in, and I'm sure it was the loudest noise that little old bowling club had endured for quite some time. Paul and Terrie had opened their fish and chip shop Swinging Seagull not long before they married. It was, without a doubt, the best fish and chip shop I've ever seen. As always, Terrie gives 100% to any of her ventures in life, and this was no exception. The decor was all black and white, and set in the 60s era. She had a record player playing rock and roll very loud, and the shop catered for everyone's likes and dislikes. The uniform was embroidered with swinging seagulls on the back, and the caps were black with a yellow peak to resemble the beak of a seagull. During the first few weeks, she gave free lollies for the kids and delivery thanks to Paul and his friends. The atmosphere was amazing. The fish and chips were more amazing, and business was booming.

Terrie and Paul worked well together, but Paul was also working as a supervisor during the day at the abattoirs, and Terrie was managing the shop, home and three children. Busy times. Although having such busy times, they have remained strong and united against all that has been thrown at them.

Terrie has never wavered with her total devotion and support for me throughout her life, and fortunately for me, her husband, Paul, right from the start, has also given me support, kindness and love. It is hard to put into words just how much it means to me to have this love from my daughter and son-in-law. Thank you with love.

Yes, let me get back to the walkabout part of this story.

Paul and Terrie's family was growing with grandchildren arriving and girlfriends and boyfriends and extra friends of friends moving in and out, swelling their house to the limits at times. As you know, Terrie always longed for the country life, and always dreamed of living on a farm, thus giving her own children/grandchildren, the same understanding and love of farm life as she herself had experienced with her Nan and Pop on Sunnyside farm. With this in mind, Terrie gradually planted the seed in Paul's mind that she would like to buy a farmhouse on a small property, to which Paul was not totally adverse to. However, it had to be close to his work. They found a beautiful property, and as always, called us to have a look and give our opinion.

In actual fact, they needed my Paul's advice, as they had full trust in his business knowledge. It certainly was a beautiful house and property, but unfortunately, this didn't have the outcome that they would have liked. So never give up. They started looking again. One day, Paul thought he would play a trick on Terrie and called her to look at the house of her dreams that he had come across whilst browsing the For Sale section of the real estate page. Naturally, Terrie couldn't wait to see a photo of this house. Paul laughed as he pointed to an old, run-down stone house with a broken roof and no verandah one side of the house surrounded by rubbish and dead trees.

To his astonishment, Terrie wasn't tricked at all. In fact, Paul had tricked himself. Terrie at once fell in love with this 100-year-old house, and said, "Paul, ring the agent quickly. I want to see inside this house. I love it."

You better believe it, the next day, Terrie and Paul were at least an hour early for the appointment to meet with the agent, and before they had walked down the passageway of this house that had been unlived in for ten years, Terrie was asking the agent for the contract so she could sign to purchase the house of her dreams. Terrie said the feeling was so powerful that she had to buy that home. Paul, on the other hand, wasn't sure at all, as all he could see was work and more work.

This beautiful old home was full of history, and some of the history had direct connections to our family. Some of the tiny threads from way back in our family's Web of Life may have possibly been walked upon by owners of this old home. My mum's grandmother, Agnus McNeil, was born in Scotland and came out to work as the first school teacher in Wagin, and she married George Watson, and they had a daughter, Jess Watson, who is my Nanna Jess. When Terrie was going through all of the paperwork that had been left in the home, she found many references to the Watsons and Agnus. We are not sure if they ever lived in the home, but certainly the documentation found referred to them.

The beautiful old home was situated on five acres of land on the outskirts of Wagin, and as far as Terrie was concerned, she had found the home of her dreams.

Excitement plus. I must say, both my Paul and I felt a strong connection to this home also, and we could see past the work that had to be done, which, thankfully, we didn't have to do ourselves. We did, however, help as much as we could.

Within a very short time, the old tin roof was being replaced, the power was reconnected, and water was running into the kitchen. What else would you need? Both Terrie and Paul were still working full time, but every moment they could spare, they worked on their home, trying to bring it back to its past glory. As the Grand Old Lady of Wagin, the whole town was interested, and people would slow down as they were driving past, congratulating them on their achievements. A truly wonderful time.

But of course, farms need animals. No worries for Terrie. Before very long, the old, dilapidated chook pen, which incorporated the old dunny out the back, was resurrected and became home to twelve or more chooks, two roosters, ducks of all varieties, and a discarded peacock. Paul, Terrie's husband, also helped with this venture, as he built at least five bird aviaries, and within a short time, numerous very beautiful birds felt right at home with the freedom of a large, warm aviary complete with specialty seed on demand. They already had their dogs and cats from their home in Narrogin, but one day, a beautiful ginger cat appeared from under the side verandah, and within a very short time, became king of the cats and became the special one and loved by all. This was a wonderful home for all of Terrie and Paul's family, with room to run and play bikes to ride and sheep to feed. A dream come true for everyone, certainly including me.

But there's always a but!

All was wonderful until Paul and Terrie booked a holiday to Scotland and Ireland. This was one of Terrie's dreams to perhaps find some of the family history, or at least understand from where our family had originated from.

"Hi, Mum," was the phone call. "Just wondering if you and Paul would like to have a holiday down here in Wagin as we're going to Scotland and Ireland for about two to three weeks, and thought you might not mind having a holiday here to look after our home." Of course, we laughed knowing just what this would mean, but both Paul and I knew we would enjoy the break, even if it did mean a little bit of work.

A little bit of work was certainly an understatement. To this day, I still laugh about this holiday with a lightness of heart and happy memories. Our darling mum was 95 years of age, and we needed to convince her that it would be a lovely holiday and we could make her comfortable, and she would probably really enjoy being in Wagin. And this, of course, was easier said than done.

The bathroom in the old home consisted of a shower over an old, deep bathtub, totally unsuitable for Mum to attempt to get into. Just as well, I've been blessed with the ability to compromise in life when required, and just as well, I didn't throw out the grandkids' little paddle pool. Yep, all sorted. I pumped up the paddle pool to one rung, placed it on a non-slip mat in the middle of the bathroom, placed a chair in the middle, sat Mum on the chair, and used an extension hose with a shower head attached to shower my very nervous and very unamused darling little mum – a picture no artist could paint.

There was a little bit more to this holiday break, as you can imagine. Yes, only one dog, but he was a very big, heavy, powerful Bloodhound, and impossible for me to take for a walk, that is, unless I was happy to be dragged along the dirt whilst he ran full speed, drooling from his mouth and only stopping when it suited him to cock his leg on a tree. No, no walks, just a repeated throw of a spit-sodden rope and the risk of being knocked clean off my feet if I was too slow to get out of his way. He was only a puppy after all. The garden was all newly planted and required watering every second day. Thank goodness, Paul and Terrie hadn't extended the garden too far from the house, as it was a complete day's work to get everything wet enough in the clay soil. But don't worry, we didn't have much to do with watering the six sheep, as Paul had put a self-watering trough in their yard, and it was just a matter of throwing them some hay and oats.

My Paul had decided he would need something to do whilst we were 'holidaying' in Wagin, so he kindly began painting the passageway. This was a massive job, as the ceilings in the Grand Old Lady were extremely high, and the ladder was needed even with an extender roller. Believe it or not, this *was* a wonderful, happy holiday, and one I will certainly never forget.

All told, we looked after one dog, four cats, twelve chooks, two roosters, one peacock, six ducks, thirty-four birds, six sheep, and … wait for it … a hand-fed baby pig. Yes, just before they left, Terrie's maternal instincts couldn't let a little runt of the litter be put down, so took it home as a pet.

The baby pig lived. The passage was painted. Mum was showered, and we had a wonderful holiday. Happy memories of the Grand Old Lady.

*Cody, Shoo (Tsung), Ash and Zac*

*Shoo's aunty, holding Ash, Lin (Shoo's mum), Cody and Shoo*

*Ash* *Zac*

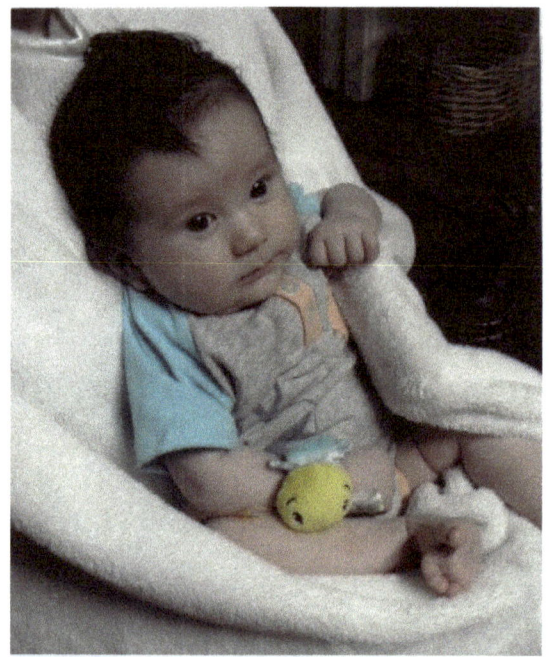

*Ash*

*My great-grandchildren just having fun*

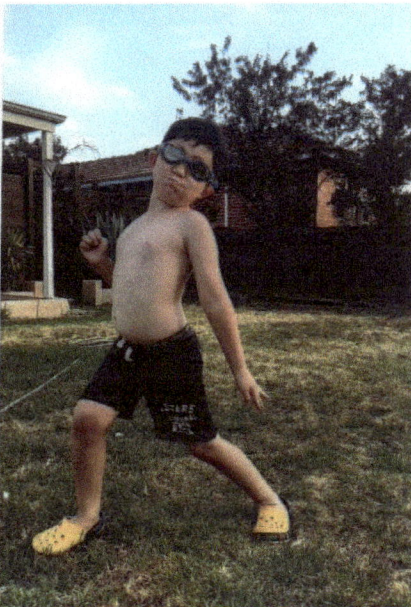

*Ash, Bohdi, Cody, Deegan*        *Ash*

*Kaelyn, Ash, Van, Bohdi, Jamal, Deegan, Quade*

*Left: Kaelyn*

*Right: Quade*

# Blast from the Past

After selling Bedroom Trends, I was able to acquire a wonderful job with a company called Pine Discount. Once again, I put my energy into selling, although it was not only bedroom furniture. The variety was also exciting for me as I found it a great challenge.

On arriving home from work one day, Paul, showing signs of excitement, told me that a friend of his from Africa was coming out to Australia to visit us. He went on to explain that he had boarded with Anne's family when he was first working, and Anne's family were wonderful and supportive of him when he was first starting out on his own. I was thrilled to bits; having someone from Africa visit would be fantastic. I couldn't wait to meet Anne.

We hit it off so well, and Anne and I laughed and joked and spent hours and hours chatting. I was like a sponge, soaking up every bit of information about her life in Africa, sometimes drifting off in an imaginary state when she was telling me about her unbelievable adventures. Paul and I spent many happy hours walking along the foreshore and just sitting, relaxing with Anne as Paul spoke of his time since arriving in Australia. It was certainly a blast from the past for them both, and I was delighted that they were able to spend time reminiscing. How special.

We introduced Anne to as many of our ever-growing family as possible while she was with us on holidays. We were able to travel to Bridgetown so she could meet Paul's daughter, Marika. This was a special day, and the weather was kind. Anne had married an African Airways pilot, and they had two daughters. Anne's visit with us was a short stay, and a very sad goodbye. However, the promises of lots of phone calls, letters and even a promise that we would visit Anne in Africa one day, somehow softened the farewell and somewhat excited me.

Could my second childhood wish come true?

# Dark Clouds Approaching

Paul and I were kept very busy with families, golf and caring for Mum. Paul was a wonderful son-in-law to Mum, and always insisted I go down to Mum's granny flat and say hello the moment I arrived home from golf or shopping. Mum also loved Paul, and was not happy with me when I left Paul home on my golf day without leaving him a fully prepared lunch. In Mum's eyes, a wife should always make sure her husband has his meals ready, no matter what. It became a bit of a joke between Paul and me, as many times when I arrived home, Paul would say, "Mum came up to say hello, and I'm sure it was to check if you had left me lunch, as within a short time, she brought me some lovely mock snapper to eat."

Paul was playing golf three times a week and insisted on playing 18 holes as well as walking. Many times, if it was going to be a very hot day, I would waste my breath, I know, but I would suggest that he take a cart and just play nine holes, as I knew he was pushing himself, which could be dangerous.

Sadly, pride would not allow him to be one of those nine-hole players. Also, using a cart was an indication to others that he wasn't feeling well. Paul was too private for that.

Unfortunately, because of his fear of showing any sort of weakness, he quite often arrived home from golf in an exhausted, unwell state.

One day, Paul was sitting in his chair doing his Sudoku when I noticed he looked very pale and not well at all. My heart began to pound. Fear and sadness took over, and I held back my tears. I had seen that illness before. When I asked, "Darling, are you okay?" His reply was such that I knew immediately that he was far from okay. I said, "I'm sorry. I'm very sorry, but this time I'm calling the ambulance. I think you're having a stroke."

For the first time ever, his response was such that he knew himself that he needed help.

Paul was very fortunate and recovered better than expected. The MRI did indicate a large intracranial aneurysm, and also showed a smaller aneurysm, which had occurred earlier. The doctor could not believe that Paul showed very few effects from such a large bleed, but did insist that Paul take medication and have regular checkups. I became so much more anxious and worried, but always inwardly, as I didn't want Paul to feel any more pressure than he already was dealing with himself. The clouds lifted. How blessed were we?

# A Wish Comes True

Within months of Anne visiting from Africa, we received a wonderful phone call from her inviting us to visit her in Bethulie, a small town in what was once referred to as the Orange Free State of Central Africa. I could hardly believe my ears. I was actually going to Africa. My excitement was unimaginable.

We arrived in Johannesburg to be greeted by Anne's brother, David, and his wife, Wynne, who had kindly offered to put us up for the night and drive us back to the airport the next day to catch our flight to Bloemfontein. We were greeted with such warmth. It was like I had known them for years. The drive from the airport was such an experience for me, without anything else. I was mesmerised by the never-ending number of tents, humpies and campsites all along the road and on the median strip of the busy road. People were everywhere and running up to the car with handmade artifacts. I asked David if we could stop and buy some of these amazing carvings and wares, but was politely told that it would not be wise to stop the car under any circumstances. This was the first sign for me of the dangers we could meet in some areas of Johannesburg.

David drove us to their home, which was not too far from the airport. As we slowed to turn into the carport, he said, "When I open the garage door, please quickly go into the garage and through into the back garden, and I will follow with the car and lock the door before I take it out your luggage. Can't be too careful."

Oh, my goodness. When we arrived to open the fly screen door, it was very clear that security was at a high level. The windscreen door was made from heavy metal bars and heavy wire. Obviously, no one was worried about flies getting in at all. Another little shock to my system. My heart went out to these beautiful people who were obviously accustomed to enduring this way of life with little or no hope of things improving for them or the many other families in the same situation. A cup of tea, a pat of the family cat and happy conversations can take away from things we can't change. This was a wonderful reunion for Paul and David as they could reminisce about their days in the Kenya regiment, recalling many mates and events which I found very interesting to say the least. Wynne was an amazingly talented seamstress and worked from home with the lounge room converted into her sewing room. I was astonished to hear that Wynne actually handmade many of the bathing costumes for the Miss World competitions, and was known throughout the world for her costumes. Who would have thought this possible? One thing I did realise was that the two-piece costumes were very small indeed, certainly not much material required. Wynne and I chatted about our children, and it was astonishing how much we had in common, even though we had never met before. Although we were all enjoying catching up and chatting, Paul quickly faded from our long flight, and it was time to say goodnight. Not as simple as that. David calmly explained to us that he would have to bolt a heavy barred door between the bedrooms and the front of the house for security reasons. He went on to say, "We experienced shootings in the street last night, so if you hear gunshots during the night, get on the floor on the other side of the bed and stay down."

What can I say? This was a bit scary, to say the least.

The next morning, on the way to the airport, David asked if we would like to experience the real Johannesburg.

"Yes, please," was my answer at once.

Paul, on the other hand, knowing what David was talking about, was not so keen, and even suggested that we might not have time, but, as I had not experienced seeing Africa before, Paul reluctantly agreed.

We drove for a short time when David said, "Please put your handbag out of sight and hands by your sides, and as we drive, do not look directly at anyone, even if they come close to the car. Just look straight ahead. But don't worry, I will not stop the car under any circumstances."

I must say, even the way he was talking frightened me more than I would let on. Before very long, we were driving faster than before, down a narrow dirt road with thousands of tin humpies to the right and left of the road as far as the eye could see, and even more, thousands of people wandering in between and on the sides of the road. More than once, I held my breath as I was sure we would hit some of these people, but miraculously, we didn't, and after about fifteen minutes, I began to breathe again. For me, this was possibly a once-in-a-lifetime experience.

The flight from Johannesburg was a little scary as a couple we were talking with whilst waiting to be called made a joke and said, "The propeller plane is okay. It's whether or not the plane has got enough fuel to get you to Bloemfontein or not." They laughed. I, on the other hand, felt sick. I have never been keen on flying at the best of times, and these comments certainly didn't make me feel any better. Paul sensed my anxiety, and in his usual calming manner, just tapped me on the hand and smiled.

Anne and a friend met us at Bloemfontein airport, and after a cup of coffee and many hugs, we headed off through the city towards the town of Bethulie. Although the road we were travelling along was not a busy road, I was somewhat alarmed at the speed at which we were travelling. Before long, beautiful Africa started to show its wealth of surprises, and my heart was pounding with the need to experience more. My eyes were dry from straining to appreciate every little animal, flower, tree and bird as we drove along the dusty road. At one stage, Roy, Anne's friend, did slow down as a hundred or so monkeys ran across the road in front of us, cheekily looking up the road at us as they bolted at high speed to the safety of some bushes on the other side.

The drive was long, bumpy, fast and dusty, but when we arrived at the gate of Anne's beautiful home, I only remember the amazing sights and smells I had experienced, and couldn't wait to see more. Anne tooted the horn of the car, and a darling old man quickly opened the gate to allow us to pull into a large shed. This old man had been working for Anne for many years, and although it was something I felt awkward with, I also respect that when in Rome do as the Romans do. Anne also employed a housemaid, and this took time for me to adjust to also. The town was similar in size to perhaps Merredin, and the population was mainly African people, with only a few white African families, such as Anne and some close friends of hers who lived nearby. At night, I would sit on the large verandah and listen to the amazing voices of the African people singing. It was breathtaking, and something I will never forget. Anne's home was not far from the allotment, as the housing estate was referred to. It was here where the families would sing for hours, and their voices carried clearly on the warm, sweet-smelling breeze, enriching the atmosphere for all to enjoy. Heart-warming memories.

One special memory of our time spent with Anne was a day we visited the local aged care home to support the community with their annual Open Day. A variety of local foods were on sale as well as a variety of stalls selling handmade products. This was right up my alley as I appreciated the work and effort that had gone into these never-ending pieces of jewellery, handcrafted clothes, bags and much more. After working in some aged facilities in Perth, I have always felt that, in some cases, there are many areas that need improvement, but after visiting this aged care facility in Bethulie, I remember thinking, *if I ever needed to go into care, this would be the place to go.* The Bethulie Aged Care Home was spotless, with fresh flowers everywhere, one or two carers attending to each patient, with everyone upbeat and happy. Of course, I realised that the African staff's wages are substantially less than here in Australia, but aged care means Care, and in Bethulie, the patients were cared for in every respect. It was so refreshing to be in an aged care facility where perfume came from freshly cut roses rather than a stale smell of urine-soaked, unchanged underwear. Less fortunate people in other parts of the world have so much to offer. One day, ever hopeful.

Anne's daughter and son-in-law were Rangers at one of the wildlife sanctuaries north of Bethulie, but because they knew we were visiting from Australia, they had very generously organised a four-day stay, including the use of a private Landie, and included guided tours at the Addo Elephant Reserve situated east of Bethulie. This kindness was overwhelming, to say the least, and to even see an elephant in the wild was something I had only ever dreamed about. Jillianne, Anne's daughter, had organised a friend of the family, Renarta, to drive us the 500 kilometres to Addo. How very grateful that I didn't have to drive; the road was not only narrow, but also very windy and uphill for most of the trip. Once again, although confidently, I know Renarta drove very fast, and I can only say it wasn't easy holding my breath for that length of time.

The Lodge was breathtaking, and our accommodation was second to none. What an amazing gift. Thank you. We even had our personal sentinel at the front door. When I first stepped outside, I thought it was an ornament, but on second glance, I realised we had the biggest tortoise I have ever seen in my life. Silly me. I had only ever seen one in real life at the zoo. Nevertheless, there he was, big, dusty and motionless at the front door.

The first day, we were given a guided tour in a purpose-built, large Land Rover to see as many animals as possible in their natural habitat. We weren't disappointed. We saw lions, giraffes, warthogs, hippos, birds of all sizes, and never once did I feel in danger. 'This must be a dream' were my thoughts over and over again.

Our evening was spent beside a beautiful pool and dining in luxury. Our bed was a king/king, and the room was enormous. In fact, everything in Africa appeared to be big, fast and over the top. The next day, we had to be at the Landy very early to attempt to see a herd of elephants. The tour guide explained that most of the herd were tolerant of sightseers, but one of the elephants was transferred from another sanctuary to breed, and he, sadly, was not accustomed to attention, so he asked if we could talk quietly and make no quick movements. He explained he would have to leave if the situation became dangerous.

Certainly, the highlight of my time at Addo was that day we drove along a track in an area which I remember thinking 'elephants couldn't be here. The trees are too small', when all of a sudden we came over a small rise, and lo and behold, there in front of us was a large herd of elephants. The guide slowly came to a stop, and I remember an eerie silence, except for the occasional crack of a tree branch as a hungry elephant chose his tasty meal. I remember the occasional snorting noise with huge ears flapping, and occasionally an inquisitive trunk reaching out towards the Landi. All of a sudden, things changed, and the elephants seemed to rush together, and I thought two elephants were squashing a baby elephant, but they were actually holding him tight between them, so if they had to run, he would be taken with them. How extremely clever.

Our guide, quietly but firmly, said, "We might have to leave. Hang on," and with that, he reversed and turned around all in one movement, and we drove off with one or two elephants appearing to follow, but only momentarily.

Paul had a wonderful surprise and reunion with a friend from his past, who drove all the way to Addo to join us on the last night. Thanks to Grant and Gillian, we enjoyed a holiday of a lifetime. Unfortunately, I wasn't able to meet Anne's other daughter, Paula. She was away when Paul and I visited.

A shhhh moment here.

Saying goodbye to Anne was not easy for me, but of course, much more meaningful for Paul. There were some quiet, thoughtful moments as we began our long journey back to Johannesburg.

My wish comes true.

# Life Has Many Twists and Turns

It is always good to be home, but returning from a wish-come-true holiday did take a little time to recover from, to say the least. Thank goodness for our wonderful family and friends who quickly brought us back to normality.

Need I say more? Paul was back playing golf, reading his Bible and doing Sudoku with one or more great-grandchildren perched on his knee, helping Poppie Paul solve the Sudoku game, and I was also back playing golf and planning meals for our regular family weekend get-togethers. We were in a happy, contented place. I had finally retired from work at 66 years of age after trying to retire twice before, but was unable to let go of what I loved and my friends from work. I loved mixing with people, and my customers were my friends, as were my work colleagues. When I left work the first time, I found myself in a state of sadness, and I did nothing but cry, so back to work, and all was hunky dory.

Again, a similar situation occurred the next time I tried, but eventually, third time lucky, and I settled into spending more time with my great-grandchildren and, of course, caring for Mum. Paul's health had deteriorated in some areas, and he was having more tests for his kidneys.

One particular day, I was driving him up to Hollywood Hospital to see the specialist. Paul was not well at all, and many times I asked him if I needed to stop. It seemed to take forever to finally park the car and walk to the back entrance of the hospital. Paul was walking very unsteadily and finally, almost collapsed onto a bench near one of the entrances. I was terrified as to what was happening, and ran into the hospital calling for help. Fortunately, a staff member was just inside and came running out to help.

Within seconds, another nurse helped Paul into a wheelchair and said to me, "Can you walk fast? to which I answered, "I am a golfer. I can walk fast." With that, the nurse wheeled Paul through that hospital at warp factor one, until we arrived at the cardiac ward. Paul was having a heart attack.

So many thoughts were flooding into my mind: 'Please, dear God, no. Please help my darling Paul." I felt cold and couldn't stop shaking. Tears were uncontrollable, running down my face as I phoned Marika, not knowing how to make the situation sound not so serious. And to be honest, I can't remember what I said, only that I would let her know if anything changed.

I sat alone in a little room for what seemed like hours, and suddenly an alarm sounded. I froze as I knew what that sound meant. I had heard it before. I couldn't breathe, and within minutes, a nurse entered and gave the rehearsed speech, knowing full well that the alarm may have added to my fears.

"Hi, Mrs. Maxwell, now your husband has suffered a heart attack, and he's in the very best of care, but it might take a little longer. Would you like a cup of tea?"

I looked up at her and said, "I know what that siren means, and I don't think a cup of tea will be of any help at this stage, thank you."

Fearing the worst, I could do nothing but wait.

The doctor eventually walked into the room and explained that Paul had suffered a blood blockage and his heart stopped for seventeen minutes before they could revive him. He went on to say that he was in intensive care, and there was a chance that he may not recover fully, but once the intensive care unit had Paul settled, I would be able to go and see him.

Marika arrived from Bridgetown very quickly, and we spent the next five days in the intensive care unit, reassuring Paul we all loved him and he was getting better. Paul was sedated almost all of the time, and we weren't sure if he could hear us, but we never gave up and continually thought of ways to encourage him to stay strong and get better. Remembering he had actually gone to the hospital for a kidney checkup, he was also continually on a dialysis machine.

Terrie and many family members visited with love and encouragement, but we had to wait. Marika played some classical music for him. With all our love, we wished him better. We arrived one day to be told the decision had been made to remove the breathing tube, telling us that if Paul couldn't manage, they could replace it. My darling, strong husband must have heard that and decided he was going to be okay, and no, he was not going to have that breathing tube inserted ever again.

What a wonderful sight when we entered the room: Paul was sitting up, sipping water through a straw, with tears of relief in his eyes. Our prayers had been answered. Our tears flowed with happiness.

Paul was in hospital for quite some time, but slowly recovered enough to come home to a loving welcome. It was very difficult for his sisters and family in England, as all the details had to be relayed by phone. I can only imagine how much anxiety they must have gone through. There is no doubt that their many prayers had been answered.

*Paul, me, Brian, Mum and Gail*

*Lovely photo of Brian and Gail*

*Top left: Wayne, Banksie, Rhys, Gail, Lyn, Brian*
*Front: Tara, Oaklin, Peg*

*Gail, Pat, Lyn, Brian, Peg, Paul*

*Mum and Todd*

This next photo was taken at my 70th birthday. My darling Paul had arranged this wonderful surprise for me.

Thank you with love. XX

*My wonderful, mixed-up, crazy, best family anyone could ever have.*

***I LOVE YOU!***

# Relentless Storms

Fortunately, life's ever-moving, ever-changing situations don't allow us to dwell on the bad times, and we always look forward to happy, new, exciting times. Thank goodness for that. Paul and I were very contented with our life, but often talked about visiting his sisters in England again – perhaps their more frequent phone calls and concern for Paul's health prompted these considerations.

Paul started spending more time with his friends from the Baptist Church, and even attended Bible reading once a week. Paul wanted so much for me to join in with his church activities and follow his beliefs. This was very sad, because as much as I wanted to please Paul, I knew it would be untruthful for me to do so, not only to Paul, but most importantly to God. Paul's beliefs were embedded in him right from childhood, which I respected. It made me very sad the day Paul told me of his pain as he knew I wouldn't be able to meet him in heaven. My heart is heavy remembering this, not for me, but for the sincerity of Paul's love, which he was showing me with his eyes.

One Saturday, Paul left for golf as normal and told me he was hoping to play as well as he had done on the Thursday. As always, Paul was very competitive with his golf and always aimed to improve and lower his handicap. I was home doing normal washing/cleaning things when I received a phone call from one of the pros at the golf club.

"Hi, Lyn. I wanted to let you know that Paul collapsed on the golf course, and I've called the ambulance."

Before I had time to think I was on my way to the golf course. As I drove into the car park, one of the ambos came running up and said, "Are you Paul's wife? If you hurry, you can ride with us. We are on priority one."

Paul was being attended to, and all I could do was call out to him and let him know I was with him and tell him I loved him. The ambulance driver was only young, but was an amazing driver. I felt completely helpless. My mind was like a washing machine. My heart was pounding as I waved and thanked verbally all the wonderful drivers who went out of their way to allow the ambulance to get to the hospital as quickly as possible.

The entire journey, Paul's condition was being monitored by the hospital and the ambulance officer who was treating him and kept relaying his deteriorating condition over the two-way, which, of course, heightened my worst fears. On arriving at Fiona Stanley Hospital, I was able to run to the back of the ambulance so Paul could see I was with him. How can I explain the pain, and fear, as Paul reached out for me to give him a gentle kiss. Within minutes, I was waiting in a small room with another couple who smiled at me knowingly, but also without realising it, showed that look of heartache.

This storm was relentless. During the twenty years Paul and I had been married, I had steadily strengthened my ever-changing Web of Life to a point where I felt each vibe was now strong and we together could withstand the never-ending little storms which occur as a normal part of life. But sadly, some storms are catastrophic, and this was one.

I have no idea how long I sat motionless with millions of jumbled thoughts running through my head, when suddenly my worst fear: the once heard, never forgotten, blood-curdling sound of the alarm pierced not only the once quiet corridors, but my heart also. My Web of Life was torn to shreds as the doctor explained that he did all he could to save Paul's life, but sadly, he had passed away. I felt myself being blown from side to side by the storms relentlessly breaking every fibre I reached out for until I could hang on no longer.

Once again, I knew I could not be selfish with my grief as I struggled with the ability to inform, first and foremost, Paul's adored daughter, Marika, of the passing of her darling dad, followed by his sisters and all of our children and grandchildren and great-grandchildren. In the twenty years we were together, we built a lifetime of memories, with our Web of Life extending far beyond the years, and these memories will live on.

My darling Paul, with love. Very special 'shhhh moments.

Although I had known this heartache many times before, there is no way of making the pain any less just because you've experienced it before. In fact, the emptiness and confusion of mind is so relentless that you feel a need to curl into a ball somewhere and wake up to find it was only a dream. But, no, it was not a dream, and you once again have to be strong as others are suffering also.

Paul's funeral service was held at the Baptist Church, and with combined efforts and loving intent by all of our family members, my wish, with all the love in my heart, was that we were able to give Paul a service that he would have thought was "Good, dear."

The church was full, and his favourite hymns were sung. His family joined to speak the eulogy. And as I've mentioned before in my book, there is always one person at the funeral who tugs at my heartstrings until they ache. This time, it was Paul's brother. This darling man was himself very unwell, but because of his faith and love of his brother, he stood upright, hardly able to fight back his emotion as he worded his eulogy for his brother. There were no dry tears – the pain I heard in everyone's voice as they told of their love and respect for Paul, the wonderful dad, brother, uncle, brother-in-law, stepdad, Pop Paul was something I will hold in my heart forever. My friends from the golf club all formed a guard of honour as he was carried from the church, a touching honour. Thank you.

The days that followed the funeral of a loved one are always just a blur, with people coming and going and so much food arriving at the door, all wonderful gestures by friends and family who care. Time does not heal. It just allows you to be able to readjust and work out how you're going to keep your pain hidden and adapt to some form of normality to avoid others worrying about you.

We all do this in different ways.

Rest in peace, my darling, Paul. XX. Loving, 'shhhh moment.

# Building New Threads in My Web of Life

Once you've fallen completely from life's web, it takes all of your strength and willpower to reach up and commence climbing the storm-shredded fibres, which are the only threads that remain to enable you to start the difficult task of building new, never-walked-upon threads in your Web of Life.

One of the ways I endeavored to do this was to keep myself so busy and completely tired that I didn't have time to feel sorry for myself, and when I went to bed, I fell asleep, which gave me the strength to start again the next day. I also surrounded myself with family, friends, and grandkids, and the busier things got, and the noisier they became, the better it was for me to move forward. Another quick way I cleared my thoughts was to get in the car and turn the music up so loud that I felt like I was going to blow my brains out. Told you, I'm queer, odd, but this worked for me.

What better way to achieve all of the above, other than doing a complete renovation of the kitchen and lounge room. Great idea. But I did, of course, need a little help from, you guessed it, my best support in life, my daughter, Terrie, of course. Poor Sophie got dragged into the massive amount of work that was needed to be done. Within days, they were both in the lounge room scraping black rubber off the concrete so the new carpet could have fresh underlay. What a job! I worked with them for days, and eventually, not a skerrick of black rubber was to be seen anywhere.

Cody, my grandson, was staying with me at that time. He lived in the country, but was working in the Rockingham area during the week, and went home on weekends. One morning, after thinking about it for some time, I mentioned to Cody that I was going to knock out a brick wall that partitioned off the dining area from the family room. Cody raised his eyebrows, looked at me and said, "I don't know, Nan, that's a pretty big job. I don't think you'll be able to do that."

Cody. Cody, Cody, you shouldn't have said that. I've always loved a challenge, and if someone says I can't do something, something inside me just makes me want to do it even more.

Within two minutes of him driving off to work, I had bashed the polished wooden top off the bricks and had commenced smashing down the bricks with a sledgehammer. Thank goodness I still have many of the tools that Dad used on the farm many years ago. I worked all day with the hardest job being that of taking the bricks outside. Although I thought I was pretty clever, I had to admit that I came across a stumbling block when it came to the bricks closer to the concrete floor; they were well and truly glued and concreted down, and my strength was not enough. Bless his heart. Cody, though totally exhausted from his own job, worked for days getting the floor cleaned from concrete and level. Thank you all.

Within a few weeks, my home looked fresh, different and helped me so much with all of the adjustments needed to rebuild my life, thread by thread again. Mum has been living in her attached granny flat with me since she was 86 years of age, and how truly blessed I have always been to have Mum as part of our life.

Mum has been able to be part of her grandchildren's, great grandchildren's, great-great-grandchildren's lives for many years, which has been wonderful for not only Mum, but for the children as well. We have celebrated birthday after birthday, all with Mum included. We have enjoyed a very large family Christmas every year with Mum as the matriarch of the family. Mum has seen more candles being blown out and more wobbly birthday cakes being spat on as an excited birthday child endeavours to blow out all the candles in one go than anyone else I've ever known. Mum has been able to go to school assemblies to watch her great-grandchildren receive their first achievement certificate, and watch how proud another great-grandchild was when they put their face underwater in the swimming pool for the first time.

Of course, she's also seen more tantrums than I would like to remember, and more sibling rivalry than any of us need to see. But most of all, Mum has been part of our busy lives. Please, don't think we've tortured her with all this chaos. Fortunately, Mum has had the advantage of going down the passage and shutting her door behind her if she needed peace and quiet. All good.

Because we live in the metro area, Mum has also had the benefit of being able to go to the many happy functions held by Brian and Gail, Keith and Gloria, Gordon and Diane, as well as family get-togethers with her nieces and nephews and friends. One memorable get-together was a family reunion held at Brian and Gail's. This was very special, as family members came from as far as Queensland and Adelaide for this wonderful family reunion. Mum, her sister and two sisters-in-law, and nieces and nephews were all with us on this special, never-to-be-forgotten day.

Mums will always be mums, as the saying goes. My mum is where this saying comes from, I'm sure. She did all in her power to ease the pain I've carried within, sometimes a little too much, but Mum's love is unconditional love, and for this, I will always be truly grateful.

Once again, my friends were always there for me and certainly helped me rebuild my Web of Life.

*Below: Normal small family Christmas*

*Cousin John, Derry, Mum, and sitting Felix Sainsbury (Dad's cousin)*

*Cousin Leigh, Mum, Jessica, Kessi, and baby Lucas*

*Gordon, Gloria, Diane, David Marsland, Keith and me*

*Left: Julianna, me, Jonathon          Right: Sebastian and Julianna*

## Tip-Toeing Past Threads

I tried to catch up with my friends as much as I could, although, as we all know, with everyone trying to manage their own hectic lives these days, it is not always easy to keep in touch. I did, however, manage to find a time to see my friend Rose from the deli where I spent many happy years working. Rose was as bubbly and happy as always when we met up, but this time for another reason. Rose and her husband had parted many years prior, and therefore Rose had been extremely busy working herself at the deli, keeping up with the increasing demands of her large family, with schooling, sporting activities and normal children's needs. The first exciting news was that Rose had met the man of her dreams, and couldn't be happier. Hearing this news gave me tingles, as this beautiful friend deserved every happiness possible. 'shhhh moments.

"But there's more," Rose explained. "I've finally been able to find my biological father, and I've met him."

"Oh, my goodness!" I was so excited for her. "What about your mum? Have you been able to find her?"

Rose explained that they were getting very close to finding her birth mother as well. Rose's eyes were glistening with excitement, and I felt so happy for her.

My next question, and her answer was enough to knock me off my feet. I casually asked, "Where did your dad come from?"

Rose's reply made me very interested, as I went to high school in that town. Without hesitation, I asked, "What was his name?"

Rose's response left me speechless for a second, which Rose noticed, and said, "You know my dad, don't you?"

"Yes," was my reply. "We went to the same school. I know him well."

How could this be? I had worked with Rose for years, knowing that she had always wanted to find her biological parents, without realising that I had known her father and had, in fact, been at the same high school all those years prior. Rose deserves all the happiness in the world.

*Bernie and Simon enjoying Dragon Boat Racing*

*Simon, Bernie with Luke and Bec*

*Bohdi, Jayke, Van and Mum*

*Mum, 99 years of age, with great-great-grandson Deegan*

*Deegan, Jamal and Van*

*Van*  *Paul (Gar) and Bohdi*

*Michael and Jaing*

*Oaklin and Ben*

*Such a happy photo.
Lisa, Amy, Max, at one of their every year Birthday parties.
Warm memories*

*Kaelyn, Quade, Sophie, Jamal*

*Mum and Sophie, forever the protector of Grandma*

*Eldest girl five generations. Sophie (Mum's great-granddaughter), Mum, Terrie (Mum's granddaughter), Me (Mum's daughter), and Kaelyn (Mum's great-great-granddaughter)*

*Mum at her 99th birthday*

*Mum with seven of her eleven great-great-grandchildren*

*Terrie, with Quade, Kaelyn and Jamal at a NAIDOC day, Coolangup Primary School*

*Terrie, with some of her students at one of the Nation Aborigines and Islanders Days, Safety Bay High School*

# Quick Glance at my Favourite Things/ Least Favourite Things

Paul Bayless would often refer to me as his queer, odd girl, which always gave a happy, warm flutter in my heart. Some people would be upset, I know, being called queer-odd, but from Paul, these were affectionate words. In fact, many of my different ways attributed to the special love we shared.

I love; remember, love has many depths, as I see it, and the expression 'I love' in the following certainly includes all different forms of love.

I love.

I love the smell of the rich soil associated with freshly ploughed, damp straw-enriched paddocks. In fact, I love rolling in this dirt. This is something that, of course, comes from my childhood, and to this day, nothing has changed. I love the smell of rich dirt.

I love the heat from the wood fire on a cold day, inside or outside' there is nothing nicer than being up close to a crackling wood fire, even if you have to rotate regularly to avoid your bum burning, or your tits freezing off. Wood fires are so soothing, and even mesmerising, but they also give off a beautiful smell of their own. Now I am remembering my childhood again with the unique smell of a Mallee root fire.

I love eating an apple when it's brown, not 'off' brown, fresh brown. I eat some of the skin from the apple, then leave it for a while, and when the white of the apple has gone slightly brown, I enjoy the flavour of the apple. Queer-odd, I know.

I love heaters in cars. This, I'm sure, comes directly from my childhood when travelling in our FX Holden with its vinyl seats, which were colder than sitting on a shelf on the inside of our kerosene-fuelled refrigerator.

I love chocolate. Nothing much to be said here.

I love Utes. I think they are sexy cars. Not sure why. I've always noticed them more than other cars, but involuntarily, I seem to always take a second look, especially if the ute is sporting a deep-throated exhaust system.

I love listening to the rain on a tin roof. It is so soothing.

I love the smell that is released from dry stubble when a summer rain pounds the dusty, dry paddocks as it tries to quench the thirst of our sun-burnt countryside.

I love looking at the moon through a telescope or binoculars. I find it so fascinating and thought-provoking. Incomprehensible to imagine that someone has walked on the surface of the moon.

I love looking at the Evening Star on a clear night. I am always filled with a spiritual feeling of drifting off in my own world, but the Evening Star gives me a direct line to my beautiful daughter Nicole, in heaven. Very precious 'shhhh moment to lock in my heart.

I love upbeat music. I love all different types of music. But, of course, the 60s music has many heartfelt memories. I love bagpipe music, pan flute music, but most of all, upbeat, feel-good, makes you want to dance music.

I love intimacy, sex, whatever you choose to call it. Without a doubt in my mind, orgasm is nature's way of resetting and alleviating nervous tension, certainly the most scrumptious, yummy way I know to do this.

I love walking on the golf course after the rain, when the sun sparkles like silver on the wet leaves of the trees, with the perfume of nature captured on a gentle breeze.

I love that everyone is different, and I take pleasure in listening to how they manage life's challenges.

I love my mum, brother and sister-in-law. There are no words to fully show the depth of this love.

I love my daughter Terrie, and my daughter Nicole, now in God's arms. I love all of my children, grandchildren, great-grandchildren, sons-in-law, daughters-in-law, and it goes without saying, this includes my stepchildren, who I am blessed to have in my life.

I love all of my sisters-in-laws, brothers-in-law, nieces, nephews, in fact, all of my in-laws and outlaws and cousins. After three marriages, I feel absolutely privileged to still be part of the lives of my crazy, mixed-up families. With all my love. XX

I love being able to enjoy a hot shower and feel very fortunate to have this pleasure. This also goes back to my childhood, when water was so precious that we all bathed in the same bath water. By the time I got into the bath, I was bathing in mud-coloured cool water.

I love swimming nude. Oh, what a feeling!

I love sexy perfume. I remember running after a complete stranger in Kuala Lumpur airport to ask what perfume she was wearing. Paul sat quietly, embarrassed, and was $200 out of pocket when the very kind lady who could hardly understand my English took me to the perfume shop and showed me which perfume she was wearing.

I love the fact that my daughter Terrie has embraced her Australian First Nations heritage. She is working as an Aboriginal and Torres Strait Islander officer and is studying her mob's language, Whadjuk, to also become an Australian First Nations language teacher. I am so proud of you, darling.

I love the fact that our family is multicultural, including English, Irish, Scottish, Scandinavian, Polynesian, Spanish, Taiwanese, New Zealander, Cook Islander, Slavic, Polish, Australian, First Nation, Anglo-Indian, Chinese. And I'm sure if everyone did their DNA, we would find more wonderful surprises.

I love life itself, and will always give 100% and a bit more to enjoy all the blessings that have been afforded to me.

I love cats. I've always loved cats. They are so intuitive and know when you are sad, always giving a gentle nudge of affection.

I love dolls. From a very early age, I've been fascinated by dolls – baby dolls, Cupid dolls, rag dolls, old dolls, walkie-talkie dolls.

Wheat, the smell of wheat, the feel of the grain, the look of wheat on the stalk, chewing wheat grain until it resembles chewing gum.

I love Freesias, the highly perfume flowers that grow wild on the verges.

## Dislikes

I dislike cruelty of any description, especially to children and animals.

I dislike being forced to do everything online with the depletion of services across the board, including banks and post offices. I'm sure I'm not the only person who struggles with navigating online banking and filling out important documents, etc. 'Hate' is the big word that I don't use very often, but certainly the frustration I feel with not having trust in my ability to do these things right is enough to make me use the H word. Intimacy to the rescue.

I dislike arguments over trivialities. We are all strong-willed, and arguments are a complete waste of time and energy. If someone thinks someone something is black and another person thinks it's white, why argue? Each will always think they are right. Utter waste of time.

I dislike tripe. Nothing more to be said here.

I dislike racism, homophobia and judgmental arrogance.

I dislike our throw-away society. I feel very sad when I see so much waste by many, when others are in need; it just seems so wrong that it is cheaper to purchase new rather than fix anything. It all seems back to front and I am sure many other baby boomers cut their teeth on 'waste not, want not'. Still, sounds right to me.

I dislike/hate drugs and what the use of drugs is doing to our families and lives. This is one time I can use the H word with no regrets. My heart goes out to all who have suffered as a result of this curse.

I dislike goats' cheese. To me, it smells and tastes gamey.

I dislike many other things, I'm sure, but I would prefer to put my thoughts and energy into my loves in life.

*Rhiannon, Ceri, Paul, Amelia*

*Left: Luke and Bec
Love and Happiness*

*Right: Me with beautiful
Savannah, Adam's and
Rhiannon's daughter*

*Paul, Terrie, Susie, Greg, Paul, Amy Lisa, Max, me, Ceri*

*More happy photos of us all.*

*Josh and Sophie*
*Congratulations XX*

# Time Waits for No One

'Time waits for no one' is an expression I've heard many times in my life, as we all have, I'm sure. I always thought Mum was being silly when she said, "I don't know. Time just flies as I get older."

This was hard for me to believe when I was young, as waiting for a special occasion such as Christmas holidays or a birthday, was where I felt time went very slowly indeed.

As with most things in life, we don't understand until we experience situations for ourselves. And yes, for some unknown reason, time does go by very quickly as we get older. The most obvious reason to me is that when we are younger, we only have ourselves to consider, but throughout our lives, we gather a multitude of family, friends and acquaintances, which in turn gives us a multitude of thoughts and actions to fit into the same timeframe.

My life is no different, and I've managed to pack my life full of much to do with my adored family, including caring for my darling mum, spending time with my daughter and sons-in-law and their children, grandchildren, great-grandchildren, stepchildren, step-grandchildren, step-great-grandchildren, extended families, cousins and all. How blessed am I? Who would have thought that I'd still have the privilege of taking my great-grandchildren to the movies or to the beach or even to school on the odd occasion? 'Never a dull moment in our home' is one of Mum's most used expressions these days. God love her at 99 years of age; it must seem all too much.

With all of this much-loved chaos in my life, it is hard to believe that I could possibly feel lonely. When speaking to a friend one day about my busy times, she asked in a concerning manner, "But how are you, Lyn?"

I replied honestly, "I'm never alone, but sometimes I feel lonely."

I'm very sure many have felt this emotion.

A few weeks later, my friend rang and asked if I would like to meet a very nice man she had known for many years who had expressed a similar sentiment to her. I thanked her for her concern and said I would think about it.

A short time later, I spoke to Avery and we arranged to meet for a coffee.

Both of us, being young at heart, had experienced almost a lifetime of happy, sad, hectic, busy times in our past, and were both able to freely be honest as to what we needed in a friendship with each other. I was completely honest and explained that I didn't want or need commitment, but a friendship where I could feel like Lyn, the person, every now and again, would be nice. He agreed that it would be nice to have a friendship where we could be ourselves.

At first, I felt like I was doing something wrong/bad/wicked even, for embracing my emotions at my age, as I felt like no one would understand. Surprisingly enough, when I finally felt brave enough to confide in a friend at golf, I realised that people did understand and to my dear friends and my family, thank you for your understanding and support.

It was difficult for me to have a normal relationship as such, because I couldn't leave my mum on her own.

Avery was very compassionate and understanding of the situation I was in, and was happy to visit for dinner, go for a walk or watch a movie with me. He was an avid dancer and often expressed how he would love for me to go dancing with him. I would have loved to be able to enjoy some of these things also, dancing, camping, weekends away. But leaving Mum alone for any length of time was not an option. Sometimes, Terrie or Sophie would stay with Mum so we could go out for a meal or show or even enjoy a game of golf, which gave some normality to our friendship. A few 'shhhh moments here! We were very compatible, and it was beautiful to feel the intimate love that is so important for all of us, that special level of love that fulfils and satisfies like no other.

Avery was able to take me to such great heights where I could mindlessly step away from reality and immerse myself in selfish fulfilment. It is, however, very difficult to feel that closeness with someone without all the other levels of love and commitment becoming stronger.

We spent many very happy times together, but unfortunately, our needs and wants and situations couldn't allow us to continue our friendship in this way. We have parted, still as friends, but with a mutual appreciation for the short time in our later years of life where we were able to drift back to feeling like teenagers again. Yes, there is a love word for this – 'yummy' comes to mind,

# Revisiting Some Precious Threads 50 Years Later

It has only been in the last decade or so that I have fully understood why this time spent at Sunnyside was so vitally important to my children. My darling Terrie has never been able to settle completely in the city. Her uncontrollable yearning to return to the country has been evident so many times. In fact, we often make a joke about the twenty or so times we've helped Terrie move house, from the city to Nungarin, Merredin, Cunderdin, Southern Cross, Darken, Wagin and Narrogin, Williams and other moves back and forward within those towns and back to different city areas also. Oh, my goodness, so many trailers hired, cars loaded to the hilt. Laughter by the truckload as one house was emptied and another filled to the brim, sore backs, black toes, sweaty armpits, but much more than that, love and laughter and family helping family.

Terrie's heart belongs to country, and this has been evident throughout her life. Terrie is very proud to be a descendant of many bloodlines – Scottish, Irish, Spanish and indigenous Australian. The love of the land is something that I understand completely, but the need for country is inherited. Terrie is happily married with grandchildren of her own, working as an Aboriginal and Torres Strait officer at a city high school, plus is currently studying one of the Noongar languages. As her mother, I am so happy that Terrie has found fulfilment, and I could not be prouder of my daughter and her achievements in life, and who herself has her own massive story to tell. As her mother, I also know it always pays to have the phone number of a trailer hire company handy. Love you with all my heart, darling.

# Reflections of My Book ... Closing Chapters?

One day, without rhyme or reason, an overwhelming feeling of excitement came over me to revisit my Web of Life (as I refer to my life's journey) by writing a book to ensure that my grandchildren, great-grandchildren, and even, God willing, my great-great-grandchildren, could learn a little about their heritage. I felt a need to write about the life-changing, happy, sad, traumatic, elating, devastating, and everything in between, memories that had been forever embedded in my heart and soul. I feel so blessed that I have always been able to follow my heart to achieve without the fear of failure crossing my mind. The Power of Positive Thinking is one of my most-used sayings.

It was during one of these deep in thought moments when I mentioned in passing to my darling husband, Paul, an avid book reader all his life, that I was going to write a book.

Paul, normally a person who controlled his visual emotions, couldn't hide a look of sheer amazement. "Write a book," he said, "but you don't even read books."

My quick answer to that was, "Just because I don't read books doesn't mean I can't write one."

The response from Paul can be best described as a look for those who knew him, would know exactly the look he gave, followed by a slight smile and back to his Sudoku.

I commenced writing my Web of Life in 2015 and enjoyed passing each page I had written to the most qualified editor ever. To my delight, Paul praised me and encouraged me always. My heart jumped for joy sometimes when I watched his expression change while reading what I had written, and many times as he handed the pages back to me, he would smile and say, "Very good, dear." As his sisters often told me, if you get a 'very good, dear' from Paul, you can feel well pleased.

However, because of my somewhat foolish enthusiasm, I didn't for one moment take into consideration that whilst writing about these life-changing moments, life itself goes on, and more and more life-changing moments would occur daily. Obviously, the many tiny fibres of my Web of Life were and are still changing, and others are being revisited many times over.

I had planned the many stages and chapters in my book, with, obviously, the last chapter being a soft, gentle, contented, Happy Ever After life with Paul and me sitting up in bed every morning having a cuppa and chatting with love and warm memories. This had always been my dream. Devastatingly, my darling Paul could not stay with me to complete this chapter in our life, but I know his gentle love will always be the encouragement to keep me going and his love will somehow give me my Happy Ever After ending. Loving memories to my darling, Paul Bayless, locked in the special part of my heart forever.

## My Web of Life

Thank you for reading my interpretation of how I've maneuvered my way through the ups and downs of life's journey. We all have our own Web of Life, and how we manage to hang on is entirely up to each of us to discover and achieve in our own way. As you know by now, if you've read my should-not-have-given-up-my-day-job of a book. I, like many others, just struggled on doing my best. And fortunately, thanks to the strength I was afforded by my parents when I first commenced building my own Web of Life, I've been able to hang on.

Being able to build very strong threads right from the start is vital, as we need this strength when we add more and more threads. We also need to be able to retread these older threads many times throughout our life. Thus, we need the strength of these first threads over and over again during our lifetime; our web must be able to withstand the ever-increasing, ever-strengthening storms that occur during our lives, battering the myriad valuable threads, until the sun shines through as it always does, blessings us with sunshine and happiness. I am now ready to stop fighting with my laptop, find the most comfortable thread in the sunniest part of 'My Web of Life' and dream about my future happiness a lifetime ahead.

Yes, I have retired from recalling my past life's experiences, but I will never give up on life itself.

In the shadows of darkness, I am, with joy in my heart, embracing a truly delightful shared emotion with an extremely caring, kind person. Happiness finds us when we least expect it. '*I know no mushy stuff*'. But beautiful emotion can be unspoken.

Whispering warmest thoughts.

Shhhh!

# My Queer-Odd Way of Writing

Throughout my book, you will have noticed that many times I've written a silly, not even a word thing, "shhhh', however, that silly, little not-even-a-word-thing, does perhaps have more meaning to it than any other word in my Web of Life.

In the main, it stands for an emotion, feeling or love, true love, unconditional love, intimate thoughts, secret thoughts of the heart and sometimes little wicked things. 'shhhh is simply my way of reaching out to those who are within that secret without betraying their trust. 'shhhh can, however, mean something so bad that it is never to be spoken about, or just for those who are involved to know about.

Unfortunately/fortunately, however you yourself feel about it, there are many regretful, hurtful, wrong, very wrong, dare I say it, unlawful, things that have occurred in almost everyone's life which cannot be erased or repaired. Therefore, they simply go to the grave with that person. Very big 'shhhh moments.

I am very aware that whilst tiptoeing around and around my Web of Life, there have been numerous more 'shhhh moments, too many to mention, in fact, so I've decided to leave those moments for the future generations to write about.

Shhhh.

## The Depths of Emotion, Love

During my life, I have been blessed with the ability to explore many depths of emotion of love. I have been able to find beauty and kindness everywhere, and I have tried my hardest to find the emotion that is within everyone.

I have experienced love in many different and fulfilling ways, and every one of these emotions of deep love, I will carry in my heart forever.

More importantly, I have always been overwhelmed with the emotion/love extended to me by so many, especially the thoughtfulness and caring visits and phone calls from my nearest and dearest, always showing kindness, encouragement and unconditional love. Thank you, my darlings.

With all the threads of love in my Web of Life, one special 'shhhh love will forever shine in my heart.

*'Shhhh.'*

## Dreams Do Come True. Shhhh Moment

For one very short, precious time during the wee hours of the night, when my most personal and intimate thoughts controlled every inch of my body and soul, I experienced the most gentle, caring, sincere love making I could have ever imagined. It is very difficult to believe that this fulfilment of a lifetime wish could be anything but a beautiful, orgasmic dream. I experienced overwhelming emotions, gentle touches, and deep love, which was real and profound, heightening every part of my being as I tingled like a giddy schoolgirl, deeply in love, revisiting the tiny threads of my Web of Life. A love like no other I've ever experienced, a dream come true, my heart is now completely cradled in the arms of my life's true love.

Sometimes dreams we experience are so real that we can never free them from our thoughts, and sometimes our real experiences are so overwhelmingly beautiful that they seem just like a dream.

After experiencing a high such as this, there can only be an even deeper and more heart-wrenching low to follow. During my lifetime, I have endured many different types of lows. Most were the saddest kind, but this time, the low I'm feeling is of an emotional kind, which brings a deep, real ache within which I am finding so hard to control. I am finding it difficult to concentrate and find myself going to bed at a certain time with thoughts of nothing else but the possibility of a reunion with that special dream time. I know I must and will get the strength to push the heartache to one side eventually, as I truly know that I have been blessed to have been given the joy of having my dream come true, be it for such a short time, and know, I have been more fortunate than most, but for now, my heart burns for the return of this love.

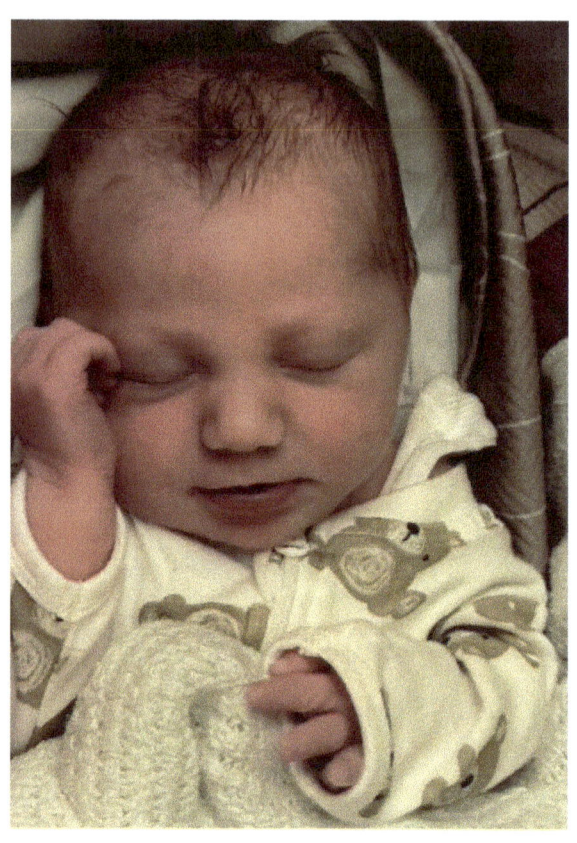

*"Am I too late, Grandma?"*
*"No, little darling, you're in!"*

Introducing Montie June Tutevera, born just in time to make the print. Welcome to our wonderful family Xxxxxxx.

*85 Family and friends celebrating Mum's 100th birthday*

*Happy 100th Birthday, Mum*
*31/1/2025*

www.ingramcontent.com/pod-product-compliance
Lightning Source LLC
Chambersburg PA
CBHW061213070526
44584CB00029B/3816